Trump and the Media

Trump and the Media

Edited by Pablo J. Boczkowski and Zizi Papacharissi

The MIT Press
Cambridge, Massachusetts
London, England

This book was set in ITC Stone Sans Std and ITC Stone Serif Std by Toppan Best-set Premedia Limited. Printed and bound in the United States of America.

Library of Congress Cataloging-in-Publication Data is available.

ISBN: 978-0-262-03796-9

10 9 8 7 6 5 4 3 2 1

Contents

Acknowledgments

It always takes a village. But sometimes more than others. This was one of those times. This book took six months from conception to final delivery of the manuscript, which is quite a feat for scholarly publishing. This would not have happened if it were not for the support and contributions of a large number of people.

We are extremely grateful to our editor at the MIT Press, Gita Manaktala. Her unfailing commitment to this project from the very first email exchange, her insightful advice at every step of the way, and her always warm presence have made our collaboration not only possible but also a true pleasure.

Our authors were a blessing to work with. They trusted us to shepherd a project that was unique not only because of its fast production cycle but also for the unusual genre format we asked them to work with—a 2,500-word essay, something of hybrid between an op-ed and a paper. They took on these speed and genre challenges with intellectual rigor, a strong work ethic, and a great sense of camaraderie.

We could not have pulled this off without the incredible behind-the-scenes work of Jamie Foster, a first-year doctoral student in the Department of Communication at the University of Illinois at Chicago. Jamie went above and beyond the call of duty, dealing with all kinds of issues in a timely and efficient manner. We also acknowledge the financial support received from our respective departments.

We thank the staff at the Cherry Circle Room in the Chicago Athletic Association. Perhaps, if it weren't for the delicious food and drinks they served us on a cold January evening, the book you now have in your hands might have only been a figment in our imaginations.

Last but not least, this project has been a team effort in which both of us contributed equally. Editorship order is just a function of the arbitrariness of alphabetical order.

Pablo J. Boczkowski (from Berlin, Germany) and Zizi Papacharissi (from the beautiful beaches of the Greek Islands), July 30, 2017

1 Introduction

Pablo J. Boczkowski and Zizi Papacharissi

Donald J. Trump's ascendancy to the presidency of the United States took the world by storm and became a key moment of the still nascent twenty-first century. Analysts, pundits, politicians, and members of the public have feverishly tried to make sense of why this happened and what it might mean for the future of democratic life. Lots of explanations have been proposed and an even greater array of potential future scenarios have been floated in public discourse. This has naturally led to many disagreements that probably will be sorted out only with time. Beneath these disagreements, however, there are two ideas around which significant consensus has emerged.

First, the electoral victories, initially in the primaries and then in the general election, of Trump are to a certain extent extraordinary within the context of the American political system. While the electoral contests were unfolding, most observers in leading think tanks, the media, and the academy thought of them as relatively improbable outcomes. When he was finally declared the winner of the presidential contest on November 8, 2016, the dominant feeling in the establishment was one of deep surprise.

Second, there is a certain sense that the media played an important role in this extraordinary turn of events. This applies to both the news and social media individually, and even more so to the combination of them. From the apparent disconnect of the agenda-setting media with a vast segment of the American voters to the deluge of fake news circulating on social media, and from the intensity of the confrontation between President Trump and these media to his constant use of Twitter to promote alternative—and often unsupported by facts—narratives, there is a sense that the matrix that used to tie politics, media, technology, and the citizenry in fairly predictable ways has moved far away from equilibrium.

This book was born from the premise that these two ideas are connected, and that probing that connection provides a powerful window into broader transformations that mark the information landscape of the twenty-first century. We take the extraordinary character of the ascendancy to power and the leadership style of President Trump not as an exception or a fluke. On the contrary, we think that it that makes visible the fault lines underneath ordinary processes that have been evolving during several decades but were more difficult to ascertain during periods in which both electoral outcomes and political communication followed conventional, and therefore quite foreseeable, patterns—in the same way that the malfunctioning of a technological system does not create but reveals underlying design problems that were present long before the system breaks. Furthermore, this also applies to the news and social media: they did not become unsettled all of a sudden, but as part of evolutionary processes that are now easier to see and assess.

Making sense of these processes is challenging due to the complexity of the phenomena at stake and the recency of the main events in question. But it is also imperative to begin the discussion in order to contribute to ongoing scholarly and public conversations that can shape future trajectories in a constructive fashion. We tackle this challenge by asking a series of renowned scholars of communication, technology, and politics to contribute accessible essays focused on a key aspect of how the coming to power of Donald Trump intersects with the dynamics of information production, distribution, and reception in the news and/or social media. We do not aim to offer a comprehensive or definite account—much more time will have to pass before any text can accomplish that. By contrast, our goal is that, taken together, the essays in this volume can illuminate in a kaleidoscopic and timely manner some of the most critical and distinct dynamics that account for the nature of this president's relationship to the media, provide historical context, and lay out possible future scenarios.

Thus, our aim is to present a collection of chapters that informs readers about questions lingering in the collective mind regarding such issues as the role of the press, digital information infrastructures, and social media; the character of a media and political system increasingly removed from a common ground and fragmented into disparate cultural enclaves; and alternative futures that might emerge from major shifts in media, politics, and the ties that bind them. We rely on the current populist moment to explicate, and contextualize, tendencies and tensions that have been developing for some time. Moments change and situations evolve. What is normal may gradually turn into a new normal between the time we write this introductory chapter and the moment the book is published. This does not negate our ability to do relevant work; quite the opposite. It invites us to produce work that addresses, yet is not trapped in, the moment. This is how we see our stance as scholars in general, and as editors of this volume in particular. We employ the present, long moment as an opportunity to rethink our roles as researchers, journalists, and citizens. In other words, we take advantage of the present, but do not fall prey to it. The chapters in this volume all take inspiration from, but move beyond, the contemporary situation so as to attain and retain their relevance for future analyses.

A lot can change in the next few months or years. A lot can stay the same. Therefore, our emphasis is on the Trump candidacy and the initial phase of his presidency as critical instances of more geographically and temporally extended phenomena, and certainly not the cause of the present media condition. In the chapters that follow, our contributors trace the roots of the dynamics that reinforce the contemporary impasse in journalism. As a result, we write about the relationship between truth and politics; editorial practices and conventions; facts, events, and reality; media and historicity; the economics and business of journalism. We use theory, previous research, and history to understand. These are our interpretive lenses as we consider the more contemporary vocabulary of fake news, alternative facts, clickbait headlines, and bot farms.

The volume is organized in four sections. The first one is titled "Journalism in Question" and considers the present position journalism finds itself in, the historical context that led to the current situation, and the role that the news media play in the business of truth-telling. The second section, "Emotion, Populism, and Media Events," tackles these three topics as they relate to both our platforms for storytelling and the democratic process. The following section, titled "Why Technology Matters," sheds light on the place of technology in news storytelling, social media conversations, and political communication strategies. The closing section, "Pathways Ahead," outlines how the present context can either entrap us in state of embattled passivity or dynamically drive us to reinvent media practices and democratic life.

A number of themes coalesced as our contributors parsed these important issues. We want to conclude this introductory chapter by highlighting
three of them: (1) the benefit of historical hindsight permits us to understand that our experiences are neither entirely new, nor a mere continuity
of what came before; (2) the importance of situating the current moment
within a preexisting crisis in journalism that exacerbates systemic tensions
but also opens up new opportunities; and (3) the emergence of a distinct
digital culture that has been shaped by longstanding social transformations
and has also contributed to major social and political changes.

First, several contributors emphasize the deep historical roots of key tendencies and tensions in the relationships between Trump and the media
that many commentators have treated as mostly novel. These tendencies
and tensions have long occupied a certain place in the media and political
landscape. Areas of continuity range from how current press–government
confrontations draw upon notions of enemy formation that shaped editorial practice during the Cold War to the extent to which the commercial orientation of American journalistic institutions during the twentieth century
prepared the ground for a news and social media system overly focused on
profit and unable to contain the spread of false information, among others.
This shows how contemporary tendencies and tensions have not developed
overnight.

However, a historical sensibility also helps put in perspective significant
discontinuities, such as how particular uses of social media have shifted
to the frontstage of campaign messaging a lot of what used remain in the
backstage of political communication, and how the democratic ideals
embedded in the design of a platform like Twitter were subverted into a tool
well suited for the spread of populist rhetoric. This is because, as Melvin
Kranzberg famously remarked in his first law of technology:[1] "technology
is neither good nor bad; nor is it neutral," thus its use can have divergent—
and sometimes unforeseen—consequences when deployed in different historical eras and sociocultural milieux. The past survives in the present but
does not determine it.

Second, as several of our contributors argue, it appears that the contemporary moment caught journalism rather unprepared, and in the middle
of its own crisis. The social media metrics that favor clickbait headlines,
eyeball economics, and bot-supported storytelling further confused a voca-
tion that was already experiencing an existential conundrum of its own.

Social media afford journalists ambience—an always-on presence. In addition, they offer seemingly direct connection to politicians and the public. But they also imply that journalists are no longer the first ones, nor the only ones, with access to the story. Journalism no longer has a monopoly on deciding what's news—and perhaps, it never really did. As a result, facts are semantically renegotiated to a greater extent than before, and fake news and alternative facts have become part of our everyday vernacular. In order to move forward and, potentially, out of the matrix of misinformation connecting and confusing politicians, the media, and the public, journalism must reconsider its place in society. Social media enable journalists to have a connection to the public that can be employed so as to transform ambience into higher degrees of vigilance and relevance. It is through these heightened states of vigilance and relevance that journalism can rebuild networks of trust; give voice to diverse stories; reconnect publics that feel displaced, misunderstood, and insecure; and restore the fractured sociocultural fabric connecting diverse publics together.

Third, what has been happening to journalism is part of a larger transformation that is critical to the Trump and the media nexus: the emergence of a digital culture that combines high levels of top-down algorithmic power concentrated in the hands of a few corporations with equally high levels of bottom-up insurgency capabilities distributed among a myriad of individual and collective actors. If the former might give the impression that a few technological giants can determine our present—after all, what media corporation in history can boast reaching over a quarter of the population in the planet, like Facebook now does?—the latter should remind us of the vitality of avenues for contingent resistance and change. For instance, a social movement such as Black Lives Matter would not have the same ability to shape the national conversation about racial justice by relying solely on the information infrastructure of the past century. This tension between increasing level and concentration of top-down power on the one hand, and renewed strength and tactics for bottom-up intervention on the other hand, opens up a broad range of novel opportunities for action, from regulatory efforts taking place in Europe to street demonstrations of unparalleled scale and scope like the Women's March that took place in cities around the globe on January 21, 2017. The potential future trajectories of our societies will depend in part on how this emerging digital culture is designed, governed, and appropriated in everyday life.

Taken together, the issues addressed in the chapters that follow invite designers, policy makers, journalists, and citizens to reconsider their ethos toward technology, communication, and civic life. Ethos includes ethics, but also evolves beyond ethics to speak to *a particular sense of purpose* when designing, governing, and using the digital infrastructure that subtends our societies. Thus, the events that culminated with the election of Donald Trump as the 45th President of the United States afford a unique opportunity to reflect on what kind of media ecosystem we want to build as a collective and why. An alternative ethos for journalists, designers, and politicians may be challenging to arrive at, because it requires working cooperatively. This runs contrary to the prevailing news media mentality of securing scoops and not sharing information. It also runs counter to a strong mindset in technology firms, which places emphasis on proprietary rights and locks up access to the algorithmic process that rules automation. And, finally, it defies the personalized nature of electoral processes, which more and more invite voters to choose increasingly simplified personas over complex projects that can only be realized collaboratively. Yet, in light of how high the stakes are, we are hopeful that journalists, technologists, and politicians can find new common ground. If anything, the present moment, lasting or fleeting, calls for a new ethos to take form.

Notes

1. Melvin Kranzberg, "Kranzberg's Laws," *Technology and Culture* 27 (July 1986): 544–560.

I Journalism in Question

2   Why Journalism in the Age of Trump Shouldn't Surprise Us

Barbie Zelizer

In the months since Donald Trump ascended to the US presidency, unexpected obstacles have been held responsible for preventing better coverage. This essay[1] argues, however, that journalism in the age of Trump is far more predictable than assumed, and that its analysts and observers would do well to assess why. It argues that deep mnemonic cues about enemy formation, consolidated and entrenched during the Cold War, have undermined coverage of the Trump phenomenon. Until their influence is more fully exposed, there is little chance of journalism moving beyond these cues.

On Enmity and Politics

Enmity is instrumental in political discourse, used by political leaders to help articulate who they are by defining what they are not. Although the notion of an enemy—he or she who is not us and who threatens us—constitutes what Kenneth Boulding (1959, 130) called "the last stronghold of unsophistication," it nonetheless permeates in times of political uncertainty, disarray, and crisis, promoting behavior that sharpens distinctions between what is and is not seen as appropriate for the time.

A set of representational patterns launches this dynamic. Requiring clarity and simplicity and provoking anxiety over an imminent threat, enmity "turn[s] established values upside down," with "the otherwise forbidden" newly encouraged (Beck 1997, 66). In so doing, enemy formation activates a range of negative behaviors—distrust, polarization, negative stereotyping, black-and-white thinking, aggression, deindividualization, and demonization (Spillmann and Spillmann 1997)—while fostering ethnic intolerance, racism, and political or religious fundamentalism (Beck 1997). Central to enmity are dichotomies, which reduce complex, unmanageable, and often indecipherable realities into binaries between "us" and "them" (Finlay, Holsti, and Fagen 1967). Often taking the shape of mirror images that position the two sides as opposites of each other, dichotomies produce a range of antithetical values—good/bad, right/wrong, moral/immoral—that keep the binary in place. Predictably, when enemy formation becomes the aim of one institutional domain, it is often introduced into other domains cohabiting the same institutional culture. This puts journalism in the direct path of enmity that is driven by political, economic, or other institutional concerns, leaving it subject to external objectives that may contradict its own.

Cold War Enmity, Cold War Journalism

Such was the case during the Cold War. Although not the only period in which journalism had been tasked with reflecting enmity crafted elsewhere, an entrenched set of newsmaking cues emerged during this period that were rarely thereafter questioned. In large part, this had to do with journalism's centrality in driving the Cold War, whose prosecution depended on journalism's buy-in.

The Cold War was driven by a deep mindset sustained over nearly five decades of international conflict between the US and the USSR and intensified domestically via McCarthyism. More an idea than a war, it took shape via populist impulses that were uniform, internally consistent, and steadfast in nature. As its ideological contours offered Americans unambiguous cues about what made an enemy, how one recognized its presence, and how one minimized the threat it brought, a very particular kind of journalism evolved in the war's early years, much of it taken up with establishing and disseminating enmity (Zelizer n.d.). That enmity cast the war's central antagonists—the US and the USSR—as polarized, mirrored opposites of each other and propelled a hunt for the enemy within US boundaries. In this mindset, neutrality disappeared.

Unusual here—and a direct precursor to current circumstances—was journalism's instrumentality. With no battles, physical destruction, or corpses on its main front, the Cold War needed instructional, exhortative, propagandistic, and pedagogic efforts to instill and maintain the necessary mindset of war. It was thus up to actors on the mediated landscape to intensify the psychic distance between a democratic US and a communist USSR so that everyone remembered the conflict at hand.

Echoing journalism's predilection for clear, dramatic, and simple formations of conflict, the larger ideological environment of the time easily displayed what Hofstadter (1964, 3–4) later called "heated exaggeration, suspiciousness, and conspiratorial fantasy." The need to emphasize the conflict between "absolute good" and "absolute evil" remained high:

What is necessary is not compromise but the will to fight things to a finish. Since the enemy is thought of as totally evil and totally unappeasable, he must be totally eliminated. (Hofstadter 1964, 82)

Although ideological stridency raised different kinds of problems across institutional culture writ large, it was particularly problematic for journalists, who were torn between two dissonant goals—maintaining independence or servicing an ideological anticommunist environment.

The latter goal took precedence over the former. As many journalists became Cold War navigators—relying, in one view, "less on facts" and "more on moral assumptions about how the world was to operate" (Adler 1991, 43)—they readily sustained the binary between "us" and "them," strengthening rhetoric about US democracy and fostering a negative image of the Russians and communism. Political pressures—tendered via red-line edits on news copy, subtle censorship, loyalty oaths, dismissal, and special favors in exchange for sympathetic coverage—reminded journalists to mind their perspectives carefully (Liebovich 1988); economic trends toward corporatism and consumer capitalism made bucking the line more difficult (Hixson 1996); and television's technological predilection for briefer and more formulaic relays readily cohered with Cold War aims (Bernhard 1999), to say nothing of a public largely indifferent to the news. It thus became easier for journalists to downplay the problematic aspects of current events and overstate those consonant with Cold War enmity.

But none of this would have succeeded had Cold War enmity not rested on longstanding journalistic conventions and practices. The embrace of enmity firstly required deference and moderation, which helped turn journalists into eager spokespeople for those in power. Self-censorship and currying favor happened regularly, as when *Look* magazine featured a cover story titled "How to Spot a Communist" (Cheme 1947). As the trade journal *Editor and Publisher* proclaimed in 1948, "Americans are Americans first and newspapermen second" ("Security Problem" 1948, 36).

Second, enmity relied on cronyism, close ties between officials and journalists that ensured officialdom would remain the preferred information source. "If McCarthy said it," one reporter later remembered, "we wrote it" (cited in Broder 1987, 138). Not only did this uphold proven patterns for accommodating elite sources of authority (Gans 1979), but it also facilitated intricate and sometimes incestuous sharing of personnel, resources, and information across news organizations and government agencies like Voice of America or Radio Free Europe, setting boundaries around what was permissible and appropriate to say.

Third, enmity invited understatement, euphemism, and false equivalences that obscured clear articulation. Many reporters showed timidity about the topics broached and provided qualified observations of what they thought they saw, sorely misreading what was happening: Slow to recognize McCarthy's impact, journalists at first treated him like a joke, dismissing him with labels like "Senator McThing" (Markel 1953, 26). As late as 1955, the American Society of Newspaper Editors voted McCarthy one of the most overplayed stories of the preceding year ("Second-Guessing" 1955, 1).

Finally, enmity rode on accommodating objectivity, neutrality, impartiality, and balance. Broadcaster Eric Sevareid dismissed his colleagues for "our flat, one-dimensional handling of the news" (cited in Broder 1987, 138), while another reporter said journalists had been no more than "recording devices" for officials (cited in Broder 1987, 138). Believing that a valueless perspective and reporting from nowhere would offset political interference, journalists maintained the illusion that they were acting independently. The tools they relied on, however, tied their hands.

What all of this meant was that Cold War mindedness succeeded in driving journalism for two related reasons. First, it rested upon already existent predilections among journalists, securing their widespread conformity by playing to long-held occupational and professional mores and conventions. Simultaneously, it made journalism central in the entrenchment of its ideological contours, where journalists became irreplaceable navigators of Cold War enmity. Although holding journalists captive to these circumstances undermined autonomous newsmaking, it made simplified and polarized enmity a necessary part of their coverage.

How Cold War Enmity Has Reemerged with Trump

Today's journalism builds upon Cold War enmity with a remarkable degree of consonance. In a way similar to other deep mnemonic structures, Cold War cues inhabit a silent backdrop for journalists facing the unfamiliar circumstances prompted by Trump.

In part, this is because enemy formation has itself been central to Trump's rise. Mobilizing fear, anger, frustration, and resentment like most populist leaders to divide the public into in-groups and out-groups (Wodak 2015), his rhetoric insists upon the demonization and necessary elimination of an external other. Thus, much about longstanding extreme versions of us versus them motivates today's circumstances: unexpected exits from conventional political alliances, hate speech as it takes on local flavor across multiple locations, entrenched divides between political formations. In the words of the *New Yorker*, "outsiders are in, insiders are out" (Lepore 2016, para. 13).

In part, too, economic pressures and surrounding institutional structures continue to reward outrageous reports and cut back support for more nuanced and time-consuming coverage of conflict. With negative, simple, provocative, and emotional events driving the news and its ratings, Trump's indignation and drama render him newsworthy, underscored by his media savvy. Coming from years of reality TV, tabloid coverage, and gossip shows, he repeatedly turns journalistic activity into evidence of his own victimization, even when he contradicts himself. In Rosen's (2016) terms, the consequent asymmetry that characterizes contemporary politics works to mute journalism. The uneven delegitimation of one political side by the other—normally recognized as polarization—cuts to the heart of journalists' dependence on balance as the key to political coverage, making it irrelevant when the parties are not symmetrically positioned. The resulting asymmetry thus "fries the circuitry of the mainstream press."

But it is wrong to blame only media economics, Trump's rhetoric and strategizing, or the structural relationship between politics and journalism for journalism's poor performance. For the core of the problem lies with journalism itself. How journalists of the Cold War era dealt with enemy formation—accepting it as dogma, sidestepping and underestimating its impact, pursuing a value-free ground that abdicated journalistic responsibility for addressing events with nuance and thoughtfulness even as US public life crumbled—offers a familiar precedent for covering the anger, resentment, and polarization that accompany Trump, making it easy for journalists to import enmity into coverage that might have been reported differently.

This has happened in three ways. First, journalism's hearty embrace of Cold War tools has been ongoing. The conventions that allowed Cold War enmity to flourish—moderation, deference, cronyism, euphemism, understatement, false equivalences, neutrality, impartiality, balance, and objectivity—figure largely in coverage of the Trump phenomenon. This has stretched from Trump's presidential campaign—when Fox News's Megyn Kelly and NBC's Matt Lauer soft-pedaled Trump's flaws, and then-President Obama accused the media of creating false equivalences between Trump and Clinton ("Obama Critiques Media" 2016)—to the still-resonant reluctance to call Trump's lies by name, preferring instead to label them "controversies" (Pompeo 2017). It lurks in journalistic deference and moderation, which encourages journalists to sidestep the dangers attached to Trump's assault on widely-shared US norms of the presidency, press, and legitimate elections and to stay silent in face of his rogue behavior—intolerance, name-calling, bullying, disregard for conflicts of interest, extremism, and self-aggrandizement. Much like these conventions failed journalists in explaining the Cold War, they leave contemporary journalists unable to fully contextualize, evaluate, or criticize Trump, showing that "a balanced treatment of an imbalanced phenomenon distorts reality" (Mann and Ornstein 2016). Largely because journalists are too entrenched in their own compliance with Cold War enmity, the practices it spawned, and the structures to which it responded, they repeatedly fall short.

Second, the failure of journalists to go beyond enmity in their coverage of the so-called "flyover zones" means that, just like during the Cold War, they are unable to either serve or reflect the US public writ large. Journalists' embrace of dichotomous black-and-white thinking prevents them from recognizing that the public—no longer as uniform as journalistic conventions tend to assume—differs from that which has conventionally been addressed by the news. In Glenn Greenwald's (2016, para. 3) view, journalists—reflecting "an agreement that Trump was this grave evil"—acted like elites "telling each other how smart they [are]," so that Trump supporters weren't really ever heard from … they were just talked about in contemptuous tones … sort of looked at like zoo animals, like things you dissect and condemn (para. 4).

The neglect in this regard has been significant, for in not listening across the divide, journalists treat class as a disruption rather than a fundamental flaw in their thinking. Buttressed by a feedback loop that is closed to others, journalists' reluctance to stretch beyond people like themselves, again to quote Greenwald, is legitimated by the sentiments of opinion-making elites that are "cloistered," "incestuous," and "far removed from the public" (2016, para. 5, line 5). As journalists instead remain caught by enmity's grasp, populism passes them by.

Third, journalists' inability to see that they are part of the problem makes them unable to recognize the ramifications of a changing institutional culture that undermines journalism's authority. Journalism exists as an integral part of a larger institutional culture, where its deep ties with politics, economics, the law, education, security, religion, and the military are profoundly intertwined with how the news works. That culture includes patterns of inter-institutional dependency, entrenched power sharing, corruption, concentrated or government ownership, a gravitation toward impunity, self censorship, and a resistance to change.

It stands to reason, then, that the populism that helped bring Trump to power comes with its own novel descriptors. As it has blurred longstanding distinctions between left and right, liberal and conservative, young and old, urban and rural, the enmity it spawns against Washington insiders, global interventionists, and immigrants keeps populism afloat. This challenges much of what has been a given in US politics—a symmetrical two-party system; elites positioned authoritatively across central institutions; a largely silent majority—and rattles many assumptions related to coverage. These include acting as if difference is inevitably settled by compromise; as if facts, truth, and evidence are equally revered by all players in the game; as if political culture necessarily works through symmetry; and as if journalists are not part of the political systems they cover. Because politics and the news inhabit the same institutional culture, journalism has little choice but to accommodate such change, but US journalists do not yet show their recognition of its inevitability.

Thus, journalistic judgment remains at fault here just it was during the Cold War. With many journalists continuing to act in ways that should have been retired long ago, they reveal how out of touch are many of their assumptions about covering Trump. Conditions thought necessary for journalists to do their job in more conventional ways are no longer applicable today. Journalism has been here before, but it again fails to notice.

Conclusion: Why Journalism in the Age of Trump Shouldn't Surprise Us

This essay has addressed how one aspect of the Cold War mindset—that of enemy formation—undermined US journalistic coverage of the Trump phenomenon. Journalists not only reproduced the conformity and homogeneity of the Cold War era but also oriented to its longstanding—and now outdated—cues of practice. This renders them powerless to offset the problematic coverage of Trump that has ensued. With such mnemonic cues deeply and uncritically entrenched, the past silently undergirds the conventions through which the present takes on journalistic form.

Populist passion and the strident, anti-establishment enmity it rides on erupt when something is not quite right with democratic function. When that is further unsettled by something being not quite right with journalistic function either, it is time to think creatively about journalism's reformulation. Journalism in the age of Trump should not surprise us. But imagining journalism differently can do no less than jumpstart our expectations.

Notes

1. Parts of this essay appear in N. Carpentier and V. Dudaki (eds.), Special Issue of *Communicazioni Sociali* on "Power, Contingency and Socio-Political Struggle," 2017. It was written while the author was the Helsingin Sanomat Foundation Fellow at the Helsinki Collegium for Advanced Studies.

3   Alternative Facts: Donald Trump and the Emergence of a New U.S. Media Regime

Michael X. Delli Carpini

On January 21, 2017, White House Press Secretary Sean Spicer held his first official briefing, accusing the media of deliberately underestimating the size of Donald Trump's inauguration crowd, and stating that it was "the largest audience to ever witness an inauguration—period." Two days later Trump's campaign strategist, Kellyanne Conway, defended Spicer's by-then disproven comments on NBC's *Meet the Press*, explaining that he was simply giving "alternative facts" to those being presented in the press.

The inauguration "controversy" was one of a blizzard of such surreal moments characterizing the Trump campaign and his first 100 days in office. The online news site Politico estimated that Trump averaged as much as one mischaracterization, exaggeration, or outright falsehood for every three to five minutes of speaking during the campaign. The fact-checking organization, PolitiFact, judged nearly 70 percent of verifiable Trump statements made between February 2011 and April 2017 as mostly false, false, or outright lies. And in a February 2017 *Los Angeles Times* interview, presidential scholar George Edwards concluded that Trump "tells more untruths than any president in American history." The assault on facts also went well beyond Trump and his administration. For example a BuzzFeed analysis found that the top 20 fake election news stories emanating from hoax sites and hyperpartisan blogs generated more engagement on Facebook (as measured by shares, reactions, and comments) than the top 20 election stories produced by 19 major news outlets combined, including the *New York Times*, *Washington Post*, Huffington Post, and NBC News.

It would be easy to see the current moment as an aberration. Certainly, there is much that is irreproducible about Donald Trump. And a number of factors that collectively formed a "perfect storm"—a Republican Party in disarray; an overconfident, disliked, and female Democratic opponent;

a news media that took Trump "literally but not seriously"; WikiLeaks and Russian interference in the campaign process; historic lows in public trust of both politicians and the news media; etc.—might suggest a low probability of something similar happening again. Indeed, had Clinton received just a few thousand more strategically located votes, Trump would have lost the general election, and the national conversation would likely be very different.

But this would be a mistake. Rather than an exception, "Trumpism" is a culmination of trends that have been occurring for several decades. What we are witnessing is nothing short of a fundamental shift in the relationships between journalism, politics, and democracy.

In our 2011 book, *After Broadcast News: Media Regimes, Democracy, and the New Information Environment*, Bruce Williams and I argued that political, economic, cultural, and technological changes in the United States were fundamentally altering the media environment, with significant implications for the practice of politics. Such periods of disruption, in which old rules, norms, institutions, and expectations regarding the relationships between the media, political elites, and citizens no longer apply, but new ones have yet to develop, have occurred before—for example, between the partisan and penny presses in the early nineteenth century, between the penny press and the age of realism in the mid-nineteenth century, between realism and the progressive era in the decades straddling the start of the twentieth century, and between the progressive era and the era of broadcast news in the early to mid-twentieth century.

In each of these prior transitions, a new set of rules, norms, institutions, and expectations eventually became normalized, resulting in what we called a new "media regime." In the latter half of the twentieth century, this included accepting the naturalness of a relatively centralized media system that distinguished "news" from "entertainment," "mass-mediated" from "interpersonal" communication, information "producers" from information "consumers," and—most central to this essay—"facts" from "opinions" and "beliefs." It also reified professional journalists as the gatekeepers of the public agenda, elites as the central agents of politics, and—except for the periodic act of voting—citizens as passive consumers of news and politics.

If this media regime and the set of relationships it has supported is breaking down, what might a new, twenty-first-century regime look like?

At the time that we researched our book, this was unclear, though its basic contours were becoming evident: a collapsing of the prior regime's presumed and enforced distinctions between news and entertainment, mass-mediated and interpersonal communication, information producers and consumers, and facts, opinions, and beliefs. In turn this was creating a political landscape that is both "multiaxial" (i.e., in which the gatekeeping role of professional journalists and their control of the public agenda is ceded to multiple, shifting, and often previously invisible, fringe, and/or less powerful actors) and "hyperreal" (i.e., in which the mediated representation of reality becomes more important to individual and collective political deliberation, opinions, beliefs, and behaviors than the facts underlying them).

The impact of these changes on the relationships between the media, political elites, and citizens has been happening gradually but inexorably for decades. Consider the conduct of national campaigns and elections. Evidence of small but significant ruptures in traditional mid-to-late twentieth-century campaign techniques emerged as early as the 1980s, when the Reagan campaign used satellite technology and prepackaged "video news releases" to bypass the national press and target local (and presumably less aggressive) journalists and media outlets. Other signs of change included Ross Perot's appearances on the cable talk show *Larry King Live* to jump start his third-party candidacy, and Bill Clinton's appearances on *The Arsenio Hall Show* (think sunglasses and saxophone) and *MTV* (think boxers or briefs), all in 1992; John McCain's unprecedented use of Internet fundraising in 2000; Howard Dean's insurgency campaign fueled by his (and Joe Trippi's) creative use of the Internet to motivate and mobilize young supporters in 2004; and the implosion of Senator George Allen's reelection bid (and presidential aspirations) in 2006, the result of a cell phone video that went viral (think "macaca moment").

By 2008 and 2012, the use of digital, social, and nontraditional media and technology to announce one's candidacy, fundraise, reach and engage supporters, and get out the vote had become firmly entrenched as an integral part of campaigning, more effectively by Democrats than Republicans (Kreiss 2012). But despite some prominent examples (e.g., *Saturday Night Live*'s parodies of Sarah Palin; *The Daily Show*'s award-winning election coverage; *The Colbert Report*'s satirical civic lessons on campaign finance; the viral releases of problematic comments by Mitt Romney and Barack

Obama; even Obama's ability to overtake frontrunner Hilary Clinton in 2008), the impact of this reconstituted information environment remained largely channeled within the traditional media and political parties, often in informal partnership with tech-savvy people "borrowed" from digital media companies (Kreiss 2016).

The 2016 presidential race was a more radical departure from the recent past. The success of Donald Trump's insurgent campaign would be unthinkable in the campaign structure of the mid-to-late twentieth century. To be sure, the new information environment did not *cause* his success—there were real social, economic, political, and cultural issues underlying his unexpected victory. But most of these issues have existed in some form since the nation's founding, and none were unique to this election. What *was* unique was the ability of a 70-year-old real estate developer turned reality television celebrity to exploit the contemporary information environment in ways that were unprecedented, and done outside—and against the concerted efforts of—the traditional institutions of national media and politics.

Consider the Trump campaign (and presidency thus far) in light of the first three core qualities characterizing this emerging information environment. His campaign shattered the already weakening distinction between news and entertainment, with primaries resembling nothing so much as a reality television show, debates that drew "huge" audiences in large part for the spectacle, and a national news media that provided Trump with unprecedented coverage in large part because of his celebrity status and entertainment value. His use of Twitter to bypass and/or influence traditional gatekeepers and speak directly to, motivate, and mobilize his followers epitomizes the blurring of interpersonal and mass communication. And the amplification and diffusion of his message through online social networks made his followers both consumers and producers of political information and discourse.

But it is the fourth core quality that, in combination with the prior three, is most problematic in our current moment. While disputes over the lines between facts, opinions, and beliefs have always existed, Trump took has taken this to a new level, demonstrating that a public figure can make statements that are verifiably false, be called out on these misstatements, and pay (to date at least) no political price for them. This is possible because of the multiaxiality and hyperreality of the current information environment—characteristics that Trump successfully *exploited* but that were also already in place *before* he began his run for the White House. Our multiaxial environment creates conditions in which we are always just one click of a mouse or remote control away from information that contradicts what we just heard, read, or saw. This makes it easier for ideologically committed citizens to hold fast to their prior beliefs regardless of the facts; for less politically engaged citizens to be uncertain, dazed, and confused; and for political elites to exploit this situation. In turn, our hyperreal environment creates the conditions in which the competing narratives emerging from this combination of beliefs, opinions, and alternative facts—rather than the material conditions underlying them—become the basis of political discourse and action. The result is a mediated politics resembling nothing so much as Kabuki theater.

In making this argument it is important to emphasize that there is nothing in the emerging media regime of the early twenty-first century that necessitates its political dominance by any one type of movement or person, or that necessitates a hyperreality that is uncoupled from facts. The same conditions that led to the emergence of Donald Trump's brand of conservative populism facilitated the presidential campaigns of Barack Obama and Bernie Sanders; the Occupy Wall Street and Black Lives Matter movements; the growing and more impactful role of citizen journalists as well as more "random acts of journalism"; the use of computational science methods, large data sets, and visualization technologies to create new forms of investigative journalism; improvements in government services through the use of more interactive and responsive websites; and experiments in crowdsourcing that allow citizens to discuss and sometimes even develop public policy. The current media environment has rightfully been implicated in the spreading of "fake news" and "alternative facts," but also in efforts to counter them; in growing concerns about the loss of privacy, but also in the ability to provide citizens with more targeted, useful, and useable information precisely because of this loss; in the creation of echo chambers in which like-minded people talk only to themselves, but also in the ability of people to engage each other across temporal, geographic, political, and cultural boundaries. Indeed, within minutes of newly elected President Trump's signing an executive order effectively banning Muslims from seven nations from entering the United States, individuals and groups opposed to this policy took advantage of the same conditions that elected Trump to organize large and spontaneous demonstrations at airports and in cities around the globe.

It is also important not to romanticize the past; to conclude that if only we could return to the days of three national nightly news broadcasts and a daily newspaper we would be better off. There was much in the highly centralized, corporate-dominated, and citizen-as-passive-consumer media regime (and resulting politics) of the latter half of the twentieth century that was very problematic. Indeed, one of the major effects of the current environment has been to reveal shortcomings in the prior media regime, such as the essentially contestable nature of what often passed for facts; the important and often positive role that has always been played in public discourse by emotion, popular culture, narrative, beliefs, and even myths; and the way in which facts, even when broadly agreed upon, can be used selectively to support or counter particular viewpoints. Consider Kellyanne Conway's (admittedly misleading) definition of "alternative facts" as "additional facts and alternative information." In a March 2017 *New York* magazine interview she elaborated, adding "Two plus two is four. Three plus one is four. Partly cloudy, partly sunny. Glass half full, glass half empty. Those are alternative facts." While her *actual* use of the term was in defense of something much closer to "two plus two is six," she is right that facts can be used and interpreted selectively, and that it is important to have an information environment that brings diverse, but relevant and supportable, facts to the table.

Perhaps most profoundly, the current environment forces us to seriously consider what "a fact" is and what relationship it has to "the truth." As Scott Keeter and I wrote over two decades ago in our book, *What Americans Know about Politics and Why It Matters*:

Establishing something as a fact is an admittedly problematic enterprise. One cannot state as a fact why certain people are poor and others are not. One cannot state as a fact how many people are poor in America. One cannot even state as a fact what it means to be poor. One can say, however, with reasonable assurance how the federal government defines poverty, what percentage of the American public currently lives below the federally defined poverty line, and whether that percentage has increased or decreased over the past four years. The reduction of weighty issues like poverty to clinical facts about official statistics leads many to argue that the enterprise is trivializing.

But this does not mean that facts do not matter. As we went on to say:

If the debate were to end there, we would agree. But our point is that facts prevent rather than lead to the trivializing of public discourse. Such facts as the percentage of the American public living below the poverty line, how the line is determined, and how the percentage has changed over time provide a foundation for deliberation about larger issues. They prevent debates from becoming disconnected from the material conditions they attempt to address. They allow individuals and groups with widely varied experiences and philosophies to have some common basis of comparison—some common language with which to clarify differences, identify points of agreement, and establish criteria for evaluation. They tether public discourse to objective conditions while allowing for debates over what objectivity means.

The multiaxiality and hyperreality of the media regime in which we now live provides unprecedented opportunities for such grounded deliberation, even as they provide equally unprecedented opportunities to ignore or fabricate facts. To facilitate productive conversations across sociocultural and political divides, or to retreat into ideological bubbles. To find safe spaces to resist authoritarianism of various social, cultural, and political stripes, or to create the conditions that lead to it. To develop mediated narratives and myths that while not "factual" in the narrow sense are "truthful," or to develop narratives and myths that are neither. Which path we ultimately choose is *the* question of our time, and nothing short of democracy is at stake.

4   Trump and the Great Disruption in Public Communication

Silvio Waisbord, Tina Tucker, and Zoey Lichtenheld

The victory of Donald Trump in the 2016 presidential election reflects a troubling combination of rising trends in political communication in the United States, namely, the mainstreaming of conspiracy theories and incivility in public discourse, and the commercial priorities of the news media. Although these developments have a long tradition in US public communication, they have gained new relevance amid recent changes in news production and consumption. Unprecedented changes driven by digital technologies, economics, and social habits have flattened the previous hierarchies within the news ecology. This shift has thrown off legacy news organizations from their former powerful position atop the public flow of news and information, pushed conspiracy theories into the fore of US politics, and unleashed uncivil forms of expression in traditional and digital media.

These developments are worrisome because they stand in opposition to central principles of democratic communication—reason, facticity, and civility. The collapse of news gatekeeping swings the doors open for fact-free discourse. Conspiracy theories legitimize arguments supported by personal and collective convictions more than by clear and demonstrable facts. Uncivil expression is antithetical to the kind of civil, reasoned, and tolerant discourse necessary for debating different viewpoints and developing shared agreements in a society with enormous diversity. Runaway commercialism prioritizes sellable content regardless of its public virtues or contributions to democratic discourse.

To be clear, our argument is not that Trump's successful run was a logical, expected outcome of recent trends in political communication. The Trump victory cannot be explained by a single reason. Several factors played important roles, including shifts in public opinion, campaign strategies and dynamics, voter suppression, and Trump's stronger performance than previous Republican presidential candidates in key swing states. Rather, we argue that Trump's victory has an "elective affinity" with the great disruption in contemporary public communication that facilitated the spread of fact-free arguments and uncivil discourse.

The Complexities of News Gatekeeping

The gradual collapse of traditional news gatekeeping has been one of the most remarkable, seismic developments in contemporary US political communication. The digital revolution has shaken up the quasi-monopolistic position the press held in large-scale production and dissemination of news, information, and opinion for the past two centuries. Today, legacy journalism gatekeeping coexists with multiple levels of news decision-making by different publics and social media companies (Vos and Heinderyckx 2015).

The Internet has fundamentally transformed news flows. Citizens are engaged in multiple gatekeeping roles as news consumers, messengers, modifiers, and producers. They curate, comment, produce, and (re)distribute news and information. No longer do they depend on mainstream channels for news, but instead, they have easy access to an unprecedented wealth of information on the Internet. The notion of "news audiences" passively digesting content solely determined by journalistic choices does not capture the multiple ways in which news stories are shaped and framed by the chaotic digital landscape.

Also, social media platforms have become important gatekeepers as their business calculations affect news choices. Although many have speculated on the specific interests prioritized by corporations, most notably in the cases of Facebook and Twitter, it is clear that news feeds are slanted toward constant personalization of news content based on the preferences and options of users and contacts. What type of content dominates in such multilayered, dynamic news landscapes with plenty of gatekeeping mechanisms remains a subject of debate.

The erosion of the old hierarchical gatekeeping order grounded on the news power of elites and legacy newsrooms has mixed consequences for democratic communication. Just as it has empowered citizens' voices, it has also facilitated the expression and accessibility to information and opinion unconcerned with facts and truth-telling. Just as it has leveled discursive opportunities, it has also flattened distinctions in terms of credibility, trust, and quality. Just as the disaggregation of gatekeeping allows for diverse forms of information, it also deepens the difficulties for bringing different publics together.

One troubling consequence of multilayered gatekeeping is the fragmentation of news publics into "echo chambers" of relatively homogeneous partisan opinion. Although the extent of such communication chambers remains a subject of discussion, it is reasonable to suggest that the conformation of news bubbles fosters both limited exposure to counter-attitudinal information and the reinforcement of partisan beliefs (Stroud 2011). Here the consolidation of conservative "echo chambers" integrated by cable news, talk radio, digital news sites, and bloggers is crucial for explaining Trump's rise and victory. Not only did this consolidation till the ideological ground for several themes in narratives promoted by the Trump campaign, including right-wing hostility toward the mainstream news media (Arceneaux, Johnson, and Murphy 2012), it also offered political novice Trump, the real estate magnate and reality television star, a direct link to the Republican base.

The Mainstreaming of Conspiracy Theory

Changes in news gatekeeping have brought fact-free and conspiracy-driven discourse into the mainstream. For years, partisan echo chambers have been breeding grounds for conspiracy theories, but the 2016 election saw lies and falsehoods receive unprecedented attention from both mainstream and niche circles of the political information environment. The conspiracies wielded by Trump himself not only were borne out of this environment, but also were able to spread rapidly through its interconnected structure.

To be sure, conspiracy talk is not a digital-era phenomenon (see Zelizer, this volume). In 1964, historian Richard Hofstadter (1964) observed the "paranoid spokesman" who energized political movements by wielding conspiracies that framed social conflict in apocalyptic terms and cast the enemy as amoral super-villains intent on perverting the course of history. The power of conspiracies to play on deeply held beliefs, fears, and prejudices abides across time. But the contemporary political and media environment has given new impetus and scale to conspiracies. Today, the paranoid spokesman finds his home in right-wing channels—the likes of Alex Jones, Rush Limbaugh, and Mark Levin, all of whom have made lucrative careers out of promoting conspiracies to a polarized, hostile electorate primed to distrust elites and media. During the 2016 election, their conspiracy talk managed to journey from right-wing fringes to prime time news (Benkler et al. 2017).

This was aided, in part, by Trump himself, who regularly fused conspiracies he encountered in the conservative media into his own rhetoric. Conspiracy rhetoric has been a central feature of Trump's political career since it began. The virality of his 2011 claims that President Barack Obama was not a natural-born US citizen continue to reflect in opinion polls among the Republican base (Pasek et al. 2015). Moreover, these claims set the tone for his 2016 presidential run, in which he managed to drive the news cycle with a series of loosely interlocking conspiracies built on themes that those in power have rigged the political, economic, and media systems against the common man and against Donald Trump. His go-to conspiracies ranged from claims that the US government freely allowed killers and rapists from Mexico entry across the border to claims that widespread voter fraud explained his loss of the popular vote. Often, his conspiracies were vague. "There's something going on," he said on four different occasions about the Obama administration's relationship with ISIS. The lack of details sowed seeds of doubt and allowed voters to project their own narratives onto his statements (Uscinski 2016). Furthermore, his targets—first Obama, then his Republican opponents, then Hillary Clinton—struggled to shake off the conspiracies wielded against them. Not only were the conspiracies "sticky" in far-right circles and beyond, but also attempts to counter them resulted in further exposure and impetus for the conspiracy itself (Nyhan and Reifler 2010).

Conspiracy theories fuel distrust and anger. Through their regular use, Trump helped create a political world in which "truth" can be muddied and "alternative facts" are valid. Trump's legitimization of misinformation has brought conspiracy talk out of the fringes into mainstream discourse, aided by news media incentivized to privilege talk that is norm-breaking and attack-driven.

The Mainstreaming of Political Incivility

Changes in news gatekeeping have also privileged incivility in public discourse. Just like conspiracy theories, it is misguided to think that incivility is a completely new development in US public communication. Yet, the flattening of news flows has pushed different types of discourse, including uncivil expression, into the public sphere.

Scholars have not yet reached consensus on the definition of incivility, but it can be broadly understood as a vicious form of attack that resorts to name-calling and character attacks (Brooks and Geer 2007). Findings from research on the impact of uncivil messages are varied and inconclusive but suggest that incivility can have a mobilizing effect on the electorate (Brooks and Geer 2007), solidify existing attitudes (Borah 2014) and capture audiences' interest while causing them to further distrust politics (Mutz and Reeves 2005). While incivility is engaging, it may decrease trust in the political system, increase polarization, and increase close-mindedness.

Outrage, a particularly extreme type of incivility, privileged Trump's rhetoric over other candidates' in the media. An outrage is a unique form of incivility that is used to provoke an emotional response from the audience (Sobieraj and Berry 2011). Outrage discourse is more frequently used by conservatives and in conservative blogs, talk radio, and cable news shows than in their liberal counterparts. Outrage transfers particularly well into cable news shows which are dominated by outrage media—a relatively new political opinion media genre that is growing increasingly popular and is defined by its incivility toward the opposition (Berry and Sobieraj 2014).

While the Internet has created spaces for distant communities to connect, it has also created spaces where people anonymously harass one another and political discussions devolve into name-calling. The architecture of social media platforms like Twitter allows incivility to flourish. Twitter privileges discourse that is short and uncomplicated, allows users to publish impulsively, and instantaneously spreads messages (Ott 2017).

These qualities made Twitter the perfect platform for Trump's signature blunt and combative communication style. Trump's uncivil discourse spread rapidly online and through the media during the 2016 presidential election. Using his personal Twitter account, Trump made aggressive attacks against his political opponents and the news media during the 2016 presidential election and primarily communicated with outrage. Trump communicated outrage about everything from "dangerous" Mexicans immigrating to the United States to jobs being "outsourced" to China to the way he was "unfairly" treated by the mainstream media and his opponent, Hillary Clinton. For example, when Hillary Clinton brought up Trump's mistreatment of Alicia Machado, a former Miss Universe, Trump (2016) tweeted: "Did Crooked Hillary help disgusting (check out sex tape and past) Alicia M[achado] become a U.S. citizen so she could use her in the debate?" In moments, Trump's tweet spread through Twitter, other social media channels, and news websites, triggering reaction and discussion. The mainstream media quickly latched on to Trump's tweet and debunked his accusations against Machado, but ended up discussing Trump's Twitter style instead of focusing on other issues relevant to the election—a not-unusual dynamic that showed the media magnetism of his tweets. Even when the public discussion did not reflect positively on Trump, he was able to use Twitter to keep the media's focus on him during the election. Trump's uncivil discourse echoes similar forms of expression in a vast range of digital platforms.

The Mainstream Media and Trump

It would be misguided to attribute Trump's victory only to the affinity between his message and conspiracy theories and incivility. The mainstream media also played a critical role by elevating candidate Trump above the crowded pack of candidates during the Republican primary. A *New York Times* article estimated that Trump received almost two billion dollars of free airtime during the primary (Confessore and Yourish 2016). By the end of the national election campaign, media tracking companies calculated that Trump had benefitted from almost five billion dollars of free media time. Trump's presence boosted television ratings, especially for cable news companies that reported increased ratings and profits. CBS CEO Leslie Moonves's candid assertion "It may not be good for America, but it's damn good for CBS" encapsulated the belief that Trump's antidemocratic discourse and the commercial goals of media companies are perfectly compatible. In response to criticisms about excessive media attention on Trump, CNN Worldwide president and former reality show producer Jeff

Zucker asserted that "we have all benefited" and cited the astronomical revenues of cable news in 2016.

Such statements became paradigmatic of the odd fellowship between a candidate who tapped on old conservative sentiments against "the media" and the profit objectives of mainstream news. The irony couldn't be more evident: the same news organizations long condemned by conservatives as "the liberal media" drew high ratings and high revenues from covering Trump's constant barrage of declarations, no matter how absurd or vicious. Trump's demagogic, sensationalist, norm-breaking style of campaigning proved to be tremendously appealing for the news media. His outrageous, exaggerated, distorted, baleful declarations in campaign rallies and on Twitter were perfect bait for media organizations primarily concerned with entertainment and profits.

By doing so, mainstream news not only offered highly visible mass platforms to a political novice with name recognition; they also legitimized the kind of intolerant, fact-free discourse traditionally contained within certain quarters of the right-wing mediasphere. Certainly, segments of the mainstream commentariat were aghast at the tenor of Trump's discourse—his mistaken assertions, mean-spirited attacks against various groups, and factless claims. Observers legitimately worried about the implications of his distinctive combustible discourse in the tinderbox of US politics. Some news media promptly fact-checked Trump's wild assertions. Yet candidate Trump proved to be irresistible for media organizations obsessed with traffic and profits. Runaway commercialism trumped other considerations. Media corporations got ratings and digital traffic while giving Trump a daily platform to spew factless and uncivil statements.

Trump and a New Communication Environment

As tempting as it might be, it would be too simplistic to call Trump the "great disrupter" of US news and politics. No doubt, candidate Trump represented a different brand of mediated politics. His ascendancy, however, reflects the combination of longstanding media commercialism with trends that reflect "the great disruption" in public communication in recent years (see Pickard, this volume). Trump's victory benefited from the continuous significance of legacy commercial news, new forms of news gatekeeping, and the upsurge of longstanding forms of public discourse that are emblematic of "post-truth" politics and partisan hostility. It signals the consolidation of "hyperpartisan publics" uninterested in (and perhaps relatively immune to) fact-based discourse. It endorses uncivil communication best personified by Trump himself with his penchant for name-calling opponents and stigmatizing minorities. It reflects the crisis of news authority, as expressed by abysmally low trust in the media particularly among Republican voters.

Equally troubling, the coming to power of Trump reflects the crisis of central conditions of the liberal-democratic model of public communication: the existence of the communication commons to negotiate through civil and reasoned dialogue multiple forms of difference in pluralist, multicultural democracies. Like his most fervent supporters, Trump represents the ascendancy of antidemocratic trends in public communication, namely the embrace of factually incorrect beliefs, incivility, and intolerance.

Communication researchers should not simply criticize these trends. Trump's election and his presidency force us to rethink the feasibility of facts, reason, and civility as conditions for democratic discourse in the new ecology of public communication. Understanding how these conditions are possible when large segments of the public and the media, including President Trump, flatly reject them is a challenge that awaits further analysis. Upholding certain principles as necessary, constitutive of democratic communication, such as fact-grounded conversation, the public use of reason, and the practice of civil discourse, demands engaging with the study of opportunities and actions. It should not be limited to just normative aspirations, as desirable as they might be, if they are not seriously considered in contexts of practice, especially when real-world dynamics are painfully distant from the horizons of democratic discourse.

5 Empirical Failures: Data Journalism, Cultural Identity, and the Trump Campaign

C. W. Anderson

The argument of this chapter is straightforward. During the 2016 American presidential election, the elite journalism practiced at top-tier media outlets was better than it has ever been—the most nuanced, accurate, and fact-oriented journalism of the modern media age. This journalism, however, mattered less to the conduct of American politics than ever before, for reasons only partly attributable to structural transformations in the ecosystem of news production or audience "filter bubbles." The reasons are also partly cultural: the 2016 election witnessed the clash of a journalistic tribe increasingly driven by commitments to facticity and a nuanced form of objectivity, and a populace increasingly prone to seeing data-driven objectivity as an elitist form of cultural discourse. It is not even that many readers failed to be persuaded by journalistic truth but that they found the aesthetics of that reporting to be alienating and disempowering. This chapter focuses on various forms of quantitative journalism ("data," "computational," or "interactive" journalism) as a lens through which to understand these media dynamics, particularly insofar as they relate to American political culture more broadly.

The chapter begins by briefly recapitulating the general factors that may have been at work in determining the manner by which data and quantitative journalism played out in the 2016 election: filter bubbles, the decline of the so-called "mainstream media," and general notions of our "post-truth" culture. The chapter then traces the historical emergence of data-driven forms of objectivity and discusses the manner by which data journalism came to be an "elite" form of journalistic discourse. It concludes by discussing the "audience" or "reception" side of the equation, speculating about how information and information display might be interpreted as an aesthetic style and "taste signifier," a style with deeper implications for the American public and political practice.

One final note: it should be clear that all of these explanations for the 2016 election outcome are highly mediacentric, and we should not lose sight that political press coverage does not exist in a vacuum. Alongside media narratives about candidates, *actual* candidates also exist, candidates with campaign staffs, organizational infrastructures, political skills, and professional competencies. Society may or not be undergoing what Hepp and Coultry (2017) have called "deep mediatization," but personalities and world events continue to exert an effect on political outcomes, even those buried deep within our media funhouse hall of mirrors.

Explanations for Journalistic Failures

It is important to keep in mind from the outset that observers have meant many different things when they've talked about journalistic "failures" during the 2016 campaign. Some are talking specifically about polling failures, or the fact that predictive polling outlets like the FiveThirtyEight and The Upshot gave Donald Trump low chances of winning. Others are referring to the fact that reporters somehow failed to understand the mindsets and attitudes of a large swath of white working-class voters who defected from Barack Obama to Donald Trump, giving him the narrow margin of votes that propelled him to an Electoral College victory. In this piece I refer less to any of these specifics than to the fact that many journalists (a) feel like they somehow "missed the story" of the election (a grave journalistic sin according to the canons and codes of the profession) and (b) produced fact-driven reporting that somehow failed to have a the anticipated impact on its audience. Many journalists might disagree with my assessment of the situation; nevertheless, I think the core of my argument lies in my claim that there was a disconnect between journalism and the American electorate, that this disconnect had real public consequences, and that it is partially based on "empirical tribalism."

What other explanations have been offered for this disconnect between journalists and their public? There have been, primarily, three: Facebook and other social media platforms have created digital "filter bubbles"; there has been a decline in the economic health and vitality of the more traditional, centrist, and geographically dispersed news media; and we live in a "post-truth" or "post-fact" culture.

The question of filter bubbles has received a great deal of public attention in the past six years or so, spurred on by Eli Pariser's book of the same name. According to this argument, because of the algorithmic and financial incentives of media platforms and search engines, audience members are increasingly exposed only to points of view they already agree with (Pariser 2012). This selective exposure then leads to a hardening of extreme political attitudes and a clustering of people with the same beliefs who also reinforce each other's opinions.

A second point of view, most recently detailed by Politico media critic Jack Shafer (Shafer and Doherty 2017) but also discussed widely by scholars analyzing transformations in the American news industry, points to the "hollowing out" of the American news industry. For these critics, the economic and professional decline of newspapers has led to both a diminution of critical political coverage in places like Pennsylvania, Wisconsin, and Michigan, but also to a corresponding "clustering" of news companies in cities like San Francisco, New York, Los Angeles, and Washington, DC.

The third argument is more general and cultural: we live in a post-truth or post-fact era, epitomized by the Oxford English Dictionary choosing "post-truth" as its word of the year for 2016. "Post-truth," they wrote in a blog post, "is an adjective defined as 'relating to or denoting circumstances in which objective facts are less influential in shaping public opinion than appeals to emotion and personal belief'" (Oxford English Dictionary 2016). According to many observers of politics in 2016, traditional and enlightenment-indebted journalists made a mistake in thinking that their appeals to reasoned, empirical evidence would mean much to an electorate steeped in emotionalism and irrational belief.

All of these explanations have their merits, and, as will be seen, my own diagnosis draws on elements of all of them. To understand the genealogy of journalism's empirical failures, however, I argue that it is worth taking a trip back in time to understand how some of journalism's most quantitative, data-driven forms of news came to be. In the history of this data-driven journalism, I argue, lie many of the roots of our current difficulties.

The Long History of Data Journalism

Journalists have always used numbers, statistics, and other forms of quantitative information in news reports. Indeed, for much of the early history of printing, journalism was *largely* about numbers, serving as it did of a conveyor of business, shipping, and trade records along with political gossip and rumors from the royal court. It is only with the emergence of what we know today as "modern reporting" that journalism became less material and more oral, less about numbers than words, less about documents than interviews, and transformed, in Hazel Dicken Garcia's terms, from a "record" to a "report." This is why, for me, any American history of data journalism must begin not with the first use of infographics or statistics, but rather in the early twentieth century when a more general transformation of social knowledge began to take place. This transformation was propelled forward by the dual impulse of progressive political goals (collecting empirical knowledge as a mechanism for generating political reform) and the more general professionalization of knowledge disciplines (sociology, political science, economics, and journalism all assumed their current professional forms in the early decades of the twentieth century). In my book *Apostles of Certainty: Data Journalism and the Politics of Doubt* (Anderson 2018), I make the argument that we can best understand the sociomaterial roots of journalistic epistemology by looking at it historically and also comparatively, by examining how it intersected with sociology, political science, and other knowledge disciplines.

For the purposes of this chapter, it is important to keep in mind the following general line of development. The earliest sociology in the 1910s was often indistinguishable from muckraking journalism, particularly in its focus on mobilizing quantitative information for the purposes of social reform. Nevertheless, the vast majority of journalism in the progressive era rejected the insertion of quantitative data as a source of evidence for news stories, owing to its presentist focus and its primary reliance on oral forms of evidence. As sociology professionalized, it rejected its reformist, journalistic, visualizing tendencies and focused on the statistical establishment of quantitative certainty. Ironically, at just the same time, journalism began to act much as sociology had a few decades earlier, embracing context, interpretation of structural events, and data visualization. In other words, both sociology and journalism professionalized in the 1930s, but in ways that pulled them apart and changed what it meant to be properly "scientific." When the data journalism pioneer Philip Meyer initiated his crusade to make journalism more scientific he would do so on the terrain established by sociology in the 1930s. Journalism would try to become more like social science, rather than sociology trying to be like journalism, as was the case in the 1910s.

This entire process also called into question the status of "the public" and its relationship to social science and to the deployment of quantitative information. The early reformist sociologists believed data could literally "activate" the public, that viewing or consuming data could spur people and groups to political action. Modern sociology abandoned much of this pretense, concerned far more with its own internal field dynamics and, at most, with the relationship between its experts and the policy elite. Professional journalism, for its part, largely understood the role of reporting to be the provision of information to citizens for the purposes of self govern-ment, and the crux of the debate between Meyer and other journalists in the 1960s concerned the degree to which journalism should provide a new form of information ("social science in a hurry") to the public in order to better facilitate democratic goals. Meyer's critics contended that his "preci-sion journalism" would be inaccessible to many readers and impossible for many journalists to produce; Meyer countered that computers would facili-tate reportorial capacity, and moreover, that policy makers *and* interested citizens would use this new approach for democratic ends.

Data Journalism Institutionalizes

Data journalism, then, was always pitched as a more elitist practice meant for more discerning readers, and this epistemological tendency was rein-forced by the way it institutionalized in the 1980s and 1990s. One path forward for data journalism would have been for it to find its institutional home within newsrooms themselves, with every cub reporter gaining a certain level of statistical literacy in the same way that journalists learned to write a nut graf or conduct an interview. This was not, however, what took place. Instead, data journalists began gathering under the banner of "computer-assisted reporting," a cross-newsroom group of journalists familiar with computers and statistical techniques, who largely practiced forms of the "social science in a hurry" recommended by Meyer. These computer-assisted reporters formed the group NICAR (the National Insti-tute for Computer Assisted Reporting) that later affiliated with a second group, IRE (Investigative Reporters and Editors). This, in turn, tied data journalism even more closely with forms of investigative reporting—itself one of the most respected and elite forms of newswork. This cluster of underpinnings—the link between data journalism and investigative reporting, the fact that CAR stories often won journalistic prizes, the unfortunate reality that a large number of reporters were numerically illiterate, and the fact that data journalism was always pitched to a more policy-focused audience—reinforced the elitist tendencies of data reporting.

Industry-wide changes in journalism have only exacerbated these divisions between ordinary, superficial, tabloid, emotionalist, or partisan reporting and more high-level data journalism work. As Rasmus Kleis Nielsen puts it, alongside the growth of superficial, impressionistic, and transient news items distributed through smart watches and social media, the twenty-first century has also seen

[t]he parallel and simultaneous growth in forms of digital news that are far closer to the "knowledge-about" end of [William] James's spectrum, forms of long-form, explanatory, data-enriched journalism that offers mediated, publicly available, forms of news very much concerned with questions of causality and teleology, with the relations between events, and that offers this in a far more accessible and timely fashion than other forms of "knowledge about" current affairs. (Nielsen 2017)

Clearly, the type of journalism advocated by Meyer and his followers has played a large part in this journalistic efflorescence. Digital sites that dominated the public conversation about the 2016 American presidential election—Nate Silver's FiveThirtyEight, the *New York Times*'s Upshot, ProPublica, the Marshall Project, and other forms of high-level data-driven political reporting—can be seen as the heirs to Philip Meyer as well. But how have these professionalized forms of objective communication been received by audiences? My answer is: not well, and the reasons for this problematic uptake go beyond simply providing information itself. Simply providing highly factualized discourse would not in and of itself be a problem unless there were not deeper fractures and fissures within the American polity, and if citizens were not as prone to thinking about politics in terms of identity as they were in terms of factual knowledge (see Kreiss, this volume). Filter bubbles and business model failures play a role in this, but the primary culprit, I argue, is the aesthetic style of "intelligence" and the populist reaction to it (Perlstein 2017).

In other words: in the partisan and polarized American political environment, professional journalistic claims to facticity have become simply another tribal marker—the tribal marker of "smartness"—and the quantitative, visually oriented forms of data news serve to alienate certain audience members as much as they convince anyone to think about politics or political claims more skeptically. The problem of the public discussed a few pages earlier has re-emerged under conditions of digitization. Data journalism and other forms of quantitative newswork mark the further extensions of journalistic skill and professionalism we have yet seen in the news business. Unfortunately, what is good for the journalism industry is not always good for democracy. Quantitative news, partly because of its own institutional history and partly because of political polarization in the United States, is an aesthetic style that alienates some and confuses others; it is not "value-neutral," whatever the journalists who practice it might hope for.

What Now?

Journalism theorists and critics, looking at the current state of American politics and the press, have generally offered two suggestions for how the press might produce a journalism that fairly represents more of the public and has a greater impact on political outcomes. The first is what I call the "discursive" solution: journalists ought to do a better job including the voices, perspectives, and thoughts of so-called "ordinary Americans" in their coverage. Understanding the perspectives of so-called "middle America," the theory goes, will lead to a fairer, more accurate journalism. A second solution might be called the "emotionalist" solution—rather than doubling down on facts, mainstream journalists should take a page from the Fox News playbook and, as President Donald Trump might put it, aim for the gut.

I'm skeptical that either of these solutions will be successful. The discursive solution seems to place too great an emphasis on dialogue as a process, with objective information as its input that then leads to positive democratic outputs. I also find it hard to imagine journalism ever deprofessionalizing to such a degree that it is willing to be as emotional and colorful as might be required to match the right-wing media machine and its obvious disdain for facts. Whatever it does in the future, however, it seems clear that journalism's confidence in its own professional certitude has been shaken, and that new paths forward are be required if the media is to fulfill its tremendously important democratic functions in the years ahead.

6   My Very Own Alternative Facts abou

Michael Schudson

Let's accept at the outset what Hannah Arendt wrote half a century ago about truth and politics: they are not on good terms. Donald Trump is not the first president to lie. He is not the first populist to turn out to be a plutocrat. He is not the first to surround himself with advisers and spokespeople without respect for reality (remember the George W. Bush aide who spoke of journalists sneeringly as "the reality-based community"). He is of course in an unbroken line of presidents who attack the press—including both George Washington and Thomas Jefferson.

What is original with Donald Trump is his mastery of Twitter, a social media platform that 21 percent of Americans use (24 percent of Americans who are online at all) but it is practically universal among American journalists.[1] If Joe McCarthy retains fame for having taken advantage of the 1950s reportorial norm of printing with a straight face any outrageous charges a US Senator might present to them, Donald Trump is at least as successful in manipulating the Twitterosis that US journalists suffer from.

What may also be original to Donald Trump, among presidents, is a mania or an egomania for numbers. In his first days in office, Mr. Trump— national leadership on issues of importance his to take up, a chance to charm the world his for the asking—veered off course with an effort to insist that more people attended his inauguration than Barack Obama's first inauguration in 2009, the largest in American history. Whether one looked at aerial photographs or the record of Washington subway ridership as of 11 a.m. on January 20 of both 2009 and 2017, the evidence showed Mr. Trump's position to be pure fantasy. Six months later, President Trump insisted that Congress had passed more bills (42) in his time in office than in the first six months of any previous president. This turned out to be an gure to track down and, again, Trump's claim was simply wrong. was far behind the pace of Franklin Roosevelt, Harry Truman, and Jimmy Carter, a touch behind Bill Clinton (50), and just ahead of Barack Obama (39).[2]

Of course, in a democracy, numbers matter—and they should, although the founders created the political system that they did because they distrusted numbers and they perfectly despised the multitudes.

Americans call our government a democracy. This is not what the founders called the system they brought into the world in 1789. They spoke of what they were building as "republican" government, by which they meant a representative democracy with protections built into the Constitution to prevent one-person or one-party or even majority rule. We refer to these mechanisms as "checks and balances." Add to them the system of federalism that locates power in the individual states separately from the power located in Washington, DC. Without these means for limiting the accumulation of power, even power endorsed by a (temporary) majority, ours would not be a political system worth our allegiance.

This is not something that media scholars, as opposed to most political scientists, have sufficiently recognized. Right-wing populism is ascendant in Britain and the United States, entrenched in Hungary, and in 2017 made serious bids for power in Austria, France, and the Netherlands. Right-wing populism assaults liberal democracy while communication scholars too often reduce liberal democracy to an ideal of participatory democracy and a practical reality of rule by 50 percent of voters plus one. But 50 percent plus one can be misled. They can be an angry majority, angry enough to strip the other half of the population of civil, political, and social rights. Scholars endorsed too warmly and too quickly the idea of Internet democracy—not only are people now coming to see how mythological this idea is but there is a dawning that it should have been rejected from the outset. Democracy worth defending is liberal democracy, not simply a majoritarian scheme for voting. Liberal democracy is based on majority rule (more or less), but majority rule within law, with specific and enforceable protections for civil and political liberties, particularly for minorities whose small numbers make them unable to form a majority and therefore make them especially vulnerable to what Tocqueville identified long ago as the "tyranny of the majority." That was not just a catchy phrase.

What is the role of journalism in a democracy? That is, what role should it play in a liberal democracy? Journalists literally "make" news. They do not find it. They do not publish transcripts of reality. Even if they make their best efforts, they would not provide a copy of reality, but reality in a frame, reality enhanced, reality reconfigured by being heightened on a page or a screen, reality retouched by the magic of publication itself.

Whether it is Macedonian teenagers wanting to make some money or far-right conspiracy-minded partisans trying to roil the waters, "fake news" has become part of today's political vocabulary. Just how influential fake news was in the US presidential election in 2016 is very hard to know, but the idea of fake news has certainly become a powerful part of our public discourse. President Donald Trump likes to grab headlines (as did his predecessors), but Trump regularly does so by name-calling the mainstream news media "fake news" as well as by making reckless assertions for which he has no evidence. He has repeatedly asserted that any investigation of connections between the Russian government and his presidential campaign will find nothing. At this writing, enough is known that President Trump and his defenders have shifted from saying "there was no collusion" between the campaign and the Russian government to asserting far more modestly that "collusion is not a crime." That counts as partially true, judging from a round-up of expert legal opinion that Politico published July 12, 2017, in "What Is Collusion? Is It Even a Crime?" It may be that President Trump's original "there's nothing to find" claim meant only "I myself did not meet with Russians"—but it is now known that his son, Donald Jr., did so in what arguably was a crime (in agreeing to meet with Russians close to the Putin government in order to receive information from them discreditable to Hillary Clinton), and it is likewise now known that his son-in-law, Jared Kushner, had multiple meetings with Russians that he seemed to have forgotten when filling out forms to gain security clearance.

A US president commands enormous attention around the world whenever he opens his mouth. If he places troops on a battlefield, even many Americans who saw no point in war rally round the flag. If he has a cancerous polyp removed from his colon (Ronald Reagan), thousands of people in the next few days make colonoscopy appointments. If a president can inadvertently push people to undergo colonoscopies, what else can he do by example or by words? When a president declares the mainstream news media to be the "enemy of the American people," what might otherwise reasonable citizens be inclined to think?

A journalist's job is to make news, as a carpenter's job is to build houses. Both crafts have rules. The first rule for journalists committed to their work is to put reality first. Responsible journalists learn to not produce fake news or hyped news or corrupt news. They do not subordinate honest reporting to ideological consistency or political advocacy. They do not curry favor with advertisers, or with the publisher's business interests, or even with the tastes of the audience. Nor should they bow to the consensus among their own colleagues if it clashes with what they see in the world around them— this, the bias of the inner circle, is the most difficult to avoid.

For a century now, the dominant trend in the history of American journalism has been the professionalization of a staff of reporters who gather the news. Journalism preceded reporting, but from the 1820s on, reporting became the center of American journalism. Europe was not the same; there one opined that "reporting is killing journalism"—that is, straightforward accounts of events of the day were taking the spotlight away from the discursive essays of political advocacy, theory, and philosophy that dominated much of the European press. Only in the twentieth century would the European press begin to borrow US news techniques like interviewing and US news standards that placed reporting first.

But doesn't the US model of journalism deny the truth that presumed "facts" are just opinions in masquerade? That everything is relative, it just depends on the standpoint you start from? Most college sophomores in their first philosophy class will walk in with the argument that "it's all relative" and that "that's just your opinion!"—no research, argument, or discussion can alter our preconceptions.

That's why we call them sophomoric. But none of those students truly believes everything is relative. If their computer malfunctions, they do not pray that it be fixed by divine intervention, nor do they normally kick the computer. Instead, they call tech support—they turn to experts. If one of the students, in the middle of class, feels a powerful and distressing pain in his chest, he can ask the philosophy professor for her guidance or he can ask the student at the next desk for her advice or he could ask someone else to call for emergency medical assistance. Will he choose A, B, or C? He will choose C. He will seek medical assistance. When reality insistently knocks at the door, the premature commitment to "everything is relative" is left behind. Relativist or modernist or postmodernist, left or right—all will seek out experts.

When people want to know on an everyday basis what is going on in the world, most turn to professional news gatherers who have earned reputations for reliability. But how is a person to know which of the news providers and purveyors around us can be trusted? Expertise in reporting is not certified by many years of study and training as in medicine, or by easily measured results, as with the computer tech expert who either fixes or fails to fix the computer. But there are, nevertheless, some earmarks of evidentiary quality in journalism:

1. Willingness to retract, correct, and implicitly or explicitly apologize for misstatements. The *Time* reporter who misreported in the first day of the Trump administration that President Trump or his aides had removed the bust of Martin Luther King, Jr., from the Oval Office retracted and corrected his report within hours. That is what responsible reporters and news organizations do.

2. Adherence to professional ethics—including the following:

    —Be accurate. Spell the name right. Get the address right. There's no "it's all relative" here. Joan Smith lives at 10 Maple Avenue or 20 Maple Avenue, not at both addresses, and 15 Maple Avenue as an approximation is not good enough. Write a story that tells what happened, not what you think about what you think happened, or what you wish happened, or what might have happened.

    —Dig for contrary evidence. "Report against your own assumptions," my Columbia Journalism School colleagues tell their students.

    —Follow the story wherever the evidence leads. If you are a reporter, not a propagandist, you will follow the story you catch a glimpse of even if it may injure the career of the candidate or party or cause that you personally favor or that your news organization has endorsed. The *New York Times* repeatedly endorsed Eliot Spitzer's bids for office in New York, including in his race for governor in 2006. But it also broke the sex scandal story that led Governor Spitzer to resign. A real reporter prizes a truthful story over partisan advantage or political preference, come what may.

3. Reliable journalists adopt some identifiable literary features, too, like the following:

—Be calm and declarative. No hyperventilating.

—Present multiple positions or viewpoints within a story if the topic is a controversial one and if (unlike "false balance") the various sides adhere to different values but are not separated by an acceptance of consensual scientific evidence and a rejection of it.

—Identify your sources whenever possible. And acknowledge the gaps, inconsistencies, or insufficiencies in the data you are basing your story on.

—Use commonly accepted data, databases, and reliable authorities. If you want to write about whether more people rode the Washington, DC, metro system on the day of Barack Obama's 2009 inauguration or on the day of Donald Trump's 2017 inauguration, to provide a reasonable proxy for the size of the inauguration crowd, ask the Metropolitan Transit Authority that collects this data. If you prefer to take President Trump's word for it, you are not a journalist; you are a propagandist or a sap. Personal vanity is not a commonly accepted database.

Professional news reporting is not easy. Its place in the world is still young—it really cannot be said to have existed in a full-bodied way for much more than a century. That's not a long stretch. But at its best, it has proved itself a bulwark of accountable democratic government and a thorn in the side of autocrats around the world. The economic fragility of the news media these days is troubling, and it sometimes leads venerable news organizations to prefer clicks to conscience, but reporters can and often do maintain a fierce allegiance to its highest ideals, and this is a force to reckon with. When President Trump called the mainstream media the "enemy of the people," many journalists responded with redoubled effort to hold him accountable for both his words and his actions.

Professional journalism is often a quick study. It is a "first rough draft" of history, not the last word. But it is the enemy of pride and pomposity and ignorance. When the president of the United States is a walking, talking, tweeting example of pride, pomposity, and ignorance, we need professional journalism more than ever.

And, of course, that's not all we need. We need a professional civil service loyal to its own standards of integrity, not loyal to whichever party or person happens to occupy the White House. We need an independent judiciary that, likewise, is dedicated first to enforcing the law, not to pleasing the occupant of the White House. We need the whole energy of civil society—partisan and nonpartisan organizations across the political spectrum that seek to hold government accountable. We need the decentralized strengths of a federal system with states free (within the Constitution) to make decisions for themselves that Washington has only limited authority to challenge. The news media alone are a slim reed against a determined autocrat. But the news media, alongside other essential elements of liberal democracy, have a key role without which democracy itself is endangered.

Notes

1. Pew Research Center, "Social Media Update 2016," November 11, 2016, based on a survey conducted March 7–April 4, 2016.

2. Michael Shear and Karen Yourish, "Trump Says He Has Signed More Bills Than Any President, Ever. He Hasn't," *New York Times*, July 17, 2017.

7   Who's Playing Who? Media Manipulation in an Era of Trump

Robyn Caplan and danah boyd

After the election of Donald Trump in November 2016, the denizens of 4chan and 8chan, two anonymous online forums, were celebrating what they thought was their victory. "We fucking did it lads. It's happening. Florida is ours," one user on 8chan wrote (in all-red caps). On 4chan, the party was also in full-force. "We actually elected a meme as president," one 4channer was reported to have said.[1] These celebrations resembled more of what you'd expect inside a campaign's headquarters than of voters happy that their candidate had won. On 8chan, users praised "kek"—their meme deity—and quickly took toward planning their future campaigns. By the end of November 9th, they were already discussing their next goals. One user posted an image of the earth as seen from space with a swastika embedded on its face alongside next steps to "push further right" and try to "normalize NatSoc and Fascism." Electing Donald Trump as president of the United States, in their collective hivemind, was just the first step in what could be a global movement. So, how did these online communities become so convinced they had played a pivotal role in the election of Donald Trump?

As news media and political communication, in general, have moved online, a new set of variables is influencing how ideas are produced and amplified through communities that have figured out how to make their ideas trend and become more mainstream. Far-right groups have been able to gain visibility through producing content for social media and coordinating likes, clicks, and shares over algorithmic networks, exposing a new generation of individuals to ideas through not only "hacking" into recommendation engines, like YouTube, but by also affecting what news media companies and journalists think of as "newsworthy." As a result, the newfound capacity of far-right groups to shift political consensus through online organizing has been given even greater visibility by news media companies who are vulnerable to such efforts because of longstanding commitments to cover what they perceive to be significant shifts in politics.

Dreaming of Participatory Culture

When the Internet became a mass consumer-oriented media in the mid-1990s, tremendous hype surrounded its potential for realizing a new form of political participation. Many early Internet proponents saw the rise of blogging and social media as the ultimate articulation of Habermas's "public sphere" and saw themselves in Warner and Fraser's "counterpublics."[2] Early advocates, such as Howard Rheingold, saw online communities, chat rooms, blogs and blog comments, and wiki talk pages as enabling a powerful form of bottom-up democratic participation that could challenge elitist forms of journalism. So strong were the dreams of "user-generated content" that in 2006, *Time* Magazine declared "You" the "Person of the Year."[3] For all of the excitement, few of those in the progressive and libertarian circles that dominated early Internet adoption imagined that the political power of the Internet might be most significantly realized to drive conservative and neo-reactionary ideologies under the guise of populism.

As social media helped usher most people into participatory culture,[4] a small number of companies began serving as dominant information and community platforms. While the heyday of blogging and RSS galvanized those who envisioned a decentralized ecosystem, Facebook, Google, and Twitter pushed the public in a different direction. By the mid-2010s, a huge swath of the public was consuming news through tech intermediaries. Social media had become the public sphere for a large number of people.

News media companies, seeing declines in page views, went to the digital platforms to find their audiences, and increasingly paid attention to audience preferences through analyzing data about what their audience liked and what was trending on social media.[5] Politicians, both in the U.S. and abroad, went to platforms like Twitter and Facebook to communicate directly with their constituents and to mobilize public opinion for their policies or goals.[6] Activists like those involved with the Black Lives Matter movement turned to social media to coordinate protests and engage the public.[7] Marketers sought to brand their content in line with the practices afforded by social media, such as through clever hashtags or other viral strategies.[8] And hate groups and non-state actors with violent motivations, such as ISIL, Russian propagandists, and white nationalist groups, used these platforms to identify and recruit potential members.[9] Data-driven networks became a powerful tool for those seeking to inform, persuade, and mobilize for good, bad, and ugly.

As the centrality of social media increased, scholars, journalists, and advocates began questioning the motivations and incentives of algorithmic-based platforms. Facebook was publicly scrutinized when it became clear that their system was designed to propagate posts related to the ice-bucket challenge rather than the Ferguson protests.[10] Indeed, because social media systems are designed to amplify content based on clicks and likes, the content that spreads is more likely to be frivolous and entertaining than to contain hard-hitting news. Furthermore, because most information platforms depend on advertising revenue that demands page views, these companies are not incentivized to ask users to struggle with complex topics or conflict that might push them away from their sites. Finally, the view that platforms were a more organic way of surfacing public-level concerns led to some initial confusion about whether manipulation of data-driven networks could even occur in an environment shaped by data analytics.

Regardless of the intentions of early advocates and designers, there was nothing in particular about the design of the Internet that would upend authoritarianism, conquer tyranny, and democratize the world. As it turned out, the Internet quickly became a tool for mass surveillance of populations, and authoritarian governments learned how to build walls online, often by coordinating with companies to control the flows of information.[11] Older structures of domination, norms, and values also took root in over social media and in forums. The Internet is not just a space where progressive subaltern populations can organize and find their voice against the powerful—it is also a place where labor can be de-organized, and women, minorities, and LGBTQ can be harassed, doxxed, or otherwise be made unwelcome or invisible.[12] To many idealists' surprise, the democratizing features of the Internet that enabled mass participation were actually politically agnostic, and could be used in service of any ideological aims.

Misinformation and Manipulation

After the outcome of the 2016 US presidential election, many surprised political pundits, progressives, and liberals scrambled to identify culprits. In addition to challenging the value of the Electoral College and questioning the legitimacy of a heavily gerrymandered electoral map, some also turned to the role of "fake news" and the spread of misinformation in shaping the election. News outlets quickly suggested the blame lay with powerful information intermediaries. Facebook, Google, and Twitter, they argued, had been used as tools for the spread of misinformation, disinformation, and propaganda. The phrase "fake news" emerged from the left to refer to the emergence of hyperpartisan websites and news imitators that had produced headlines like "Pope Francis shocks world, endorses Donald Trump for president."

To some degree, manipulation of online information intermediaries has always occurred. As data came to be a powerful variable in how content was filtered to users, those seeking to shape public opinion sought to influence this data. Within each stage of the Internet, commercial and political actors who have seen the political, ideological, and financial potential of gaining visibility within these networks began modifying their content to gain algorithmic traction. Digital media strategies, such as the creation of pages on Facebook and hashtags on Twitter, the editing of Wikipedia pages, and the use of SEO and metatags on websites, were already-tested mechanisms used by marketers and publicity agents to ensure their messages would be prioritized across data-driven networks.[13] Mechanisms built into platforms designed to organize content for search or social media could also be used to organize communities or people across common ideas or brands, including political ideas and hate-oriented brands.

Like "attention merchants"[14] shilling patent medicine in the past, a whole host of different actors had learned how to tap into a cultural ethos that had begun prioritizing metrics and data analytics over the content of messages. What had been done to wreak havoc online "for the lulz" became a powerful way to question the legitimacy of institutions like government and could be easily manipulated through appealing to large numbers online—whether representing "real" people or not. Regardless of whether or not they unite voters, networked strategies of manipulation are at least effective at spreading enough discord, chaos, and confusion to make seeing through the noise more difficult.

At no point has this become more visible than in the run-up to and aftermath of the 2016 election. Online communities that coordinated across forums and messaging applications like 4chan, 8chan, Voat, Reddit, and Discord used these activities to coordinate the spread of memes and messaging in support of their candidate, Donald Trump, first during the Republican primaries and then against Hillary Clinton during the general election.[15] Botnets, including those linked to Russian propagandists, also worked to amplify messages over secondary platforms like Facebook and Twitter. Media producers geared toward the production of hyperbolic and click-worthy content—even if it was misleading or false—started working within platforms to profit financially through the use of a variety of ad networks. Those with more ideological aims—often labeled collectively as the "alt-right"—began seeking to open the "Overton window" as they used platforms to get mainstream media to increase the range of acceptable topics of discussion. These diverse actors had varied motivations, but they organized around a set of tactics and strategies geared toward hacking into the logic of platforms (trending and personalizing content) and eventually into the frames of the news media industry that were also looking to these platforms to surface content from the masses.

A Vulnerable News Media

The Internet had not only ushered in new political potentials but new financial realities for the news media industry. New forms of production of news-like content from users around the world occurred in tandem with the failure of the newspaper industry to digitize and monetize their content for the Internet. By 2009, the newspaper industry had reached a financial crisis. Unable to compete with both television and online classified advertisement markets, newspapers and other media companies began selling off parts of their businesses; financial firms took over others.[16] News companies had made significant cuts, particularly to foreign bureaus and their coverage of federal and state governments.[17] The emergence of "citizen journalism"—local reports of political events posted to social media—was seen not as a political project to fill gaps and broaden participation in the newsmaking process, but as a financial necessity for many newsrooms.

With foreign, state, and local bureaus already gutted across the news media industry, many had turned to opinion-based shows and columns that took a common set of reports from wires like AP and Reuters and gave them their own spin.[18] As social media and search platforms emerged, news media companies, facing declines in print subscriptions and visitors to websites, looked to these platforms to not only find their audiences, but also to figure out what interested them.[19] These dynamics, coupled with the constantly changing rules of platforms,[20] made news media vulnerable to manipulation in new ways. Financial strain, dependence on tech companies, and pressure to move faster meant that many news companies returned to early twentieth-century norms of propagating hype, fear, and hyperpartisanship.

Dismantling the Standing of News Media

As journalists and scholars wrung their hands over the type of patently false information that spread online as "fake news," Donald Trump and his team quickly repurposed the term to question the legitimacy of more mainstream news outlets like CNN and the *New York Times*.[21] This critique amplified a longstanding tension between conservative politicians and major national news agencies, typically deemed "liberal media" by those with conservative viewpoints. By labeling them as "fake," the Trump administration sought to give a final blow to the legitimacy of news media. Only a week after inauguration, Senior Policy Advisor Steve Bannon and President Trump both declared "mainstream media" to be their "opposition party."[22]

The critiques made by Trump's team were not new to his followers, or to many on the left as well. Although declaring traditional news outlets to be the enemy was a very directly adversarial stance taken by the Trump administration, they had already worked to bypass these outlets, using social media to not only reach out directly to followers, but perhaps even to listen to their demands. Leveraging techniques of brand development, as well as the emotional effects of shock and outrage on the spread of content online, individuals seeking fame and attention—like Milo Yiannopoulos—capitalized on the weakness of both mainstream and social media to garner attention. Arguably, Trump's success as a candidate can be attributed to his ability to mobilize individuals and communities online on his behalf—or by the communities' and individuals' abilities to mobilize Trump on *their* behalf.[23] Like many of those who proudly took credit for memeing Trump into the White House by strategically manipulating the media ecosystem, the Trump administration confidently saw no need for traditional outlets because they had developed a strategy that capitalized on the new structures of media—Twitter, Facebook, and a collection of bloggers and journalists who couldn't resist covering controversy and outrageous statements.

Frustrated by the inaccurate and sensational claims made by Trump and his administration, many journalists doubled down on the need to fact check statements coming from the White House. Yet, in a polarized media landscape, an obsessive commitment to accuracy and rationality does little to assuage those who do not trust traditional news organizations; fact-checking is not read by those who distrust the fact-checkers. Recognizing the power of sites like Facebook, many progressives want to see the Internet companies who serve as intermediaries do more to address the flow of problematic content, but it is unclear that their efforts will do much to address the underlying polarization that Trump, Bannon, and right-wing conservatives know how to leverage.

News media is facing an existential crisis. Not only is its financial model precarious, but also its legitimacy is in question. Politicians, marketers, and meme-makers are all capitalizing on the news media's incentives to manipulate its agenda. Meanwhile, longstanding commitments to objectivity and an obsessive belief that they can determine what is newsworthy blind many news enterprises from being able to see the game in which they have become a pawn. In the parlance of online communities obsessed with taking the "red pill," it is time for news media to wake up.

Notes

1. Abby Ohlheiser, "'We Actually Elected a Meme as President': How 4chan Celebrated Trump's Victory," *Washington Post*, November 9, 2016, https://www .washingtonpost.com/news/the-intersect/wp/2016/11/09/we-actually-elected-a -meme-as-president-how-4chan-celebrated-trumps-victory.

2. Stuart Geiger, "Does Habermas Understand the Internet? The Algorithmic Construction of the Blogo/Public Sphere," *Gnovis Journal* (2009).

3. Adam Zagorin, "Person of the Year 2006: People Who Mattered," *Time*, December 25, 2006.

4. Henry Jenkins, Mizuko Ito, and danah boyd, *Participatory Culture in a Networked Era* (Cambridge: Polity, 2016).

5. C. W. Anderson, "Deliberative, Agonistic, and Algorithmic Audiences," *International Journal of Communication* 5 (2011).

6. Darren G. Lilleker and Theirry Vedel, "The Internet in Campaigns and Elections," in William H. Dutton (ed), *The Oxford Handbook of Internet Studies* (Oxford: Oxford University Press, 2013), 401–420.

7. Deen Freelon, Charlton D. McIlwain, and Meredith D. Clark, "Beyond the Hashtags," *Center for Media and Social Impact,* February 2016, http://archive .cmsimpact.org/sites/default/files/beyond_the_hashtags_2016.pdf.

8. Tracy Tuten and Michael Solomon, *Social Media Marketing* (Thousand Oaks: Sage, 2015).

9. J. M. Berger, "Nazis vs. ISIS on Twitter: A Comparative Study of White Nationalists and ISIS Online Social Media Networks" (White Paper, George Washington University, 2016).

10. Zeynep Tufekci, "Algorithmic Harms Beyond Facebook and Google: Emergent Challenges of Computational Agency," *Colorado Tech Law Journal* 13 (2015).

11. Ronald Deibert, "The Geopolitics of Internet Control: Censorship, Sovereignty and Cyberspace," in Andrew Chadwick and Philip Howard (eds), *Routledge Handbook of Internet Politics* (New York: Routledge, 2009), 373–375.

12. Catherine Buni and Soraya Chemaly, "The Unsafety Net: How Social Media Turned Against Women," *The Atlantic,* October 9, 2014.

13. Ryan Holiday, *Trust Me, I'm Lying: Confessions of a Media Manipulator* (New York: Portfolio/Penguin, 2012).

14. Tim Wu, *The Attention Merchants: The Epic Scramble to Get Inside Our Heads* (New York: Penguin, 2016).

15. Alice Marwick and Rebecca Lewis, "Media Manipulation," *Data & Society Working Paper*, 2017.

16. Matthew Crain, "The Rise of Private Equity Media Ownership in the United States: A Public Interest Perspective," *International Journal of Communication* 3 (2009): 208–239.

17. Paul Starr, "Goodbye to the Age of Newspapers (Hello to a New Era of Corruption)," *The New Republic,* March 4, 2009, https://newrepublic.com/article/64252/goodbye-the-age-newspapers-hello-new-era-corruption.

18. Jairo Mejía Ramos, "Reinventing the Wire: How to Prepare for Constant Disruptions" (Reuters Institute Fellowship Paper, University of Oxford, 2014).

19. Anderson, "Deliberative, Agonistic, and Algorithmic Audiences."

20. Robyn Caplan and danah boyd, "Isomorphism Through Algorithms: Institutional Dependencies in the Case of Facebook," *Big Data & Society* (2018).

21. Mark Follman, "Trump's War on 'Fake News' Is Chillingly Real," *Mother Jones,* April 29, 2017, http://www.motherjones.com/politics/2017/04/trump-real-war-fake -news-media.

22. Michael M. Grynbaum, "Trump Strategist Stephen Bannon Says Media Should 'Keep Its Mouth Shut,'" *New York Times,* January 26, 2017, https://www.nytimes.com/ 2017/01/26/business/media/stephen-bannon-trumpnews-media.html.

23. Marwick and Lewis, "Media Manipulation."

8   Lessons from the Paparazzi: Rethinking Photojournalistic Coverage of Trump

Andrew L. Mendelson

President Donald J. Trump has restricted journalistic access to the White House in ways no other modern president has, seldom holding public press conferences and limiting the number of on-camera press briefings by White House spokespeople, in addition to publicly castigating the news media as the enemy. The Trump administration clearly prefers to operate away from the interrogating gaze of the news media. As *Washington Post* reporters Philip Rucker and Ed O'Keefe wrote on June 19, 2017, "Trump even refuses to acknowledge to the public that he plays golf during his frequent weekend visits to his private golf courses."[1] The nonprofit government transparency organization, the Sunlight Foundation, summarized the Trump administration's first six months: "This is a secretive administration, allergic to transparency, ethically compromised, and hostile to the essential role that journalism plays in a democracy."

Photojournalists have seen their access curtailed as well, both during the campaign and since Trump took office. They have been excluded from documenting meetings with foreign dignitaries and other representatives; they are restricted from photographing at Trump's many clubs; and they are limited from where they can photograph at the President's public appearances. In one extreme case, photojournalist Christopher Morris was body-slammed for trying to leave the press pen while photographing a campaign event.

Such restrictions require photojournalists to rethink the way they cover this president. They are outsiders now, and they should embrace this status. One approach can be gleaned from the paparazzi, those uninvited celebrity photographers who monitor the daily activities of the famous. This chapter builds on a previous journal article of mine, "On the Function of the United States Paparazzi: Mosquito Swarm or Watchdogs of Celebrity

Image Control and Power?,"[2] where I argued for the need to reimagine the paparazzi less as invaders of privacy and more as photographers who challenge the manicured images of the powerful. This would position photojournalists as visual fact-checkers, providing evidence of how and where the President spends his time and with whom he meets. Fact-checking, the journalistic practice of testing the veracity of statements made by politicians, has taken on new significance during the Trump administration. No previous president has uttered as many falsehoods, according to leading fact-checking sites like PolitiFact and the *Washington Post*'s Fact Checker. This testing can be extended to photographic coverage of the White House. Before examining several exemplars demonstrating a paparazzi approach to political photography, I will briefly discuss the nature of political news photographs.

Deconstructing Political News Photography

Photography plays an important role in shaping our understanding of politicians. This is especially true for the President of the United States, a person who exists for most people only through media representations. Photographs of presidents inform our sense of who they are and what they stand for. These pictures also tell us about more intangible qualities, such as leadership and authenticity, success and failure. It has become essential that presidents control how and when they are seen, leading to an increase in the size and importance of the staff devoted to managing a president's communication strategy.

News photographers have the task of documenting the president's daily schedule, including speeches, meetings with dignitaries, press conferences, and other official duties. They also try to provide audiences with more personal, behind-the-scenes views of the president at work. Ultimately, as Associated Press photojournalist Evan Vucci said in a July/August 2012 *News Photographer* article: "The job of a photojournalist is to cut through all of this, and to find something that's 'real.' A real moment that isn't scripted, or a real moment that gives viewers an idea of who the candidate really is." In essence, it is the job of political photojournalists to push beyond an image a politician presents in order to reveal the more authentic person, regardless of whether it is positive or negative.

Photographs of politicians can be deconstructed along two continua: power—whether the content and look of the photograph are determined more by the politician or by the photographer; and location—whether the event being documented occurs in a public setting or in a private, behind-the-scenes one. The power dimension emphasizes that a photograph results from an interaction between photographer and subject, ultimately shaped by who is able to exert more control. On one end of this continuum is a subject who is unaware of being photographed. In this situation, the photographer has almost complete power over how the subject is portrayed. On the other end is a situation where the subject takes a selfie or hires a photographer. In this case, the subject controls the photographic moment and the resulting images. Most photographs reflect competing or negotiated amounts of power.

To gain control, politicians attempt to shape the nature of coverage by creating events—photo ops—that when photographed by journalists will amplify the desired message. The independence of journalists imbues the recorded events with a veneer of authenticity and objectivity. The politician's communication staff predetermines locations, lighting, backdrops, and the angles from which events will be photographed. Depending on the importance of the politician, news outlets feel both journalistic and competitive pressures to cover photo ops, as media scholar Kiku Adatto has argued in her book *Picture Perfect: Life in the Age of the Photo Op* (2008). In the case of a president, almost everything he or she does is by definition newsworthy and must be documented. Of course, staging the perfect event does not mean a president will appear positively. Awkward moments and gaffes can occur despite the best planning. Reagan was a master of appearing dignified and presidential at such events. Trump, on the other hand, seems uncomfortable posing for photographs, often having an odd expression, such as his broad smile when posing with the Pope, or being photographed pretending to drive a truck. In addition to shaping the nature of public appearances, presidents also exert their authority by establishing rules, both formal and informal, about how photojournalists conduct themselves. Photographers face the threat of denial of access for violating rules.

The second dimension for understanding political photographs is the location in which the photograph is made, public or private, or in the language of sociologist Erving Goffman, in his classic 1956 work,

The Presentation of Self in Everyday Life, the front- or backstage. The frontstage or public region is where we present our polished selves for an intended audience, knowing we will be seen and judged. The backstage or private area is where characteristics that might contradict the desired image are kept hidden. Politicians often try to blur the line between public and private, frontstage and back, by providing access to a highly polished version of behind-the-scenes activities to reveal a seemingly unposed, "real" person at work. These two dimensions—power and location—suggest that photojournalists should not just document politicians as they desire to be seen in public, but also attempt to push backstage, reasserting greater control of the photographic interaction.

Asserting Control; Pushing Backstage

Most news photographs of presidents are made at planned, highly controlled events held in public. Yet, in politics, it is backstage where the work of government happens, the proverbial smoke-filled rooms, out of sight of the press and the public. It is backstage where presidents potentially reveal aspects of themselves at odds with their more public personae. The paparazzi offer one approach for how photojournalists can push backstage in order to provide citizens with an alternative to controlled situations. The paparazzi are photographers who focus on making candid photographs and videos of celebrities, emphasizing everyday activities or activities the celebrities would prefer to keep secret. They seek the opposite of the glamor imagery of red carpets and other star-studded events. The resulting photographs challenge the polished images presented by celebrities. Underlying all paparazzi images is surveillance, monitoring those in power, looking for mismatches between frontstage and back, public and private.

Such an approach was actually anticipated well before the first paparazzi in the 1950s by one photojournalist, who brought audiences into the hidden world of politics. German photographer Erich Salomon documented Europe's political elite throughout the 1930s, as they negotiated treaties, discussed policies, and attended galas. He would gain access to these events through guile, subterfuge, and charm, armed with a small, unobtrusive camera. The photographs provided the public with a sense of how Europe's future was being shaped and how politicians behaved out of sight of the public. Politicians and diplomats were shown engaged, exhausted, or bored. If he could not gain access, Salomon would photograph through windows. As photography historian Mary Warner Marien (2006) states in her book, *Photography: A Cultural History*, "Salomon's work ... implied the importance of the public's right to see behind the scenes of important political events."

A Political Paparazzi Approach to Trump

A behind-the-scenes view of politics provides citizens with a more complicated and nuanced sense of how government works and of the people involved. The lessons of the paparazzi and Salomon in challenging the public images crafted by the powerful speak to the need for contemporary political photojournalists to circumvent restrictions placed on them by the Trump administration and to continuously monitor the activities of the White House. Despite the restrictions photographers currently face, a few examples of political paparazzi have emerged, produced by professional photojournalists, and at times, by citizen journalists and actual paparazzi.

Photojournalists

Although Trump criticized then-President Obama for golfing too much or at what Trump felt was inappropriate times, the Trump administration has restricted journalists from photographing President Trump on the golf courses of his clubs. When he golfed with Japanese Prime Minister Shinzo Abe and two professional golfers in February 2017, journalists were limited to a room whose doors had garbage bags taped over the windows. Associated Press reporter Jill Colvin and Bloomberg News reporter Jill Jacobs both tweeted photographs of this situation. In April 2017, CNN producer Kevin Liptak posted two photographs of the President golfing despite the White House again blocking the press pool from documenting Trump golfing.

Even when denied access, photojournalists can monitor activities in the White House from a distance, providing valuable information to citizens. Photographs that ran in the *New York Times* and the *Washington Post* in early May 2017 show Trump walking outside the White House with Keith Schiller, his director of operations, carrying folders and loose pieces of paper. One stickie-note, visible in both photographs, reveals the Secretary of Defense's personal cell phone number. Such a photo challenges claims of professionalism made by the White House and questions their handling of sensitive information.

In May 2017, photojournalists were excluded from documenting a meeting Trump had with Russian foreign minister Sergey Lavrov, even though official Russian photographers were allowed to photograph the meeting. A Getty photograph that ran in Politico did show the foreign minister getting out of his car, providing evidence of his presence at the White House.

In another case of surveilling the President, Getty photojournalist Chip Somodevilla captured a discussion between Trump and Shinzo Abe outside the White House. In the photo, taken from a distance, Trump leans over the shorter Abe. As Somodevilla said, in an article from CNN.com, "I was too far away from the leaders to hear what was being discussed, but Trump was expressive and Abe—the political leader of a country of 127 million people that Trump was frequently critical of during the 2016 presidential election—stands close with fists clenched."[3] This photo presents viewers with a sense of how Trump interacts with other leaders.

Citizen Journalists

A paparazzi approach isn't just the purview of professionals. Much can be gleaned from amateur photographs taken behind the scenes. In February 2017, when President Trump dined with Abe at Mar-a-Lago, no photojournalists were able to photograph inside the club. Still, at least one club member took photographs of the President meeting with his national security team in the dining room in view of everyone, discussing North Korea's recent missile launch. These photos were picked up by a number of outlets, including the *New York Times, Business Insider,* the *Washington Post,* and CNN.com. The same individual also posted selfies with an official who supposedly carries the President's nuclear codes.

Another individual posted a picture in late March 2017 that was picked up by *Time* magazine of the President at another Trump golf course posing in golfing attire, including a golf glove, at a time when the press pool had been told he was working. In another late March 2017 moment, a social media producer at CNBC noticed an Instagram image of the President appearing to be watching the Golf Channel with two other people, again when the press pool had been told that he was in meetings. In early May

2017, an amateur photographer posted an image to Twitter of the President golfing in New Jersey, again out of sight of the White House press corps. As *People* magazine reporter Tierney McAfee argued, in a May 9, 2017, article: "The tweet gave White House reporters exiled in Branchburg, New Jersey— six miles away from Trump's golf club—their only glimpse of the day into what the president was up to."[4] All of these photographs help keep tabs on the President when he is "officially" out of sight.

Paparazzi

Not to be outdone at their own game, an AOL News piece from late April 2017 suggests that paparazzi are getting into the game in Washington, DC, finding it lucrative to photograph members of the Trump administration, especially First Daughter Ivanka Trump and her husband Jared Kushner. As Buzzfeed reporter Claudia Rosenbaum wrote in March 2017 describing DC with the presence of the Trumps: "Unlike the photographers in the White House press corps, for whom fear of retaliation or being blacklisted still runs rampant, paparazzi are under no such restraints."[5] At least one paparazzi agency, FameFlynet Pictures, has photographs of Trump and Abe golfing.

In January 2017, the *Daily Mail* published a series of photographs of members of the Trump administration arriving for Shabbat dinner at the Kushners' DC home. In one photograph, Wilbur Ross, Secretary of Commerce, is welcomed by Jared Kushner. In February 2017, the *Daily Mail* ran a series of photographs showing Wendi Deng, ex-wife of Rupert Murdoch, paying a call at the Kushner house. While none of these photographs are aesthetic masterpieces, they serve a monitorial function in documenting the comings and goings of the Kushners—two very influential people in the Trump administration.

Conclusion

The *Washington Post*'s media columnist Margaret Sullivan, in her April 28, 2017, column, suggested the media need to "scrutinize, not normalize" the Trump administration. A paparazzi approach to political photojournalism supports this notion by positioning photographers as visual fact-checkers, monitoring the Trump administration for mismatches between what is claimed or presented publicly and what occurs backstage. This expands our understanding of fact-checking sites, which generally focus their attention on verbal claims presented by politicians, not visual ones. The paparazzi suggest a model for how to incorporate visual fact-checking in photojournalism. Just as it is essential for reporters not to accept the utterances of a president at face value by looking deeper for obfuscations and contradictions, it is imperative that photojournalists look behind the publicly presented images of the President for visual contradictions. This is not to suggest that photojournalists not document the President as he chooses to be seen, just as reporters need to report what the President says publicly. Doing so provides a baseline for when photojournalists push backstage.

Fact-checking sites represent a version of the watchdog function of journalism, holding politicians accountable for what they say. Political communication scholars Kathleen Hall Jamieson and Paul Waldman argued in their 2004 book, *The Press Effect: Politicians, Journalists, and the Stories That Shape the Political World*, that journalists need to see themselves as "custodians of fact." A political paparazzi approach does just that by allowing photojournalists to take back some control from the President about how and when he is photographed. The resulting photographs provide citizens with a more nuanced understanding of the Trump White House: who is visiting the President, how the President spends his time, and how the backstage image of the President lines up with the frontstage version. For example, if Trump claims to be heavily engaged in policy meetings, photographs can show otherwise. Of course, unexpected moments can happen even at the most scripted events—an odd expression or gesture, or a gaffe—but paparazzi moments are ideally when the President is less conscious of being photographed, and thus more authentic.

Moreover, the lack of artistry in paparazzi-style images may increase the journalistic authority for viewers, as facts are emphasized over aesthetics, in a way similar to citizen journalism of breaking news events shot with camera phones, as I argue in my 2013 chapter, "The Indecisive Moment: Snapshot Aesthetics as Journalistic Truth."[6] With the prevalence of Instagram, Twitter, Facebook, and Snapchat, citizens are used to seeing poorly composed photographs that circulate immediately when news occurs. To that end, photographs that look too crafted may be viewed as less truthful than something that is more raw.

Ultimately, this approach functions to serve notice to politicians that they will continue to be watched. As communication scholar James Lull wrote in a September 2, 1997 *Los Angeles Times* op-ed piece: "When a princess or a president wants media attention, he or she gets it. But if we allow media celebrities—political figures, sports heroes, movie stars, billionaire businessmen, pop musicians, and yes, members of the royal family—to limit the context in which they are viewed and pondered, then we would miss out on lots of important history."

Notes

1. Philip Rucker and Ed O'Keefe, "In Trump's Washington, Public Business Increasingly Handled behind Closed Doors," *Washington Post*, June 17, 2017.

2. Andrew L. Mendelson, "On the Function of the United States Paparazzi: Mosquito Swarm or Watchdogs of Celebrity Image Control and Power?" *Visual Studies* 22, no. 2 (2007), 169–183.

3. Benazir Wehelie and Kyle Almond, "Turning the Lens on Trump," http://www.cnn.com/interactive/2017/04/politics/trump-100-days-cnnphotos.

4. Tierney McAfee, "Instagram Proves Key to Exposing the Rounds of Golf President Trump Tries to Keep Secret," *People*, May 8, 2017, http://people.com/politics/president-trump-playing-golf-instagram-photo.

5. Claudia Rosenbaum, "The Paparazzi Are Flocking to Cover Trump's Dramatic Presidency," *BuzzFeed*, March 17, 2017, https://www.buzzfeed.com/claudiarosenbaum/making-the-paparazzi-great-again.

6. In *Assessing Evidence in a Postmodern World*, edited by Bonnie Brennen (Milwaukee, WI; Marquette University Press), 2013.

Part II   Emotion, Populism, and Media Events

9   The Importance of Being a Headline

Zizi Papacharissi

Imagine, if you will, a news story without a headline. Picture yourself reading that story. The topic of the story becomes unclear. Its focus is vague. Context is absent. You are reading a news report of some form, but you are not reading a news story. Headlines introduce, frame, and contextualize. They award significance, communicate gravitas, and reinforce status. Headlines inform and misinform. They are a crucial part of how news turns into a story. In the long durée, they play a part in how stories are retold and recorded, thus eventually turning into memories and histories.

The present growth of populism prompts us to reconsider news coverage of the world and the events that surround us. With populism in the United States came trends like the rise of fake news and notions like alternative facts. But it is also important to remember that before populism, many countries experienced waves of civil unrest, ranging from short-form protests, to movements, to long-form revolutions in the making. And prior to these waves of unrest came a deep financial crisis, precipitated by a couple of dot-com bubble bursts (the most severe in 2001). The financial crisis spread through a variety of sectors to land in the real estate sector and the investment firms that supported it. So, while this book uses the ascension of President Trump in the US as a starting point, the questions it addresses are not unique to the Trump presidency. For a long time, these tendencies and tensions have accumulated and have led citizens to feel cynical (e.g., Capella and Jamieson 1996), disillusioned with politics and journalism, and deeply insecure. This volume presents a variety of perspectives on what journalism can do about that. I focus exclusively on headlines, with emphasis first on the grammar of headlines ("How Headlines Read"), then on the feelings headlines evoke ("How Headlines Feel"), and finally on the economics of headlines ("How Headlines Pay"). I thus look at the economy of language, the economy of emotions, and the economy of profit that headlines are structured on. For each of these sections I consider conventional knowledge first, then explain how newer technology platforms inform the equation, and conclude with a look at how these aspects render the contemporary context. This is an essay about the meaning of news headlines.

How Headlines Read

The presentation of headlines may have changed over time, but the form remains the same. The language is meant to be short, summative, and sharp. The words bring the crucial elements of the story to the forefront, and the grammar and syntax drum up intensity, if needed. The verbal economy of headlines is tight and it must work quickly and efficiently. It is meant to capture the attention of the reader without, ideally, compromising the essence of the story. Because headlines not only lure, they also direct the attention of the reader, and in doing so, they frame a story. They offer a lens through which to understand it. They kick-start the cognitive process. They frame the issue at hand by selecting "some aspects of a perceived reality [to] make them more salient in a communicating text, in such a way as to promote a particular problem definition, causal interpretation, moral evaluation, and/or treatment recommendation" (Entman 1993, 52). Framing is guided by news values that prioritize recency, urgency, and proximity; the economy and political affairs; and privileged nations and dominant ideologies, while also appealing to viewers by being commonsensical, entertaining, and dramatic (see Hartley 2002, 166, for the comprehensive typology of news values). News values are about turning events into stories, and headlines present the first step in doing so.

Newer technologies do not radically reorganize how headlines are framed and which news values guide the framing process. But they do amplify visibility and pluralize access. Therefore, a directional lens offered through a frame becomes more visible by reaching greater audiences more quickly. In following suit with the ascent of the 24/7 news cycle that cable TV ushered in, new media platforms reinforce and reproduce an obsession with instantaneity in news reporting. Headlines must always be current. Headlines can now be revised without waiting for next day's edition, so they are. Because they can be revised, they are constantly revised, lest the attention of readers drifts off. And so we live in a news ecology of the ever-changing, always-updateable news beat; headlines are always already new.[1]

As a result, headlines become clickbait for a broad variety of news organizations and are used to attract eyeballs. Hashtags become headlines, and tweets are reported as both the headline and the story. Headlines are algorithmically generated and propagated by bots, leading to news—actual or fake. Importantly, newer platforms afford anyone the opportunity to craft a headline, and subsequently a news story. While this pluralizes the news ecology, it does not necessarily democratize the process. Actors, engaging in independent or coordinated acts of journalism, have a say in what story is told, and how it is introduced to the public arena. We might understand this process as a form of networked framing and gatekeeping, where a variety of actors—both human and nonhuman—work, together or on their own, to crowdsource news content to prominence via the use of conversational, social, and digitally enabled practices that symbiotically connect elite and masses in framing what is relevant (Meraz and Papacharissi 2013). This means that headlines about civil rights issues gain greater attention (#blacklivesmatter) at the same time that fake stories are elevated to prominence (#pizzagate). Technology is not neutral; it augments exposure. But it also does not discern between truth and fiction. Citizens, journalists, and politicians can.

How Headlines Feel

Headlines are part of the magical allure of news reading. In the early days of newspapers, newsboys yelped them out to attract passersby. When newspapers were not affordable or accessible to all, headlines would form the basis for conversation as people gathered and read them in cafés. From the food trucks of New York City that displayed above fold among coffees and hot dogs to the kiosks of Europe and South America enclosed by newspapers attached to wire with clothespins, people would gather around, peruse the day's headlines, and engage in casual social conversation with one another. There is a cognitive element to how we process the news, and framing addresses how the cognitive process is engaged. But there is a soft drama to the process of reading the news, which is always engulfed in our everyday routine, whether that involves reading the newspaper in print form or browsing through a news site on one's phone on the train to work. There is emotion involved in how we approach and become entranced by the process of following the news; this is both a social and information-seeking process. And it is a process called into being via headlines. The affect of headlines, that is, the mood, the atmosphere, the feelings headlines evoke both draws us in and further moves us emotionally.

How do newer platforms reorganize the news experience? They fold into and further extend the effect of the 24-hour news cycle, and thus further cultivate and reproduce a fixation with instantaneity in news reporting. There are multiple ways in which digital and networked platforms of news storytelling amplify the prevalence of headlines, and I have referred to some in the previous section. Here I want to focus on how technology lends texture to our affective reaction to the news. One key term in doing so is premediation. Premediation describes the form events take on, *before* they turn into stories (Grusin 2010). Premediation is thus connected to processes of events in the making, to anticipating what the news is going to be like, to how the headline is going to read. Grusin (2010) makes the point that premediation has dominated news storytelling post-9/11, a time when many of us, including news organizations, were struggling to make sense of what happened. He points to the news scroller, which became a staple of news storytelling during that time, as an example of this anticipation of the new, conveyed through the anxiety of constantly updating headlines. The form of the news scroller has dictated the stylistic and visual presentation of news online. It is a form that induces anticipation, and with that, anxiety—a state of always expecting the new.

Elsewhere, I have described this form of news storytelling as affective news. It is not a form of news storytelling that invites cool reflection, thoughtful fact checking, and in general, slow news. Affective news is native to ambient, always-on architectures that utilize a variety of social media, including Twitter, Facebook, and Reddit in particular. It blends news, fact, drama, and opinion into one, to the point where discerning one from the other is impossible, and doing so misses the point. Affective reactions are not news, nor are they headlines. They stem out of social experiences of reading the news and are a way for readers to feel their way into the story (Robinson 2009). Problems arise when affect, or an affective reaction, become the story. And so instead of news, we get mere headlines, repeated to the rhythm of the news scroller, our social media feeds, constant news updates, and always-breaking news. When headlines are repeated affectively, with no follow-up story or context, then we hear a lot about Secretary Clinton's emails without ever finding out exactly what happened. We constantly receive news alerts about President Trump not making his tax returns available, but we are spared the specifics of how this is possible. We become alarmed about #brexit, but we never manage to learn about the complexities that led to that particular development. In other words, we get intensity, 24/7, but no substance. News becomes flat.

How Headlines Pay

The economics of attention has never been absent from the business of news storytelling. Headlines are central to the economics of attention, as they are the lead mechanism of drawing in readers. Assuming this is a new problem, or even a problem, is devoid of any understanding of the business of newsmaking and the ways in which decisions are made in the newsroom. Headlines must work in a way that is financially viable for the news storytelling business. News is a business, and the people who are tasked with reporting the news function within the market economy of newsmaking. The contemporary business of newsmaking exists within the scope of late capitalism and operates within its confines in order to be financially sustainable. Reconciling economics with the politics of truth-telling is no easy task, and has always complicated life for journalists and news organizations. These difficulties are not insurmountable, but they require maintaining a delicate balance in the newsroom—a task that frequently falls into the hands of editors who must be clever and resourceful.

Social media do not simplify this equation at all. On the contrary, because newspapers are in the business of selling information and newer media make sharing information exceptionally easy, social media augment longstanding tensions of treating information as an economic good. Information is an abstraction. Unlike other commodities that are bought and sold, information does not possess a tangible material basis.[2] So do a lot of services, but what makes information unique as a commodity is its abstract nature. Information cannot be sold, produced, or distributed in distinct units.[3] Unlike other goods, it cannot be completely used up or consumed. Even when sold, it still remains with the producer. Most importantly, its relevance varies for each consumer, in ways that affirm the liminal nature of information valuation. For all these reasons, information remains an elusive commodity; "it wants to be free." It remains a subjectively defined entity with a particular kind of "lightness" that makes it difficult to trade. Crowded markets further augment the consequences of the unique character information possesses as a commodity. In this context, headlines are used to both frame the news and lure readers in. While not new, this phenomenon is amplified through technologies that connect clicking on headlines to raising potential revenue margins for news organizations.

For networked, globally-active or locally-specific news organizations, information is a key variable to prosperity and growth. But failure to realize that information is ultimately an abstraction, and not a commodity, frequently leads to efforts to compartmentalize information and sell it in bits or bytes, package it in the form of lists and clickbait content, and auction off its most attention-grabbing elements, even though those are often not the most valuable ones. There is no easy way out of this conundrum. Change would take patience and cooperation. It would require (a) leading news institutions coming to an accord on the market principles that will define the news economy and (b) news institutions becoming partially or wholly financially independent.

What to Do about Headlines

Newer media technologies afford innovative ways for news storytelling that may go a long way toward reconnecting politicians and the media with a disaffected public. Unfortunately, they are typically co-opted into conventional economics of production, thus producing clickbait headlines, bot-friendly ledes, and drama-inducing angles. These tendencies and tensions further augment tensions in the chasm that Hannah Arendt had identified between truth and politics. In an article originally published in the *New Yorker* in 1967, Arendt had famously stated what many knew but few openly advertised: "Truth and politics are on rather bad terms with each other. … Lies have always been regarded as necessary and justifiable tools not only of the politician's or the demagogue's but also of the statesman's trade." The distance between politics and the truth played its own part in the recent 2016 US presidential election, but certainly not in ways that are new, or specific to a single political context.

In a sense, journalism has always been in crisis; a crisis brought on by the difficulty of reconciling the necessities of truth-telling with the priorities of politics. Journalists are the ones confronted with this almost impossible task daily, and newer media both amplify its magnitude and offer a way out: literacy. Above all, networked platforms offer opportunities for connection and expression. They afford openings to reach out to others to fight, troll, converse and also listen, learn, and educate (oneself, and others).

So in the end, what to do about headlines? Learn how to read them.

Notes

1. I borrow this phrase from Lisa Gitelman (2006) and apply it to the context of news headlines.

2. I do not wish to ascertain here that information does not possess its own materiality, or, in the contemporary era, digitality (see Dourish 2017; Papacharissi 2014). But it does not possess the same tangible material form that other conventional goods do.

3. To this point, efforts to compartmentalize and trade information into news stories involve monetizing schemes that offer questionable monetary gain and have yet to produce a self-sustaining model for news organizations.

10   Public Displays of Disaffection: The Emotional Politics of Donald Trump

Karin Wahl-Jorgensen

At a time when our news headlines are dominated by the US President's latest Twitter rants, impulsive political decisions, and blustering denunciations of foes and former allies alike, this chapter tries to make sense of the emotional politics of Donald Trump. It suggests that Trump has ushered in an emotional regime of anger, driven by "public displays of disaffection." Trump's presidency has rendered anger a salient framework for understanding public life, with significant consequences for politics and how we view it.

In taking an interest in the emotional politics of Trump, this chapter is part of a larger project, which assumes that emotions are central to political life—and the media's reporting of it—and that we ignore them at our peril. Such a project goes against the grain of longstanding traditions of thought about politics, embodied in the liberal democratic approach. Political actors are supposed to be informed by purely rational and dispassionate considerations. However, scholars interested in politics now acknowledge that emotion plays a key role in shaping political motivation and participation. Citizens involve themselves in political causes because they *care* about an issue or, in many cases, because they are *affected* by it. Attachment to an issue might be fueled by a range of emotions, positive *and* negative, including hate, anger, and fear, *and* love, compassion, and happiness. Likewise, for politicians and their parties, emotional appeals are central to the building of solidarities.[1] These solidarities can be inclusive—based, for example, on compassion for refugees and ethnic minorities—or exclusive— based on intolerance directed at groups such as women, homosexuals, and migrants.

Recent right-wing populist movements around the world share the cultivation of such exclusive solidarities through appeals to emotions such as fear and anger. Trump is a particularly interesting example of a populist politician who relies on negative emotional appeals for the creation of exclusionary solidarities. Sociologist Arlie Hochschild studied disenfranchised conservative voters in the U.S. to explain the rise of the Tea Party Movement and, subsequently, Trump. For Hochschild, "Trump is an 'emotions candidate.' [...] Trump focuses on eliciting and praising emotional responses from his fans. [...] His speeches—evoking dominance, bravado, clarity, national pride, and personal uplift—inspire an emotional transformation."[2]

If Trump was an "emotions candidate," it is clear that the emotions he embodies and articulates are highly unusual in the history of American politics. Here, I want to suggest that the emotional politics of Donald Trump is premised on what we might call "public displays of disaffection." The appeal of Trump relies on giving voice to a narrow cluster of emotions, centered on anger.

Anger is particularly interesting to consider as a political emotion. It forms the basis for the articulation of shared grievances in the public sphere. Social movements scholars have studied the role of anger in the mobilization of marginalized groups, for whom it has been seen as an empowering emotion.[3] At the same time, liberal-democratic theory has been suspicious of anger because of its close association with violence and aggression.[4] Anger, political thinkers hold, is anathema to constructive political discourse. So why, then, do we hear so much about the anger of Trump, as well as of his supporters and opponents?

The importance of anger to Trump's appeal and rhetoric certainly stands in stark contrast to traditions of American presidential rhetoric, which has tended to be reliant on positive emotions. Both Obama and Clinton drew heavily on the emotion of hope as a central trope. By contrast, Trump's injunction to "Make America Great Again"—a slogan that embodies hope for the future and the possibility of change—has consistently been accompanied by angry rants about the present, resonating with disaffected voters. As David Remnick wrote in a *New Yorker* editorial on Trump's first 100 days in office:

The Trump presidency represents a rebellion against liberalism itself—an angry assault on the advances of groups of people who have experienced profound, if fitful, empowerment over the past half century. [...] [H]is language, his tone, his personal behavior, and his policies all suggest, and foster, a politics of resentment.[5]

A study I conducted of Trump's inauguration coverage identified anger as a central theme.[6] This goes against the strong consensus orientation that typically characterizes these events. Inaugurations seek to cement the dominant narrative around the president. They are mediated public rituals, organized around the spectacle of affirming the new president. Inaugurations channel mainly positive emotions, while the expression of negative emotions is structurally limited.

It is, therefore, all the more striking that coverage of Donald Trump's inauguration was marked by the prominence of anger. What is particularly interesting is the frequency of descriptions of Trump himself as being angry—such descriptions appeared in 23 percent of all inauguration stories that mentioned anger.[7] Anger is not usually a feature of mediated representations of presidents—particularly not their inaugurations. In a comparative sample examining the role of anger in coverage of Obama's first inauguration, there were *no* references to Obama being angry.[8]

Historically, the successful management of emotions has been vital to successful presidential candidacies, while poor control has derailed campaigns. The Democratic primary candidacy of Howard Dean in 2004 collapsed after the infamous "Dean Scream." At the end of his spontaneous speech reacting to his third-place result in the Iowa Caucus, Dean made a high-pitched scream, which he later attributed to a sore throat. This moment was captured by several media organizations and then circulated widely. Following on from the media frenzy, Dean was denounced as unpresidential and uncontrolled. His display of odd nonverbal language served as a marker of uncontrollable emotionality, and effectively put an end to his race.

By contrast, Trump's outbursts and gaffes have been too numerous to account. During the election campaign, they attracted attention when they fit into a broader narrative around his candidacy, as in his mocking of the disabled reporter Serge Kovaleski; when he appeared to call for the assassination of Hillary Clinton; and when his "grab them by the pussy" interview came to light. The blatant disregard for "emotion rules"—or rules governing displays of emotion in particular situations[9]—might have terminated any other candidate at any other time. Instead, Trump sailed onward, constantly emoting in socially inappropriate ways.

Of course, Trump's blustering performance cannot be simply understood as constructed through the discourses of mainstream media, but rather as emerging within a hybrid media system.[10] Trump, like other populist politicians, has been highly successful at mobilizing support through Twitter, and his tweets have, in turn, attracted extensive media coverage. The increasing prominence of social media shapes not just the content of mainstream media, but also their affective style. According to a number of observers, the affordances of Twitter facilitate a discursive climate which is more extreme, divisive, and polarized.[11] Trump appears to be a beneficiary of this affective shift by crafting his charged messages on Twitter in a way that spills over into mainstream media.[12]

Here, I want to focus particularly on Trump's *anger* as politically significant. My study showed that a high number of references to anger—a total of 20 percent—in the inauguration coverage did *not* identify a target, and that the subject of this anger was, in the majority of these cases, Trump himself. Trump was not only frequently represented as being angry, but *angry about nothing in particular*. This was also true of some of the coverage of his supporters. As the literature on anger suggests, anger normally requires a target for it to matter politically.[13] Going against this pattern, the angry Trump was newsworthy in his own right:

The 16-minute inaugural address that President Trump delivered was Trumpism distilled to its raw essence: angry, blunt-spoken, and deeply aggrieved.[14]

Donald John Trump intends to govern as the same fiercely angry man who inspired the discontented but aroused the worries and fears of so many other Americans.[15]

Describing anger as having a particular target both explains the anger and contributes to legitimizing it. By contrast, the generalized anger of Trump and his supporters suggests that they are angry without a cause. The image that emerges from the media coverage is that anger is essential to their identity and their worldview. Analysts suggested that Trump appealed to voters in large part because he saw the appeal of a new and angrier form of political discourse. As Doug Criss noted in a CNN inauguration update:

Donald J. Trump identified, long before anyone else did, the anger and desire for change that millions of Americans craved. He addressed that in frank, blunt terms that deeply resonated with millions who were fed up with Washington's political class and felt left behind in the globalizing economy.[16]

Trump became an emotional performer, acting as the advocate of the people and the impersonator of their anger. His anger mattered because it became a political force in and of itself.

The First 100 Days of Angry President Trump

If we look at the coverage following on from Trump's inauguration and up to the end of his first 100 days in office,[17] we see frequent references to the angry Trump. This is particularly prominent in the period immediately following his inauguration, as well as in reflections on his first 100 days in office. Just like the inauguration, the landmark of the first 100 days in office provided an opportunity to make broader statements about the character of the new president. In a widely syndicated column published on May 1, 2017, Jennifer Rubin argued that "President Donald Trump remains an angry, irrational figure, someone who still must stir up hatred against the press, against immigrants, against Democrats to enliven his base."[18] The president is here constructed as fundamentally and essentially angry—though the anger is directed at particular actors, including the press, immigrants, and Democrats.

The media coverage after the inauguration also frequently pointed to specific targets of Trump's anger, including the media, elites, and attempts to block his travel ban:

President Donald Trump is angry at all the news coverage about the people who stand to be hurt because of the Republican plan to repeal and replace the Affordable Care Act.[19]

The legal and legislative pushback has left the White House frustrated and angry. Trump slammed the court orders on his travel ban as "unprecedented judicial overreach."[20]

The U.S. has a robust, free, and fair media. No wonder that makes Donald Trump angry.[21]

Over the course of Trump's first 100 days in office, his anger was not only established as an essential feature of his character, but also as a guiding force in policy decisions:

Donald Trump's election was propelled by the wave of anti-globalization anger that is sweeping the United States and other Western advanced economies. Trump has echoed that anger in his rhetoric. And now he is responding to that anger with policy.[22]

Furthermore, Trump's anger was represented as having a contagion effect, as it spread across the population—sometimes for what was described as legitimate reasons, at other times for no reason at all:

Before last year's presidential election, Donald Trump was solidly the candidate of anger. [...] Now Trump and his motley crew have taken over the White House and those who were angry before are no longer quite so. [...] Thus the mantle of anger has passed to the left. The Women's March and the protests against the immigration ban fiercely demonstrated the resistance Trump can expect to his blundering policies.[23]

Other observers highlighted how Trump has driven a shift toward generalized public anger, among both his supporters and his opponents. Political scientist Michael Berkman, writing in the *Daily Cardinal* on February 13, 2017, suggested: "His tweets show his supporters what he is thinking, directly and unvarnished. Less well appreciated, but apparent in our research based on new polling, is how Trump's anger and its targets are quickly adopted and internalized by large numbers of his followers."[24]

Conclusion

So, what are the implications of this? The historian William Reddy suggested that we need to see practices of governance as driven in part by the way we speak about emotions in public. He introduced the term "emotional regime" to refer to the "set of normative emotions and the official rituals, practices, and 'emotives' [emotional speech acts] that express and inculcate them; a necessary underpinning of any stable political regime."[25] The media are central to the construction of an emotional regime by reporting on these normative emotions, rituals, practices, and "emotives" as articulated by the president. The emphasis on Trump's public displays of disaffection—and his appeal to an aggrieved public through it—has had significant consequences in shaping public debate. It suggests that anger is a viable interpretive framework for understanding political discourse and its performance, along with the motivations of political actors. Trump's anger can be seen as representing a shifting emotional regime, one which heralds a broader change in public discourse and the terms of public life, spurred on in part through the affordances of the hybrid media system: anger has been legitimated as a political emotion, and one which has concrete consequences for democratic practice. What we now need to understand is what forms of action this anger enables.

At the same time, the emotional regime of Trump has been met with contagious anger, and this anger itself forms the basis for resistance. The question remains whether such anger is necessary and sufficient for political action, or whether we must invent a new emotional politics to challenge the Trump regime. Such an emotional politics is unlikely to emerge solely through structurally constrained mainstream media, but rather may surface through the dynamic "affective news streams" of social media.[26]

Notes

1. David Ost, *The Defeat of Solidarity: Anger and Politics in Postcommunist Europe.* (Ithaca, NY: Cornell University Press, 2006).

2. Arlie R. Hochschild, *Strangers in Their Own Land: Anger and Mourning on the American Right* (New York: The New Press), kindle location 3712.

3. Deborah Gould, "On Affect and Protest," in *Political Emotions: New Agendas in Communication*, ed. Janet Staiger, Ann Cvetkovich, and Ann Reynolds (London and New York: Routledge, 2010), 18–44.

4. Mary Holmes, "Introduction: The Importance of Being Angry: Anger in Political Life," *European Journal of Social Theory* 7(2): 127.

5. David Remnick, "One Hundred Days," *New Yorker*, May 1, 2017.

6. Karin Wahl-Jorgensen, "Media Coverage of Shifting Emotional Regimes: Donald Trump's Angry Populism," *Media, Culture & Society* (forthcoming).

7. Wahl-Jorgensen, "Media Coverage of Shifting Emotional Regimes."

8. Wahl-Jorgensen, "Media Coverage of Shifting Emotional Regimes."

9. Arlie R. Hochschild, *The Managed Heart* (Berkeley: University of California Press, 1983).

10. Andrew Chadwick, *The Hybrid Media System: Politics and Power* (Oxford: Oxford University Press, 2013).

11. Tamara Shepherd, Alison Harvey, Tim Jordan, Sam Sruay, and Kate Miltner, "Histories of Hating." *Social Media + Society* 1(2) (2015).

12. David Karpf, "Digital Politics after Trump," *Annals of the International Communication Association* 41(2) (2017): 198–207.

13. Mervi K. Pantti and Karin Wahl-Jorgensen, "'Not an Act of God': Anger and Citizenship in Press Coverage of British Man-Made Disasters," *Media, Culture & Society* 33(1) (2011): 105–122.

14. Mark Barabak, "Raw, Angry and Aggrieved, President Trump's Inaugural Speech Does Little to Heal Political Wounds," *Los Angeles Times*, January 20, 2017.

15. Doug Criss, "5 Things for Friday, January 20, 2017: Donald Trump, Inauguration Day," CNN, January 20, 2017.

16. E. J. Dionne Jr., "President Trump's Angry, Bleak Vision," *Hartford Courant*, January 21, 2017.

17. I did this by carrying out a Nexis UK search on US Newspapers and Wires in the period 01/21/2017 to 05/01/2017. Trump's first 100 days in office ended on 04/29/2017, and by including the two following days, I captured reflections on this traditional landmark period. I used the search terms "Donald Trump" (major mentions) and, within 5 words, "anger" (major mentions) or "angry" (major mentions). This yielded a total of 234 articles. By contrast, a search on Obama's first 100 days in office yielded only 84 articles. Other, less-narrow searches (e.g., removing "within 5 words" or major mentions for any of the keywords) yielded results too large to display in Nexis.

18. Criss, "5 Things for Friday."

19. Jennifer Rubin, "This Is Not a Normal President," *Washington Post*, May 1, 2017.

20. Julie Pace, "Analysis: Trump Learning that in White House, Words Matter," AP News, March 16, 2017.

21. Jill Richardson, "The Press is Essential, Whether Presidents Like It or Not," *Eureka-Times Standard*, March 12, 2017.

22. Pankaj Ghemawat and Steven A. Altman, "Is America Enriching the World at Its Own Expense? That's Globaloney," *Washington Post*, February 3, 2017.

23. Alex Davies, "The Stewardship of Anger," *Cornell Daily Sun*, February 27, 2017.

24. Michael Berkman, "When Trump's Tweets Are Angry, the Mood of His Followers Darkens," *Daily Cardinal*, February 13, 2017.

25. William M. Reddy, *The Navigation of Feeling: A Framework for the History of Emotions* (Cambridge, Cambridge University Press, 2001), 129.

26. Zizi Papacharissi, *Affective Publics: Sentiment, Technology, and Politics* (Oxford: Oxford University Press, 2015).

11   Facts (Almost) Never Win Over Myths

Julia Sonnevend

Deep in our hearts we all hope that our beliefs are based on facts, rationality, and a nuanced balancing of conflicting expectations of reality. Among the very few things media scholars have been able to "prove" is the ubiquity of selective perception, namely the phenomenon that our desire to support our claims is so strong that we literally see only the evidence that confirms our established views. Facts in public discourse are still frequently evoked as stable foundations we refer to in times of need. And when the world seems less stable than we would hope for, we tend to think that facts could be our saviors.

President Trump's surprise win in the 2016 American elections has triggered a passionate debate over "fake news" as a contributing factor in his electoral success. In the mindset of those making a causal link between fake news and the Trump win, surprise outcomes are linked to nonrationality and a state of misinformation, when rational minds suddenly get lost and leave the safe pathway of facts for the unknown, the mythical, the untrue. In this way of looking at the world, myths are fictions or fairytales or entertainments, something designed for the weak, the underinformed, the "stupid." Myths transcend facts and charm the public with foggy imaginings. The solution, thus, appears to be a better form of communication, a more efficient way of information distribution. New technological solutions, journalistic methods, and media systems are discussed to fix the mistake, to find the right way to "inform the public." Reformers imagine that if only people were confronted with actual "facts," they would stop believing the "myth." But why would they?

If we accept our desire to experience something larger than life, to stand for something that is beyond the weekly paycheck, then myth is the only thing that is worth living for. Myths provide belief systems that structure our experience in a world too complicated for anyone to comprehend. Jack Lule defined myth "as a sacred, societal story that draws from archetypal figures and forms to offer exemplary models for human life."[1] Myths thus create imagined realities and highlight the power of the sacred in our social lives and national politics.

The American public—like all publics—has always been hungry for myths. Think about the ongoing love affair for the Kennedys, the Reagan myth of singlehandedly beating the Soviets (never mind that it was the careful and diplomatic elder Bush who was in power during the fall of the Berlin Wall), or the inspiring campaign of Barack Obama about "change we can believe in." When presidential candidate Trump entered the race for president, many American voters were more than ready to *believe* in something. They were still recovering from a crippling financial crisis, had just experienced a series of international terrorist attacks, and had come to recognize and worry about the processes of globalization even in their own neighborhoods. Candidate Trump offered a very powerful myth embodied in three key slogans "Make America Great Again!," "We Will Drain the Swamp!," and "We Will Build a Wall!" This myth promised a successful and homogenous America within reach, in which life would be easier, dignity for the worker achievable, and globalization at least somewhat controllable.

"Make America Great Again," condensed into MAGA in tweets and on bumper stickers, imagined an America that has never existed, but was nonetheless about to be "re-created." The slogan was simple and powerful, starting with a vague action word and ending in both the promise of greatness and the imagination that we are only rebuilding what was *once already there*. The slogan also embodied the massive anxiety Americans have always experienced from outside powers threatening the country's global prominence—this time mostly from China. The fear of China stands for a fear of global competition in general, in which faraway, hard-to-decipher foreign "aliens" will score better on standardized tests, take over jobs, and occupy one crucial industry sector after the other. In addition to being an anti-global message, "Make America Great Again" had a clear racial and class message as well: greatness was linked with whiteness and wealth. "Make America Great Again" pictured an America from the early episodes of *Mad Men*, when beautiful white women in pink steel kitchens awaited their handsome husbands in a dreamlike American home, while the kids were admiring the newly bought television set.

As part of making America great again, candidate Trump also promised to provide workers with dignity again. As Katherine J. Cramer so astutely detected in her book *The Politics of Resentment*, rural consciousness was boiling with resentment against elites well before the election of Trump. Trump's promise of "draining the swamp" offered a new beginning, when hardworking everyday Americans could take back Washington and other power centers from those, as one interviewee of Cramer says, "who shower before work, not afterwards."[2] For Americans worrying about their jobs, the educational prospects of their kids, and a dizzyingly complicated global economy, Trump presented a chance of things becoming controllable again. While ironic that a multibillionaire from a golden Manhattan apartment emerged as an icon for rural resentment, somehow even Trump's extreme wealth stood for the possibility of prosperity for everyone, regardless of their current social standing.

"Make America Great Again" and "We Will Drain the Swamp" were smartly combined with another promise: "We Will Build a Wall." Note how all three campaign slogans were inherently iconic scenes, as if we were reading the Bible or other foundational myths of mankind. Candidate Trump did not talk of a "fence," a "border control regime," or something similarly technical. It was not until after the elections that he admitted that some parts of the wall would actually be a fence. Throughout the campaign, he talked about a mythical wall, an imagined barrier from a fairy tale. Political leaders after the fall of the Berlin Wall have tended to call their border barriers "fences," while those opposing the barriers have named them "walls."[3] Why? The specter of the Berlin Wall had to be avoided. While many countries have desired and more than forty, in fact, have built separation walls since 1989, they did not want the symbolic power of the Berlin Wall to work against them. Candidate Trump had a different vision. More than anything else, he wanted the mental imagination of a "wall," an impermeable barrier. Building the wall in minds was more important than building it from bricks. Other than a vague promise that Mexico would pick up the costs, Trump's proposal did not include any actual policy details, construction plans, or an itemized budget. The wall had to be imagined, whether it could actually be built was secondary at that point. The wall was above all a *symbol* of division, an imagined way to keep "them" out.

While constructing this mythical universe, Donald Trump was not without historical precedent. Many describe his win as an unprecedented triumph of "lies" over "facts." But has history ever been about the triumph of rationality over desires and dreams? Consider one of the most successful American global visions, the Marshall Plan. While the Marshall Plan in hindsight is often described as a mere economic plan to rebuild certain parts of Europe after World War II, it was, in fact, a project of hope. The Marshall Plan meant to capture the hearts and souls of Europeans and prevent the spread of communism. The United States ran an extensive communication campaign in Western Europe focused on the prospect of change and a belief in the future. At the end, the famous success of the Marshall Plan was as much about captured hearts as about well-spent dollars.

Or take another icon of "Western success": the fall of the Berlin Wall. While the fall of the Berlin Wall was part of an ongoing, confusing, and contradictory political transition in the Eastern bloc, it is still remembered as a historic moment of mythical proportions: a magical, split-second "event," not an occurrence of an ongoing "process." If any previous process is highlighted, then it is bombastic iconic scenes, like Reagan's announcement in front of the much-guarded Brandenburg Gate: "Mr. Gorbachev, tear down this wall!" The slow, clunky, and occasionally accidental political processes faded in memory and a myth of the power of ordinary people emerged as the event's dominant interpretation.

This tendency to look for hope, belief, and emotion in politics is still with us today. Just before Trump's win, another unexpected event shook the globe: Brexit. In the passionate Brexit campaign, the "Remain" (in the European Union) camp provided a toxic combination of fear, anxiety, and countless incomprehensible facts. In contrast, the "Leave" campaign envisioned a mythical "Independence Day," when a New United Kingdom (or Britain) would emerge from its ashes to be sovereign, influential, and prosperous. Many voters chose this promise over the contradictory current reality of their country.

In all these historical precedents, we see the desire for something larger than life, something people can *aspire to*. In all these examples, we see the presence of "affective publics," as Zizi Papacharissi put it, a desire to "feel" politics, events, and social processes.[4] While in common wisdom emotions may be separated from reason, in our everyday online and offline interactions these sides of human existence are deeply intertwined. Social media provide an ideal set of platforms for the spreading myths, where hierarchies are often flattened; expertise is increasingly suspect and emotions quickly run high and low. Many of our contemporary myths are born in offline settings or in legacy media, only some are born digital. Still, on social media myths get reconfigured, recycled, visualized, and spread to further communities. Social media's permanent outrage culture also provides myths with much-needed passion.

In light of these examples of mythical, nonrational power, what could have brought a different election result in 2016? On thing is clear: Trump's carefully built up mythical message could not have been beaten by a set of carefully aligned facts or a series of detailed spreadsheets. Only a powerful counter-myth would have been able to win the day. Hillary Clinton's myth of "Stronger Together" was an effort in this direction, but it only suggested that the world would remain complicated and globalization would continue, but at least we would be in it together. This counter-myth was professional, rational, and fact-based, but it was weak in its battle for hearts and souls. It was as large as life, but not larger than life as any good myth has to be. In an ideal world, a professional woman with decades of experience and relentless dedication to public service would have easily won against a man who has never held any public position before and presented quite a few major character issues. In a rational world focused on calm deliberation, his win simply does "not make sense." But once we accept the power of the mythical over the factual, it all seems to come, at least somewhat, together.

If you combine the hope of a "great America" with the promise of a protected America and a renewed Washington, the vision of Trump seems rather irresistible. Still, once this vision won on November 8, 2016, the media and other opinion makers were frantically searching for reasons. It would have been possible to blame the outcome on the naïve belief in data science and polling that dominated discourses instead of sophisticated qualitative and mixed-method studies like Cramer's. Analysts could have focused on the lack of vision on the Democrats' side. Even realizing the tragic influence of the longlasting Sanders movement on Clinton's prospects would have been a brave attempt at understanding. Instead, an unlikely candidate for blame quickly emerged: fake news.

We still do not know how many voters changed their preferences based on any false news item. Fake news may have only reinforced existing beliefs in voters who already had strong voting preferences. Still, fake news as a concept has dominated discussions of the Trump win and presidency ever since. It led to an obsession with fact-checking and a constant frustration that even the best fact-checking is not enough to convince the voter who "believes." In the meantime, perhaps unsurprisingly, President Trump has hijacked the fake news debate quite brilliantly by realizing that "fake news" is also a belief system you can use for your own purposes. If facts are in the center of discussions, it is enough for him to destabilize the source or the article, and the argument for many voters is simply "gone."

Overall the fake news debate assigned a bigger role to media in public life than it deserves, while ignoring larger processes that are influencing politics in the United States, for instance income inequality, anti-immigrant sentiment, racism, and a deep feeling of economic, social, and cultural uncertainty. The fake news debate reduced voters to failed rational beings, while ignoring the "fact" that we all desire something more from life than reason. Facts, professional experience, and reason suffered a tragic loss in the elections of 2016. But they lost against something meaningful: a mythical promise of hope, prosperity, and dignity.

Notes

1. Jack Lule, *Daily News, Eternal Stories: The Mythological Role of Journalism* (New York: Guilford Press, 2001), 15.

2. Katherine J. Cramer, *The Politics of Resentment: Rural Consciousness in Wisconsin and the Rise of Scott Walker* (Chicago: University of Chicago Press, 2016).

3. Julia Sonnevend, *Stories Without Borders: The Berlin Wall and the Making of a Global Iconic Event* (New York: Oxford University Press, 2016).

4. Zizi Papacharissi, *Affective Publics: Sentiment, Technology, and Politics* (New York: Oxford University Press, 2015).

12   The Media Are about Identity, Not Information

Daniel Kreiss

"How can you tell straight news from opinion?" I ask. "By the *tone of voice*," she explains. "Take Christiane Amanpour. She'll be kneeling by a sick African child, or a bedraggled Indian, looking into the camera, and her voice is saying, 'Something's *wrong*. We have to *fix* it.' Or worse, *we* caused the problem. She's using that child to say, '*Do* something America.' But that child's problems aren't our fault."

This exchange took place between Berkeley sociologist Arlie Hochschild and a Tea Party supporter in Louisiana in the course of her fieldwork for the book *Strangers in Their Own Land* (2016, 128). Hochschild uses the exchange to reveal how the conservatives she traveled among view the professional press as profoundly biased, with the notable exception of Fox News. The celebrated CNN international correspondent was implicitly telling this Tea Party supporter how to *feel* about global suffering, which the woman responded negatively to: "That's *PC*. That's what liberals want listeners like me to feel. I don't feel like it. And what's more, I don't want to be told I'm a bad person if I don't feel sorry for that child." The social validation and release from liberal "feeling rules" is precisely why, to many of the individuals that Hochschild studies, "Fox is family."

And it is why so many of these people were elated when President Trump came along and validated their identities as white Christian Americans, and affirmed their historical place at the center of American social, economic, and cultural life. Trump told stories about how these white Americans received the short end of the stick, a consequence of bad trade deals, porous borders, affirmative action, and welfare policies that rewarded undeserving African Americans and cosmopolitan Washington and cultural elites who sneered at flyover country. As Hochschild points out, Trump, along with Fox News, gave these strangers in their own land the hope that they would be restored to their rightful place at the center of the nation, and provided a very real emotional release from the fetters of political correctness that dictated they respect people of color, lesbians and gays, and those of other faiths.

Many of these things are surprising in light of the standard stories journalists tell themselves about the role of their trade in American democracy. Journalists, and much of public discourse more broadly, posit that citizens are rational deliberators, weighing the information the media provides to make informed decisions at the polls according to the general interest, not the narrow concerns of parochial social groups. While most practicing or studying journalism would admit that this is an ideal rarely achieved, journalists, the foundations working to save journalism, and many scholars do see a public starved of quality information as a central issue in contemporary democracy. Even more, while their theories of democratic citizens are rarely made explicit, journalists and others concerned with the profession generally assume that citizens are autonomous and independent, somehow separate and apart from the internecine battles of partisanship in Washington, DC, and conflicts over social identity more broadly.

And yet, this Tea Party supporter seemingly cared little about receiving information. She saw Amanpour, a decorated journalist who has won eleven Emmy awards for television news, as *liberal*. She also seemingly rejected the very premise that a journalist should see an overseas humanitarian crisis as important for an American to care about or even as particularly newsworthy. Indeed, in the view of Tea Party members, Fox News was less about "information" than "family." The metaphor is telling. A family provides a sense of identity, place, and belonging; emotional, social, and cultural support and security; and gives rise to political and social affiliations and beliefs.

The idea that Fox is "family" casts the role of media in social life in a new light, different from standard, informational accounts of journalism and media in America. While this Tea Party supporter described Fox in terms that emphasized a quite literal "living with" the network and compared its hosts to family members, the broader point is that the network shared an identity with her. As Hochschild argues, Tea Party supporters believe that the network's personalities share the same "deep story" of political and social life, and therefore they learn from them "what to feel afraid, angry, and anxious about."

While this account of media might look odd to a journalist or even a journalism scholar, it accords with much scholarship within political science. For over sixty years, political scientists and political communication scholars have consistently found that citizens know and often care little about politics. Citizens have little in the way of developed ideological frameworks for understanding politics or consistent policy preferences. As political scientists Christopher Achen and Larry Bartels argue in their 2016 book, *Democracy for Realists,* summarizing this literature, citizens do not rationally weigh policy information in the course of an election. They vote based on their social identities, or how they perceive themselves and others, their partisan identities, and their sense of the groups they believe the two political parties represent. As Donald Green, Bradley Palmquist, and Eric Schickler document in *Partisan Hearts and Minds* (2004), people perceive the Democratic Party as the party of the poor, working class, and people of color, and the Republican Party as the party of business, upper classes, and whites. Citizens come to perceive themselves in relation to these groups as they grow into their own social identities and partisan affiliations, especially through their family lives, and it largely shapes their lifelong political identities and ultimately vote choices.

Politics, then, is primarily an identity-based phenomenon. One way of thinking about it is akin to sports fandom, albeit with much higher stakes—citizens want their partisan and social group teams to be "winners" and the other teams to be "losers." The political ideologies or policies at stake are largely unimportant for most Americans compared with the success of the teams they affiliate with—look no further than the way that the vast majority of Republicans in the electorate were unfazed by Trump's social spending proposals on the campaign trail. When citizens tune in at all, the role of media is to provide a running account of a political, and often moral, contest, whether it is candidates vying on the campaign trail or the president battling adversaries in Congress. Citizens interpret and evaluate these contests and the media that provides stories about them through the lens of their own identities, and they especially understand politics in partisan terms, which at our contemporary moment accords with other social cleavages such as race and ethnicity. Legacy journalism conveys narratives about politics that shore up political team identification, such as being a Republican or a Democrat, helping people care about the wins and losses of their team. This is far more consequential in political life than substantive information about things such as policy, which few people care about save from learning what their own team believes.

Meanwhile, people tend to believe the elites of their team over journalists, who play for no team and are therefore suspect. This is why scholars such as Jonathan Ladd (2011) have found that elite criticism of the press leads people to distrust journalism. Again, the sports analogy is apt—are you more likely to trust the star player on your team or the referee after a controversial call? And, in politics, facts are hard to determine, predicated on the work of many different institutions, and premised on interpretation, as scholars such as Lucas Graves (2016) have pointed out.

Despite these dynamics, journalists, a network of foundation funders, and academics alike generally see the profession of journalism in the narrow and ideal terms of providing quality information to rational, general-interest citizens fulfilling their solemn duty of making informed decisions at the polls. The ideal public is such a deep-rooted myth in the United States that efforts of civil repair following failures of democracy, such as electing someone dangerous to the highest office in the land, focus on someone or some thing such as media manipulation that leads democratic citizens astray through no fault of their own. The ability of the public to self-govern is never questioned.

Look no further than the dominant story coming out of the 2016 US presidential election campaign: the concern over "fake news." Elite journalists, trade publications such as Neiman Lab and the *Columbia Journalism Review*, foundations such as Knight, and media scholars collectively raised their concerns about fake news to the level of a moral panic after Trump's election. The idea of fake news being consequential for the election outcome not only lacks much in the way of empirical evidence and overlooks the identity-basis of politics; it recalls first-generation media theory, which saw powerful media messages as hypodermic needles that turned people fascist. In the aftermath of the 2016 election, many seemed to believe that voters were collectively duped into pulling the lever for the Republican by farcical stories of the Pope endorsing Donald Trump—instead of acknowledging that white cultural and social anxiety and racism lay at the root of the president's appeal as the representative of a white political party (a claim for which there are mountains of evidence). In many ways, this makes perfect sense as the collective response of the industry and its academic interpreters to the election. It is the easier explanation, and one that preserves the myth of the ideal democratic citizen, what Achen and Bartels (2016) call the "folk theory" of democracy. Even more, our field sees the world through the lens of media and information problems, not political problems. And, journalists' tenuous hold on jurisdiction means that they and their networks of supporters have a lot to gain in re-establishing the basis for their own legitimacy and authority to produce credible accounts of the social and political world. Academics, meanwhile, gain access to mountains of grant money to tackle the problem of fake news.

It is both telling and sad that "fake news" was discussed after the election far more than identity and racism, sexism, or even partisanship, which were far more important factors in Donald Trump's elevation to the presidency. As scholars such as Hochschild and Justin Gest, as well as survey evidence, tell us, it was the deep cultural anxiety that many whites feel over pluralistic, multicultural American society and their own standing in it that fueled Trump's rise. Many whites fear changing demographics and the loss of their perceived, and deeply nostalgic, "American way of life" and their rightful place at the center of it. As historians continue to tell us, these are recurrent themes in our country since its founding and are, at root, whites as the dominant social group defining and debating the borders of civic incorporation: what *should* being an American mean, who *should* be able to be a citizen, who *should* be deserving of governmental assistance and equal protection under the law.

There is a simpler answer for Trump's surprising victory than fake news, although it forces us to confront the fact that for most people politics is about identity, not rational decision-making. Although it seemed inconceivable to many coastal elites and academics, including myself, many people applauded Trump's violations of the rules of respectful political discourse and his explicit racial appeals. For many whites, Trump's message of security, law, and order resonated, especially the calls to close the border to Mexican immigrants, combat "Islamic extremism," and crack down on Black Lives Matter protesters. Many of Trump's supporters saw the potential for American cultural and economic renewal through white nationalism, and prayed for a return to the day when white Christian Americans could speak as they wished without the scourge of being accused of being racist, sexist, homophobic, or anti-Islamic. They simply wanted to "Make America Great Again" or, in the parlance of Trump's race-baiting nationalist predecessor on the presidential campaign trail Pat Buchanan, "take their country back"—and restore their place at the political, social, economic, and cultural center of the United States.

And it is no surprise that media outlets such as Fox News and the white nationalist Breitbart were highly influential during this election, precisely because they understand their role in terms of identity, not information. What is clear from Hochschild's account, but also contemporary media dynamics more broadly, is that Fox News is the de facto identity media outlet not only for the Republican Party, but also whites more generally who perceive themselves as the victims of Christian persecution and reverse racism. It is the identity of being at the center of *their* nation's history. Former senior Trump advisor, and current and former executive chairman of Breitbart, Stephen Bannon called the media the "opposition party" of the administration, but it is clear that this animus did not extend to Fox News, which enjoyed favored access to candidate and now President Trump. Fox's appeal lies in the network's willingness to explicitly entwine reporting and opinion in the service of Republican, and white, identity. For example, Hochschild finds that Tea Partiers perceive that they are asked to have sympathy for "oppressed blacks, dominated women, weary immigrants, closeted gays, desperate refugees.…" And yet, for Tea Partiers, who perceive that they have suffered declines in social and economic status in recent years as a group, "it's people like *you* who have made this country great." This is part of the deep story of Tea Party members, and as Hochschild points out, this "deep story is also the Fox News deep story."

This is not to say that information is not important. It is, especially information that journalists provide about matters that are not already politicized. It is to say that identity comes *prior* to information. Identity shapes epistemology. People filter their understandings of information through their political and social identities. Trump was likely the most factually-scrutinized candidate in American history (undoubtedly because he lied so much) and still, he hardly suffered at the ballot box: 90 percent of Republicans voted for Trump and 89 percent of Democrats voted for Clinton. We explain this through the lens of identity. In a world where partisan identity comes prior to information, fact-checks against one's team fall on deaf ears. In a world where Republicans, in particular, see legacy journalism as biased against them and have spent eighty years building a conservative media infrastructure, Fox News becomes a safe redoubt to voice outrage. This identity-based account of media helps explain everything from the stunning failure of journalistic scrutiny to impact the election and the credibility of Trump's lies to many of his supporters. Many citizens understand politics and accept information through the lens of partisan identity, and on the right, this has largely become unmoored from legacy journalism.

The failure to come to grips with a socially embedded public and an identity group–based democracy has placed significant limits on our ability to imagine a way forward for journalism and media in the Trump era. As Fox News and Breitbart have discovered, there is power in the claim of representing and working *for* particular publics, quite apart from any abstract claims to present the truth.

13   Anticipating News: What Trump Teaches Us about How the Networked Press Can and Should Imagine

Mike Ananny

Trump seems to hold the press in a state of continual anticipation.

Would the election night drops in the futures markets be followed by financial collapse? Would the Electoral College certify his win? What would he tweet Sunday mornings in response to the *Saturday Night Live* skits? *The Atlantic* created "Tweet Tracker" to imagine future Trump tweets and put them in context. And the "Trump2Cash" bot was created to automatically buy shares of the companies that his tweets praise, sell those of organizations he disparages—and donate profits to Planned Parenthood.

His unpredictable persona is anti-establishment to supporters and dangerously erratic to critics but, regardless of your perspective, it feeds a general, undirected sense of constant expectation. What might he do next? To make or read Trump-related news is to logistically and emotionally prepare for someone who cannot be ignored or predicted using standard political frameworks. This is not standard agenda-setting in which elites and journalists steer public opinion; rather, it is more akin to a hostage-taking power that keeps journalists and audiences captive, anticipating what news *might* be.

Journalists, audiences, elites, and technologies all seem poised for Trump's next move, constituting a kind of infrastructure of anticipation with both power and peril.

In this short essay, I want to trace the ambivalence of this anticipation. On one hand, journalists and audiences may acclimate to Trump's sustained unpredictability, normalize his impulses as newsworthy, let him set news time, and largely sleepwalk from outrage to outrage. Or, his erratic behavior could dislodge the press's traditional rhythms of reaction, spurring journalists to imagine new types of accountability that use Trump's *lack* of consistency as an opportunity to articulate its own agenda of public service. Instead of its usual routines of following and indexing elites—letting Trump's erraticism set the agenda—it could reject continual anticipation and create new rhythms of public interest. The anticipatory press faces a choice: it can align itself with Trump Time (random tweets triggered by emotional outbursts, illusions of future grandeur, and lies that rely on short and selective collective memories) or it can tame the chaos, consciously focusing on what kind of rhythms publics *need*, becoming a sober metronome to Trump's staccatic cacophony.

*****

My doctoral advisor Ted Glasser told me that any good project should answer two questions: what is it, and why does it matter? I'm going to try to answer both in this short essay.

First, I want to talk about what anticipation is, how it embeds itself within journalism's cultures and practices, how it might have contributed to Trump's rise, and the places it appears in today's networked press. Second, I want to suggest what's at stake in anticipation—why it matters, and how it shapes the press's ability to be motivated by and accountable to public interests.

Before delving into either of these areas, I should clarify what I mean by "the press." Inspired by a long line of scholars concerned with *the press*—distinct from practices of journalism or the content of news—I define it as *institutional conditions* under which journalists work, news circulates, audiences interpret, and publics form. By "institutional conditions," I mean the cultures, practices, technologies, economies, laws, and norms that create news and give it meaning and power. For sure, this is a broad definition that begs further questions—Which cultures? Whose norms? What technology?—but it aims to highlight the often invisible forces that shape the press. It sees journalism and news as things that are *made,* not found—produced through action, choice, force, and resistance, not nature (another Glasser framing). This image of the press is both pragmatic and optimistic. It sees the press in people and places that can be searched for, described, and traced. Contrary to former *New York Times* Public Editor Daniel Okrent's claim that a "newspaper comes out by accident almost,"[1] an institutional view of the press foregrounds its patterns, assumptions, and structures and asks: what *could* the press be if it wasn't what it is right now and, by extension, what kind of publics *could* it help to create?

With this definition made, the only other preparatory and perhaps obvious claim I want to make is that the press convenes not only people, but moments. That is, its institutional conditions—cultures, practices, technologies, economies, laws, norms—do not just bring together journalists and sources, audiences and elites, publishers and platforms. They bring them together at particular *times*. Again, relying on a long line of scholarship on news deadlines and rhythms, we can see how news time is always made, never found. There is no *natural* reason that US newspapers were delivered mornings and afternoons, that those evening newscasts typically begin at six p.m., that radio news updates come at the top of the hour, or that some stories forcefully interrupt regular programming while others must wait. These rhythms and punctuations emerged from   indeed helped to *create*— audiences' expectations about when news was "supposed" to happen, when journalists were known to be working, when advertisers knew they could reach audiences, and when sources knew they could get a reporter's attention. These norms and rules created a press focused on anticipation. Again, there are pragmatic and optimistic aspects to seeing the press's anticipatory patterns: by understanding when news is created, circulated, and interpreted, we can imagine how it might be otherwise. To do so, though, we must understand the different types of power that control news time. We must ask whether this collection of forces creates the kind of news time we want, or that publics need.

*****

What does this have to do with Trump? I want to place these two ideas— that news rhythms are made not found, and that things can always be otherwise—in the context of Trump's power to create news time.

Trump Time has never been Standard Time. He began his run for the presidency by descending a long escalator at Trump Tower, a spectacle of anticipation that held cameras and audiences captive as they watched him slowly but surely arrive at the only place he could end up. The journey held no surprise, but the prolonged public gaze was inescapable. In a sense, this was a metaphor for his entire campaign. It was a race he was never supposed to win, yet persistent news coverage of the spectacle made a retreat from the public stage almost unimaginable and, therefore, unavoidable. This media-fed inevitability through constant, cultivated spectacle is akin to what Richard Grusin calls "pre-mediation"[2]: events become so heavily mediated—so richly and thoroughly described, so familiar to audiences, so valuable to advertisers—that nothing other than their realization can be imagined. Grusin uses the lead-up to the 2003 invasion of Iraq as an example of outcomes arrived at not through debate or deep engagement with alternatives, but through a constant drumbeat of news and commentary that made war unavoidable. Pre-mediation makes inevitable conclusions that did not *have* to become true, but become so because media capture the collective imaginations of journalists and audiences alike. It is impossible to foresee anything other than what spectacle anticipates and expects— nothing else makes sense because nothing else can be imagined. If you *do* dissent from, or advocate for, something other than the dominant, perceived wisdom, you quickly become an outcast who fails to see what everyone else expects.

The press might ask itself: how did Trump become such a central spectacle of anticipation, and did such a focus implicitly sustain his candidacy and make his loss hard to imagine? As unlikely as it might have been to pollsters and elites, did the press pre-mediate Trump's legitimacy and become so addicted to anticipating his next move that his win became almost unavoidable? Sure, polls and pundits favored Clinton's win, but was it truly possible to imagine Trump disappearing post-election?

Perhaps the press—in addition to its horserace coverage, poll obsessions, and inside-the-beltway reporting—pre-mediated a Trump presidency precisely because he was so skilled at creating cycles of anticipation that played to the press's eagerness for novelty. With each *Apprentice*-style cliffhanger— the public auditions for the vice presidential pick, the nightly cameos at the convention, announced-and-then-canceled press conferences, pundit predictions that the nomination (and then presidency) would make him anew—Trump ensconced himself in news cycles, news organizations' routines, and even their hiring practices as Trump specialists became frequent commentators on several major broadcasters. Rejecting Trump would have meant rejecting the habits, rituals, and assumptions that motivated and rationalized their coverage of his spectacles. The press would have had to imagine and cover something *other than* Trump, a reliably entertaining source of anticipation and pre-mediation. He didn't always have to do something in particular, he just had to seem like he might do anything at all.

But the press is not just what journalists do; it is also the environments in which news circulates, audiences interpret, and publics form. How might they have been fueled by anticipation? Here, there is a technological story, one that is difficult to disentangle from audiences and economic imperatives. When CBS President Les Moonves said that Trump's candidacy "may not be good for America, but it's damn good for CBS,"[3] he was expressing an economic reality that holds captive news organizations and audiences alike. Advertisers paid high fees to broadcasters to sponsor Republican debates not because the public was eager to learn more about the candidates' positions, but because they wanted to see what *might* happen, what Trump *might* do. The more he ridiculed candidates, talked about the size of his hands, coined insulting nicknames for his rivals, and gave audiences what was essentially a prime-time image of the reality television presidency he offered, he cultivated anticipation and desire that aligned perfectly with what media markets valued. Audiences became hooked voyeurs; broadcasters knew they had an addictive product and captive audiences they could sell to eager advertisers; social media platforms thrived on his trending topics and guaranteed traffic, hashtags, and live streams; commentators enthusiastically rebranded usually staid debates as improvised entertainment; and journalists showed how the standard assumptions of horserace politics could be upended by spectacular circuses with a reliably unpredictable ringmaster.

How could Trump's spotlight on the political stage ever fade when so many had invested so much in anticipating his next move? In addition to its usual obsession with horserace election coverage, was the press unable to avoid stories like the private email server, the tarmac meeting with Attorney General Lynch, and Clinton's "fainting" at the 9/11 memorial because it needed these stories to help it imagine what a Clinton defeat, and thus a Trump presidency, would look like? To be sure, many factors drove the election outcome, but one of them could have been the press's inability to imagine politics without Trump, and its addiction to anticipating his actions.

This anticipation industry only seemed to grow after his election. On election night, shortly after the press announced that Trump had won key battleground states, *futures* markets and the US dollar dropped, and volatility indexes surged. Some thought that he might never take office. As states recounted ballots, "faithless electors" considered giving Clinton the Electoral College, emoluments clause experts questioned Trump's ability to be both businessman and president, and pundits speculated on whether

Trump even wanted to be president and imagined him handing the presidency to Mike Pence.

The press prepared to cover President Trump, imagining scenarios that might unfold. The *Columbia Journalism Review* offered guidance to journalists on how to cover a president who is expected to lie; *The Atlantic* discussed how it would cover the kinds of tweets it expected Trump to post; the *New York Times* and the *Wall Street Journal* told readers they probably wouldn't use the word "lie" to discount Trump's claims, finding themselves unable to imagine a president who habitually lied. And ProPublica staffed up as people flooded them with donations, posting job openings for investigative reporters and data journalists as it ramped up to scrutinize the indiscretions it expected of President Trump.

And people adjacent to news also prepared. *Saturday Night Live* contracted Alec Baldwin to play the new president; the bots "Trump2Cash" and "BOTUS" began automatically buying or selling shares of companies Trump has tweeted about, either pocketing the proceeds or donating them to Planned Parenthood. And the website www.IsTrumpAtMaraLago.org was established to track the new president's frequent expected vacations, estimate the cost of the trips to taxpayers, and represent this expense in terms of the number of Meals on Wheels recipients who could have been fed instead.

As candidate Trump became President-Elect and then President Trump, the press—the institutional conditions under which journalists work, news circulates, audiences interpret, and publics take shape—became *anticipation infrastructure*. It became poised to make sense of what he might do, primed to respond to moves it thought he would make.

It is simultaneously dangerous and responsible to design an institution around prediction, much less predictions about one man. The press is ready to react to the debates it expects, but it is less able to see outcomes that it cannot imagine and quickly becomes structurally blind to anything except what it can anticipate. It cedes part of its public responsibility to imagine what people might *need* from their leaders because it is only willing to hold them accountable within the expectations its leaders set. Trump's accountability is limited to whatever the press can imagine him doing. This is a reactionary politics of deference that leaves much power with him. To the extent that the press bounds itself within the (arguably vast) array of petulant and erratic things the Trump administration *might* do—he might tweet the morning after *Saturday Night Live*, the White House could continue to qualify the significance of the Holocaust, Ivanka Trump might intermix her business with the state, Trump might again adopt the "presidential tone" of his first State of the Union address that so effectively disarmed the media— it weakens itself and the publics it claims to serve.

This is *meta*-agenda setting through anticipation. It is not about whether the White House or journalists lead or follow public debates (healthcare, immigration, terrorism). Rather it is about a struggle over who gets to imagine the future, who anticipates whom, which institution gets to set rhythms and force the other one to react. Practically, the press could ignore Trump's tweets or only periodically consider them as collections; it could lobby social media platforms to make their algorithms less sensitive to Trump outbursts and the resulting flurries of traffic, or it could ignore White House press briefings. It could stop falling for what Bloomberg News described as "Trump's habit of self-imposing—then missing—two-week deadlines for major announcements," repeatedly promising "major news" in two weeks on everything from tax reform to healthcare policy, failing to deliver anything, but holding news resources captive in the meantime[4]. When the press consumes itself with anticipating Trump's moves, it has less ability to imagine futures that *publics* want or need.

This is the other side of anticipation: its power to reshape news time. If the press could resist the administration's rhythms, it could create something new and publicly meaningful. It could anticipate what *it* sees as publicly significant events and invest coverage in these. It could help audiences pre-mediate alternatives that counter Trump's interests and build immunity to his outbursts. If Twitter were to put a time delay on Trump's tweets because (as many have suggested) his tweets frequently violate the platform's prohibitions against bullying and harassment, it could mute some of the frenzied anticipation that currently fuels his social media. When publishers foreground long-term beats that show Trump's ever-increasing corruption (weekly updates of emoluments clause violations, state-driven revenue to Trump businesses, or mounting evidence of his campaign's collusion with Russia), it could foster in audiences an expectation that Trump's power will be challenged. It could pre-mediate a Trump who is sanctioned, helping publics and elites alike imagine nothing other than an accountable presidency.

Such innovations may seem unconventional or unworkable—indeed, they require the press to have a vision of the public beyond one that simply reacts to elites and holds power accountable—but they suggest a way that the press might retake the phenomenon of anticipation and convert it into a tool of public service.

*****

Writing six months after Trump's election, I am reminded of Daniel Hallin's "spheres" model of the media[5]. In it he argues that while some news fits into a sphere of consensus (topics about which there is broad agreement) and most news appears in a sphere of legitimate controversy (debates we are accustomed to having and likely will continue to have), very little news materializes in the sphere of deviance (issues that are considered so taboo or uninteresting that they rarely surface). These spheres change sizes and shift boundaries as social norms and news practices evolve, but the model remains valid. We must constantly be on guard for the forces that sustain and normalize these spheres. More simply, we need to know which conversations we aren't having and the assumptions driving their absence.

I think part of this normalization relates to anticipation: to the classes of events, topics, and futures that press lets itself see as inevitable versus those that it simply can't imagine or forecast. When Trump was elected, many feared that his values and priorities would become the default—that misogyny, racism, white nationalism, and anti-intellectualism would become so embedded in both elite and public discourse that it would be difficult to see them, resist them, or imagine a world premised on anything else. This is a fear of normalized evil, a fear of the failure of imagination. Fighting these fears means, in part, critiquing the press as anticipation infrastructure—asking who sets today's news rhythms, which futures and imaginations dominate, and whether the press's powers and beats give people the publics they need.

We might learn the lessons of pre-mediation that made the Iraq invasion seem inevitable and the Trump presidency imaginable and ask: Which futures does the press anticipate—what *can* it imagine? Which futures dominate, where are they coming from, and what don't they allow for? How could the press see its anticipations as part of its public service—as a way to challenge presidential power, instead of simply reacting to it?

Notes

1. Andy Robinson, "The Public Editor's Club at *The New York Times* as Told by the Six Who Lived It," *Columbia Journalism Review*, July 20, 2017, https://www.cjr.org/special_report/new-york-times-public-editor-oral-history.php.

2. Richard Grusin, *Premediation: Affect and Mediality after 9/11* (New York: Palgrave Macmillan, 2010).

3. Eliza Collins, "Les Moonves: Trump's Run Is Damn Good for CBS," Politico, February 29, 2016, http://www.politico.com/blogs/on-media/2016/02/les-moonves-trump-cbs-220001.

4. Toluse Olorunnipa, "In Trump's White House, Everything's Coming in Two Weeks," Bloomberg Politics, June 6, 2017, https://www.bloomberg.com/news/articles/2017-06-06/in-trump-s-white-house-everything-s-coming-in-two-weeks.

5. Daniel C. Hallin, *The "Uncensored War": The Media and Vietnam* (New York: Oxford University Press, 1986).

14   Media Projections and Trump's Election: A Self-Defeating Prophecy?

Keren Tenenboim-Weinblatt

In the run-up to the 2016 US presidential elections, the media were replete with projections about Donald Trump's chances of becoming the next president and the implications of such an outcome for the country's future and its position in the global arena. Pundits and journalists ventured various projections through the news media, while mediating and interacting with the forecasts of data analysts, scientists, and politicians. A dominant line of predictions suggested a low probability of a Trump victory, ranging from FiveThirtyEight's analysis of "Why Donald Trump Isn't a Real Candidate" at the beginning of the Republican primary season to final assessments in major news outlets, such as the *New York Times*'s prediction that "Hillary Clinton has an 85% chance to win" or the *Washington Post*'s story, "A Comprehensive Average of Election Forecasts Points to a Decisive Clinton Victory."[1]

Following the results of both the Republican primaries and the presidential elections, the dominant public discourse on projections focused on the purported failure of experts and the media to predict Trump's election. A similar discourse followed the surprising results of the Brexit referendum in the UK a couple of months earlier (June 2016). Various explanations were offered for why experts and the media did not get it right: surveys and statistics were used instead of going out to actually speak with people and understand their worldview; the samples were not representative; or their elitist tendencies or political views blinded them and shaped their interpretations. Others have argued that the whole prediction enterprise is doomed to begin with and that journalists should focus instead on their primary mission of reporting on that which has already happened.

These explanations and debates have addressed different kinds of problems in the media's attempt to project the future and represent different methodological, theoretical, and normative perspectives. They also signify different approaches to the feasibility of political predictions, ranging from the claim that political realities are inherently unpredictable to the view that there are ways to achieve more accurate political predictions by using systematic probabilistic thinking that overcomes the biases of intuitive human judgments.[2] According to the latter, some news outlets and data journalists arguably did a better job than others in predicting the results of the US 2016 elections.[3]

However, all of these explanations and debates have assessed the functioning of the media from the perspective of the correspondence between projected and actual reality, namely, the success or failure to accurately predict the future. But what about other functions that media projections played in these cases, and projections other than polling numbers and other statistical predictions? Is it possible that mediated projections also intervened in the projected reality rather than just attempting, and often failing, to accurately reflect it?

Using the case of Trump's presidential bid as well as examples from the Brexit referendum, this essay explores what it means to consider media projections as a form of intervention and suggests an agenda for future research in this area.

Media Projections as a Form of Intervention

As we know from psychological theory and from daily experience, when we make projections about our own lives, we are usually not engaged in a scientific exercise of getting it right. Rather, we construct future scenarios as a way of orienting and conducting ourselves in the world: we prepare for the projected future and sometimes act in order to help bring about a desirable future or prevent a scary one.

Societies likewise prepare for the future and try to shape it through projections. For instance, as argued by Richard Grusin, the intense premediation of future scenarios following the traumatic 9/11 attacks was an attempt to avoid a similar future shock.[4] Furthermore, projections about the outcomes and implications of significant events, be they the US presidential elections, the Brexit referendum, or the war in Syria, can mobilize or demobilize multiple actors. If a predicted outcome is undesirable, it may trigger attempts to avert it, dodge its impact, or take preparatory measures (e.g., protest, arm, vote differently than planned). Conversely, a desirable projection may arouse people's hopes of benefitting from the predicted event or even motivate them to help bring it about (e.g., by donating or volunteering).

Projections are thus a form of intervention and involve both discursive constructions and behavioral implications. At the collective level, such interventions unfold primarily within and through the media, with the media serving as both a central venue where projections are negotiated and as central actors in their own right. Some future-oriented media interventions are direct and blunt, as exhibited, for instance, by the extravagant utopias and doomsday scenarios on the front pages of the UK tabloids before the Brexit referendum. For example, on the day of the referendum, evocative front pages carrying headlines such as *The Sun*'s "Independence Day: Britain's Resurgence" (accompanied by an image of a globe and a glowing sun above Britain) and the *Daily Mirror*'s "Don't take a leap into the dark … vote REMAIN today" (accompanied by an image of a black hole) were aimed at mobilizing voters in the opposing directions.

Such interventionist practices are generally not found on the front pages of US newspapers, but attempts at direct media interventions through projections can be identified in opinion columns, the predictions of cable pundits, and satirical interventions. For example, a mock front page created by the *Boston Globe* during the US presidential campaign in April 2016 carried the date of April 9, 2017. Using snippets of Trump's own words, the *Boston Globe* envisioned how the front page of the newspaper would look under a Trump presidency. The lead story, "Deportations to Begin," reported on a televised address by President Trump in which he called on Congress to fund a "massive deportation force." The other headlines included: "Markets sink as trade war looms," "US soldiers refuse orders to kill ISIS families," and "New libel law targets 'absolute scum' in press." While this satirical front page was aimed at preventing this envisioned future (as the *Boston Globe* tweeted, "the front page we hope we never have to print"), the eventual outcome and the events following the elections raise the question of whether such types of interventions were simply ineffective and inconsequential or whether they contributed to a process that led to their own defeat (and, consequently, to the fulfillment of some of these predictions).

However, in most cases, mainstream news outlets tend to rely on more conventional professional practices when depicting future scenarios, most notably by selecting projections made by other actors, such as experts and politicians, and molding them into news. At the level of selection, the media's known preference for low ambiguity often leads journalists to prefer what Philip Tetlock called, following Isaiah Berlin, the "hedgehog" style of reasoning, which derives bold predictions from broad organizing principles. The "fox" style, on the other hand, is anchored in diverse perspectives and data and, thereby, often achieves superior predictions. However, as Tetlock noted, the media are less likely to select the complex forecasts of "foxes" or invite them as experts to television shows.[5] In addition, different news outlets all too often select and amplify actors' projections that better fit their own editorial line and wishes, such as the tendency of the US liberal media to highlight projections that emphasized the low likelihood and dire implications of a Trump election.

Furthermore, through a process of journalistic transformation, journalists intervene in the content of the original projections by adjusting, amplifying, or contesting them.[6] Thus, a speech by David Cameron before the Brexit referendum, in which he warned that leaving the EU could threaten the peace and stability of Europe, was given the following headline in the Remain-supporting *Mirror*: "Brexit Could Trigger World War Three, Warns David Cameron."[7] This projection can be seen as a co-creation of Cameron and *The Mirror*. Notably, collective memory references to World War Two were also present in both critical and supportive media interpretations of Trump's campaign promise to "make America great again" through a return to some hazy, mythical past.

Finally, in addition to tabloid-like future constructions, satirical interventions, pundits' projections, and scenarios that are based on the journalistic selection and transformation of projections by experts and political actors, there is also a growing domain of statistical predictions and data journalism. This can be found in both the traditional news media—such as the *New York Times*'s The Upshot—and in specialized websites—such as FiveThirtyEight in the US or Number Cruncher Politics in the UK. The result is an emerging future-oriented genre, which might be termed "predictive journalism."[8]

The quantitative, empirical orientation of this type of journalistic predictions does not mean that they are not interpretive nor constructed from past experiences. Generally speaking, the more sophisticated the predictive models, the more they rely on various assumptions and interpretations of current developments against historical patterns. Thus, when analysts and data journalists made predictions about the results of the Brexit referendum, they also looked at past data and considered which historical precedents were most applicable to the current forecast. In the case of referenda, which tend to reaffirm the status quo, this generates very conservative assumptions, even when the polls tell a different story. Similarly, the above-mentioned FiveThirtyEight's story on "Why Donald Trump Isn't a Real Candidate" was based on data, which suggested that "Trump is the first candidate in modern presidential primary history to begin the campaign with a majority of his own party disliking him."

All of these types of projections, from the doomsday scenarios to detailed statistical predictions, can play an important role in shaping the expectations, fears, and hopes of millions of potential voters. To the extent that people's plans and behaviors are aligned with their expectations, such projections can intervene in the reality that they set out to predict via both self-fulfilling and self-defeating dynamics. Thus, in the case of both Trump and Brexit, some self-defeating processes might have been at play. In other words, people might have reacted to mediated projections in ways that contributed to the surprising final outcome.

One plausible scenario concerns the mobilization of Trump supporters (and potential supporters) and the demobilization of Clinton supporters (and potential supporters) in response to the dominant media coverage that emphasized the low likelihood of a Trump victory. These dynamics may have been facilitated by two characteristics of the media and political culture: first, polarized evaluations of the repercussions of electing Trump or Clinton, with media outlets affiliated with each of the sides portraying the implications of electing the other candidate as disastrous; and second, widespread populist sentiment which views the projecting elites, and the media in particular, as part of the detached establishment and, in extreme populist formulations, as the enemy. Such sentiments can lead voters to resist and revolt against the dismissive attitude of the media toward candidates such as Trump who represent such populist sentiments (or, in the context of Brexit, the option of leaving the EU). This process can be further reinforced when such candidates gain further support on the ground and in specific outlets (e.g., Fox News), while much of the media establishment continues to predict an almost definite win for the other side. In other words, self-defeating dynamics may be likelier in polarized environments with low trust in the media and where the media themselves are positioned as the enemy.

The Way Forward in Communication Research

How do we make sense of these various dynamics and different kinds of media projections and interventions within communication theory and research? In general, our current theoretical and methodological frameworks for understanding the complex social processes of projecting and shaping public futures within and through the media are rather limited. We have some scholarly beginnings that have engaged with conceptual and empirical investigations of future-oriented media coverage, from the notion of premediation to recent comparative studies of the future-oriented roles assumed by the media in different cultural and technological contexts.[9] In addition, literature on media effects, especially the effects of public opinion polls and opinion climate, has documented some self-fulfilling dynamics in the context of the contested spiral of silence theory and the bandwagon effect.[10] Self-defeating dynamics, such as the underdog effect, have been more elusive, both conceptually and empirically.[11]

Outside of communication and journalism studies, scholars have explored important elements in the process of public projection, from the cognitive mechanisms underlying political projections to the shaping of markets through the performative effects of economic models and predictions.[12] However, these lines of research have accorded little attention to the crucial role of the media in these dynamics, while communication research has done little to incorporate insights from these bodies of literature.

In order to achieve a comprehensive understanding of media projections and their interventions, we need a multi-layered analytical approach, an interdisciplinary theoretical perspective, and a much stronger integration between the study of media discourse and media effects. In particular, I suggest an examination of the social dynamics of media projections as consisting of four nested layers: how projections are constructed in the media; how they are negotiated among various actors, most notably, the media, experts, and politicians; how they evolve over time; and what the implications of these projections are for people's expectations and behaviors. I believe that theorizing and studying these various layers and their interconnections can significantly add to our understanding of complex social phenomena such as the Trump election and the Brexit referendum. While the theoretical and methodological challenges on this path are many, addressing them is vital if we want to better understand the contribution of the media to shaping our future—and to perhaps intervene in such processes in the future.

Notes

1. Harry Enten, "Why Donald Trump Isn't a Real Candidate, in One Chart," FiveThirtyEight, June 16, 2015, https://fivethirtyeight.com/datalab/why-donald -trump-isnt-a-real-candidate-in-one-chart; Josh Katz, "Who Will Be President?," *New York Times*, November 8, 2016, https://www.nytimes.com/interactive/2016/upshot/ presidential-polls-forecast.html; John Sides, "A Comprehensive Average of Election Forecasts Points to a Decisive Clinton Victory," *Washington Post*, November 8, 2016, https://www.washingtonpost.com/news/monkey-cage/wp/2016/11/08/a -comprehensive-average-of-election-forecasts-points-to-a-decisive-clinton-victory/.

2. For the unpredictability argument, see Nassim Nicholas Taleb, *The Black Swan: The Impact of the Highly Improbable* (New York: Random House, 2007). For a more optimistic view on the ability to predict political events, see Philip E. Tetlock and Dan Gardner, *Superforecasting: The Art and Science of Prediction* (New York: Crown, 2015).

3. Nate Silver, "Why FiveThirtyEight Gave Trump a Better Chance than Almost Anyone Else," FiveThirtyEight, November 11, 2016, http://fivethirtyeight.com/ features/why-fivethirtyeight-gave-trump-a-better-chance-than-almost-anyone-else/.

4. Richard Grusin, *Premediation: Affect and Mediality After 9/11* (New York: Palgrave Macmillan, 2010).

5. Philip E. Tetlock, *Expert Political Judgment: How Good Is It? How Can We Know?* (Princeton: Princeton University Press, 2005).

6. Keren Tenenboim-Weinblatt and Christian Baden, "Journalistic Transformation: How Source Texts Are Turned into News Stories," *Journalism* (2016, advance online publication), doi:10.1177/1464884916667873.

7. Ben Glaze and Dan Bloom, "'Brexit' Could Trigger World War Three, Warns David Cameron," *Mirror*, May 9, 2016, http://www.mirror.co.uk/news/uk-news/ brexit-could-trigger-world-war-7928607.

8. H. O. Maycotte, "Big Data Triggers Predictive Journalism," *Nieman Lab*, December 2015, http://www.niemanlab.org/2015/12/big-data-triggers-predictive-journalism.

9. Grusin, *Premediation*; Keren Tenenboim-Weinblatt and Motti Neiger, "Print Is Future, Online Is Past: Cross-Media Analysis of Temporal Orientations in the News," *Communication Research* 42, no. 8 (2015): 1047–1067; Motti Neiger and Keren

Tenenboim-Weinblatt, "Understanding Journalism through a Nuanced Deconstruction of Temporal Layers in News Narraftives," *Journal of Communication* 66, no. 1 (2016): 139–160.

10. For recent developments in this area, see Wolfgang Donsbach, Charles T. Salmon, and Yariv Tsfati (eds.), *The Spiral of Silence: New Perspectives on Communication and Public Opinion* (New York: Routledge, 2014); Sjoerd B. Stolwijk, Andreas R. T. Schuck, and Claes H. de Vreese, "How Anxiety and Enthusiasm Help Explain the Bandwagon Effect," *International Journal of Public Opinion Research* (2016, advance online publication), doi: https://doi.org/10.1093/ijpor/edw018.

11. Rüdiger Schmitt-Beck, "Underdog Effect," in *The International Encyclopedia of Political Communication*, ed. Gianpietro Mazzoleni, Kevin G. Barnhurst, Ken'ichi Ikeda, Rousiley C. M. Maia, and Hartmut Wessler (Hoboken, NJ: Wiley-Blackwell, 2016), 1627–1631.

12. For a cognitive, social psychological perspective, see Tetlock, *Expert Political Judgment*; on the performativity of economics, see Donald Mackenzie, *An Engine, Not a Camera: How Financial Models Shape Markets* (Cambridge, MA: MIT Press, 2008). Within this framework, a self-defeating prophecy belongs to the category of "counterperformativity" (Mackenzie 2008, 19).

15 Creeping Toward Authoritarianism?

Katy E. Pearce

The adjective *authoritarian* has been applied to Donald Trump hundreds of thousands of times in the first few months of his presidency. Phrases like "Trump's authoritarian vision," "Trump is drifting toward authoritarianism," and "Trump is following the authoritarian playbook" are casually used by pundits and editors seeking clicks and shares. There are certainly a number of actions in the Trump presidency that are cause for concern. However, labeling Trump an authoritarian merely because of these actions demonstrates a simplistic understanding of authoritarianism and a lack of faith in the democratic institutions as well as the American people.

Trump Is Not Consolidating Power Like an Authoritarian Leader

Pundits have cited Trump's "consolidation of power" as an example of his authoritarian tendencies. Yet, his supposed consolidation of power has not been well explained and, more importantly, the current American political climate does not resemble that of an authoritarian regime at all. When an authoritarian leaders consolidate power, they *really* consolidate power, through repression and co-optation (Levitsky and Way 2002). Co-optation occurs through patronage systems where the placating of potential rivals via distribution of limited perks is essential for maintaining power (Gandhi and Przeworski 2007; Schatz 2009; Geddes 2005). The ideal way to distribute benefits is via legislative seats, where resources can be legally transferred and regular demonstration of support for the regime is available (Gandhi and Przeworski 2007). Because votes show support for the regime, the executive gets what it wants from its legislature. So while legislatures are not window dressing, as some may believe (Gerschewski 2013), the legislature has very little formal influence. The relationship between the American executive and legislative branches is nothing like this relationship under authoritarianism. Unlike in authoritarian regimes where members of the legislature demonstrate their loyalty to the leader, American presidents tend to adapt to the views of Congress in order to advance their own agendas. Moreover, American congresspeople are beholden to a variety of interests—constituents and lobbyists most of all—not the executive. And currently, Trump's relationship with the Republican Party and Congress, in particular, is weak at best.

Another frequently noted example of authoritarian-like consolidation of power is Trump's use of executive orders. But executive orders are not unilateral power—they are limited in a number of ways. The federal judiciary consistently reviews executive orders and sometimes overturns them. And while executive orders are design to bypass Congress, Congress can refuse to fund the effort, as it did with Obama's executive order to close Guantanamo. There is also the Office of Legal Counsel within the Department of Justice that is tasked with evaluating the legality of executive orders and can prevent them from being issued, as was the case during the Iran hostage crisis. These limits simply do not exist in authoritarian states. Nonetheless, Trump's assailing of judges that rule against him is concerning, as is his call for breaking up the U.S. Court of Appeals for the Ninth Circuit. Yet, breaking up a federal court is a difficult process that requires working with Congress through a reorganization. This happened in 1980 when a single court was overloaded with cases and the creation of an additional court was justified. But it would be difficult to defend a reorganization now without a clear reason other than creating a more favorable judicial climate. Authoritarian leaders do not have such limits.

Trump Is Not Creating an Authoritarian Media System

Perhaps it is Donald Trump's relationship with the mass media that is most often cited as an example of his authoritarian tendencies. In this, he does have some strong similarities to authoritarian leaders. Attacking opposition media appears to be one resemblance, but in fact, Trump's approach is far different from authoritarian leaders. Donald Trump attacks mainstream media. When he called the *New York Times*, NBC News, ABC News, CBS News, and CNN "fake news" and labeled them "the enemy of the American People!"[1] on Twitter on February 17, 2017, and called the press "dishonest" and "out of control" in a press conference on February 16, 2017, many were alarmed. But while oppositionists are humiliated and discredited through formal campaigns in authoritarian regimes (Schedler 2002), opposition media is not discredited, rather it is eliminated so that the regime can exert exclusive control of information. Control of the mass media has been a key tool in authoritarian leaders' toolkits for centuries (Siebert, Peterson, and Schramm 1963) and is an important part of social control (Schatz 2009; Whitten-Woodring and James 2012), even on social media (Hyun and Kim 2015; Pearce 2015). An authoritarian leader can use the mass media to project images that strengthen his position (Schatz 2009), portray that the regime is doing a good job (Brady 2009; Stein 2012), suggest that there is greater support for the regime or a particular policy than there actually is (Chen and Xu 2017), and limit the diversity of citizens' opinions (Lu, Aldrich, and Shi 2014). So, while Donald Trump has tried to discredit media opposing him, and he does engage in a number of the same goals as authoritarian leaders, the fact that he has not eliminated the media is a core difference between him and authoritarian leaders.

But like in an authoritarian regime's controlled media environment, in 2017, the "truth" is hazy. In an authoritarian regime the "truth" is hazy because institutions such as media commentators are too weak to provide the scaffolding for it (Ortmann and Heathershaw 2012). This is even more powerful because citizens in authoritarian regimes live with a great deal of uncertainty already (Schedler 2013) and the hazy truth merely adds to this uncertainty. And this is important because authoritarian states draw their social control–derived power from uncertainty. By disallowing citizens the "gift" of knowing what to expect day-to-day, authoritarians keep people on their toes and discourage anyone from making plans or having the luxury to dedicate mental energy to thinking about criticism of the regime. Additionally, in such a hazy environment, rumors, scandals, and conspiracy theories are given greater weight, due to the inability to make sense of what is truly going on (Ortmann and Heathershaw 2012; DiFonzo and Bordia 2007; Huang 2017), and this provides opportunities for authoritarian leaders to demonize any opposition to their rule (Schatz 2009), especially through anonymous channels like the Internet (Pearce 2015; Pearce and Hajizada 2014).

So while there is not the same type of controlled media environment, there are elements of a hazy truth in the 2017 American media environment. It is not a coincidence that Donald Trump's victory came at a time of great change in the American media landscape. While partisan media has grown over the past two decades, the addition of Internet-based and social media news led to a 2016 presidential campaign with a host of new issues like "fake news," "filter bubbles," and increased populist rhetoric (Groshek and Koc-Michalska 2017). When considering former candidate, now-President, Trump's relationship with the media, it is impossible to ignore these changes to the media environment. While ownership of media outlets is not a characteristic of the current US administration, the challenges presented are similar to those in a hazy information environment. The proliferation of "fake news"—where source credibility cannot be easily established—in combination with social endorsement of news ("My friend posted this story, and they're smart, so it is probably true.") has had a significant impact on many US social and political issues. The 2016 presidential election notwithstanding, the role that "fake news" has had on public health alone is cause for concern. Stories like Pizzagate raise a red flag. Donald Trump's tweets are particularly interesting. He can instantly make claims such as accusing former President Obama of a crime. Many argue that provocative tweets from Trump serve other purposes such as preemptive framing, reflection, diversion, and trial balloons.[2]

Self-Censorship Is on the Rise

Another common method of social control by authoritarian regimes is making it socially risky to engage in any action perceived to be disloyal to the leader or the state (which under authoritarianism are one in the same). First, authoritarian regimes create an environment where loyalty to the rulers is the *only* path for upward mobility. Individuals interested in moving up spend much energy greasing the wheels of their networks in an effort to get closer to the top. Merit is not the primary consideration of a potential employee, rather the consideration of the networks and possible access an individual brings is paramount. Grand gestures of dedication to the rulers are essential in the performance of loyalty. This takes on greater importance because in authoritarian environments, silence is perceived as disloyalty and, as such, one must be constantly vigilant in demonstrating allegiance to the ruler. Social media provide another space for this demonstration, particularly with a larger and broader audience.

Related to the performance of loyalty is the rational decision to not share one's opinions publicly or even privately. Citizens of authoritarian regimes are trained to watch for disloyalty in others, thus engaging in the exhausting task of attending to one's expression becomes second nature. The tendency to self-censor is great, especially among those with less power. And this is, even more, the case on social media, where the ability to record and share disclosures with broad and unintended audiences, and with some degree of anonymity, has dramatically altered expression. On social media, the stakes are higher, and thus the likelihood for self-censorship is greater.

As such, deviating from the norm—political or otherwise—is dangerous in authoritarian regimes. In combination with the culture of self-censorship, keeping one's head down is a dominant organizing structure in authoritarianism, especially because reputation and connections are more important than merit. Those brave enough to dissent are severely punished, but from an unexpected source—not the state, but from their own loved ones. The reputational effects of having a dissenting family member are too great for many, and individuals are ostracized. This is even more problematic where access to resources is dependent upon connections. Once those ties are severed, it is permanent. Social media can provide a space for those that deviate to find likeminded others, but can also potentially "out" those that deviate.

In conclusion, as a scholar of authoritarianism, I am not terribly worried about the United States turning into Russia, much less North Korea. However, I am concerned about general trends in both hazy information and self-censorship, which are characteristic of authoritarian regimes and have severe consequences on individuals' ability to think critically and civically engage. There is no question that these are powerful methods of social control that are at the disposal of the best "political technologists" (parapolitical professionals with the task to set and change the agenda and "construct" politics by applying whatever "technologies" available to them, especially manipulation of the media) (Etkind and Shcherbak 2008; Wilson 2005). While I hope that the current US administration's "political technologists" are not so explicit in their aims, I fear that they may, in fact, be engaging in such actions intentionally. And it is entirely possible that some knowledge transfer has occurred between authoritarian regimes and the administration. But without the repercussions that citizens face in authoritarian regimes holding them back, American citizens *can* fight against these actions. It is once that ability is gone that the label of authoritarian may accurately fit.

Notes

1. https://twitter.com/realDonaldTrump/status/832708293516632065.

2. https://www.washingtonpost.com/news/worldviews/wp/2017/03/06/trumps -twitter-feed-is-a-gateway-to-authoritarianism.

III   Why Technology Matters

16 The Potential of Networked Solidarity: Communication at the End of the Long Twentieth Century

Gina Neff

Arguably, the twentieth century ended in 2016. Historical eras do not necessarily end with the rounding of a calendar spot, but with a moment or an event that epitomizes a collective cultural or political shift. Historian Eric Hobsbawn marked the end of what he called the "long nineteenth century" with the outbreak of World War I in 1914, which ended an age of empire and set in motion the events of the century that followed. Whether or not future historians mark the end of the twentieth century with the 2016 elections in the United Kingdom and the United States that brought the world Brexit and Trump, media scholars should. The elections of 2016 show how the twentieth-century ideals that defined the larger project of communication and media scholarship are now misplaced. From the perspective of media scholarship, the twentieth century is finally over and now it is time for new theories to catch up to new realities in the field.

The twentieth century's intellectual founders of journalism, media, and communication studies anchored their research on democratic ideals, seeing the potential for informed publics as leading to better civic engagement and stronger democracies. The dual forces of rapidly expanding higher education and increased attention to the role of propaganda and influence led to a golden era for US media and communication research. New empirical tools supported new ways to study audiences, their attitudes, and their beliefs. Our field's idealized subject was information seeking and rational, a choice-making citizen, who, when armed with good quality news, eagerly and willingly participated in the larger democratic project and had the inclination, and the time, to do so. As a field, scholars continued to rewrite a narrative that argued the strong case for the centrality of our scholarship: media make good citizens and good citizens make democracy.

Internet research, my corner of the field, also fell victim to the optimism of media scholarship in the long twentieth century. In the first twenty years of the World Wide Web, researchers asked if the Internet was making people more isolated, were we listening only to like-minded others, could the Internet be free for participation, and what roles would news editors and other cultural mediators play. Fundamentally, Internet scholars repeated an assumption about information and democracy that grounded media and communication studies in the twentieth century—namely, more information could spark more, and deeper, democratic engagement with civic life.

The project of the field of media and communication has always been about meaning-making and connection. But while the field focused on the institutions that made, or supported, democracy, the fabric of many social institutions, not just that of the media, faded. Companies broke the tacit agreements for loyalty to their employees. Membership in unions and social organizations that cut across the lines of race, class, and gender dwindled. The middle class lost the economic security that it had won during the economic expansion after World War II. As Hobsbawm phrased this slow social unravelling,

The cultural revolution of the later twentieth century can thus be understood as the triumph of the individual over society, or rather, the breaking of the threads which in the past had woven human beings into social textures. For such textures had consisted not only of the actual relations between human beings and their forms of organization but also of the general models of such relations and the expected patterns of people's behavior toward each other; their roles were prescribed, though not always written. (Hobsbawm 1994, 334)

Hobsbawm describes both a cultural and social transition, in which the logic of markets wins over social solidarity. The social institutions that supported Americans in their daily well-being weakened and fractured in this time. So too did our media. The logics of markets, although shaped by social forces, came to be seen during this time as independent of the values and needs of the communities and individuals that comprise them. In this way, markets logic tore at the threads of social life and by extension at society's ability to connect and cohere in public spheres.

Which brings us back to Trump and the media in the twenty-first century. A focus on media as the cornerstone of democracy blinded media scholars to the powerful ways that connection and solidarity were being reimagined and rewoven in the twentieth century. New media intersect but do not wholly supplant these economic trends, and yet the powerful cultural image of an Internet, "free as in freedom," renewed the possibility and the hope for communication to be relevant for democracy.

Consider Facebook and other social networking sites that now connect people in unprecedented ways, provide new forms of connection, and enable rapid dissemination of information in times of political crisis and upheaval. Social media sites fundamentally reshape how we feel, not think, our way through news and shape our response to it, creating what Zizi Papacharissi (2015) calls "affective publics." They provide the social infrastructure that can be activated in times of political crisis. Our news is increasingly mediated by our social networks and consumed in what Pablo Boczkowski, Eugenia Mitchelstein, and Mora Matassi (2017) term as brief, interrupted, and partial ways, which is the biggest transformation of consumption, reception, and circulation of news since the advent of the World Wide Web. These partialities, fragments, and affective moments result in the lack of shared and coherent narrative in how we approach news and political life. More importantly, this fractured new media landscape cannot possibly reweave the threads of "social textures" long stretched thin by free markets, and now pulled to breaking.

As news mediation shifts from professional newsrooms to Silicon Valley algorithms, we have seen the problem with media and the problem is us. Trust in our social connections has now supplanted trust in the sources of news, creating a teeming environment for virulent and forged news to propagate. We are living in media and, to use Neil Postman's (2006) words "amusing ourselves to death" with the affective pull of media designed to be enticing, exciting, inciting, addicting, and stimulating. The lines between news and entertainment are indistinguishable to readers, even if that line still matters in some newsrooms. At the same time, the affective pull of social media news slowly eats away at the capacity of another social institution—journalism—to be a source for the social empathy necessary for civic life.

Perhaps a corrective for this moment of declining social connection can be seen in the writings of a nineteenth-century sociologist, Emile Durkheim, whose work has not been used widely in media and communication. Durkheim wrote about the shifts occurring in early industrial societies and the impact on what he termed "solidarity." In *The Division of Labor in Society* (1893), he posed a puzzle: how did modernity make individuals more loosely connected to their existing social arrangements but more tightly integrated into economic life? The "mechanical," as he termed it, or automatic solidarity of pre-industrial life was predicated on a lack of personal autonomy over who one knew, married, and lived near, and on an excess of shared common values, norms, and feelings. In contrast, the "organic" solidarity that emerged with industrial society depended on the expanded economic roles of the division of labor in society, a connection to a larger economy that helped give people meaning through their work, while they found themselves at the same time confronted with more choice in personal "associations," like who to marry, where to live, and how to comport themselves. Compared to fellow nineteenth-century social thinkers Karl Marx and Max Weber, Durkheim is, perhaps, less known outside of sociology. But his ideas are rooted in something that feels quintessentially right for assessing the media landscape of the long twentieth century—that the modern, depersonalized social institutions like the economy and the news anchored society until they no longer could. Liberal democracy once rested on sets of social connections that now no longer hold. Durkheim's notion of organic solidarity was that through our positions in industrial society we could learn to see empathy and connection to one another. But the irony of late capitalism is that its most fervent supporters attacked the empathy and social connection that holds capitalism together. The free market, Hobsbawm wrote, "claimed to triumph as its nakedness and inadequacy could no longer be concealed" (1994, 343). Capitalism, "took for granted the atmosphere in which it operated" and "had succeeded because it was not just capitalist" (Hobsbawm 1994, 343). In other words, Durkheim was right: without "organic solidary," industrial society would devolve into tribalism, traditionalism, and nationalism.

Where does that leave us now? The culture wars waging in American politics between traditional, isolationist values and pluralistic, cosmopolitan values reproduce the anxieties over social solidarity that raged in Durkheim's time. Trump as a candidate expertly tapped these anxieties and amplified them with his messaging. What is missing in our historical moment, however, are the sources for the trust and solidarity on which Durkheim's notion of modernity relied. The division of labor in society can no longer be counted on by social theorists to save society, when it has in fact has doomed many to lives of poverty, disconnection, and mistrust.

In such a society, the news is potentially one place to increase empathy for others, help provide recognition of multiple publics, and create social cohesion and solidarity at a moment when society needs these things the most.

Perhaps the long twentieth century proved that Durkheim's faith in the power of labor markets to provide meaning and social cohesion was misplaced. Or perhaps the unrelenting cultural and political attacks on the American working class were organic solidarity's undoing. Regardless of the reason, media scholars have work that we must do next. The powerful and positive connections that people can make online show that to some extent society has the capacity to reweave the social connections that formed the basis of solidarity in the last century. Three Canadian communication scholars, Enda Brophy, Nicole Cohen, and Greig De Peuter, have put forth the concept of "networked solidarity" as reclaiming communications infrastructure for the goals of the benefit of labor, for the "recomposition of a disconnected, flexible, yet altogether digitally adept labor force" (2015, 321). I would argue we could extend this concept to think of networked solidarity as the next step after mechanical and organic solidarity and as one way to conceive of the social organization that is to come, and the multiple roles that media have for helping people to establish it. Networked solidarity could be one way to reweave the connections that individuals in societies have to one another, but the existing social and technical infrastructure for connection will need to be reconfigured. Will online connections guide us to trust likeminded others or help us to create empathy for those who are different from us? Will these connections and affinities reinforce politically pluralistic and classically liberal connections or will we see the reentrenchment of nationalism and the reemergence of tribalism? These are open questions as we see the extent of media manipulation and intentional subversion of free and civic discourse online. But networked solidarity and the connections that constitute it may be the last best hope for repairing the type of solidarity that must be in place to hold contemporary societies together.

Might we imagine, together, new possibilities for the evolution of the connections and dependencies of modern societies that Durkheim pointed out? The personal connections of our social networks, supported by new media, have already created new pathways for collective action and social cohesion. Might the new rituals of incidental news consumption be used for building new types of social connections and solidarity? Or will we continue to fuel economies of outrage with our attention and clicks?

Our sense of public is shrinking and we must reinvigorate our online conversations if we are to reweave the fabric of social solidarity. The lesson for media scholars from the Brexit and Trump elections of 2016 is that we must challenge the outmoded liberal assumptions at the twentieth-century foundations of our field and work to identify and cultivate networked solidary for the next century.

17 Breaking the Rules of Political Communication: Trump's Successes and Miscalculations

Susan J. Douglas

Writing about the presidency and the media in 2017 is a perilous enterprise, with Donald Trump violating virtually every rule of presidential messaging, decorum, and press management while the news media, in turn, struggle to adapt and keep pace with the near daily barrage of controversial and thus newsworthy events, while also clinging to—and revitalizing—traditional journalistic practices. This essay analyzes the extent to which Donald Trump and the news media, especially the broadcast and cable news channels, departed from precedent and violated many of the basic rules of campaign and presidential coverage. To appreciate the extent of Trump's rule-breaking—especially via his favorite mode of communication, Twitter—and the news media's response to it, we need to review over one hundred years of precedents that have accrued around campaign and especially presidential news coverage. Twitter also revived the question about whether new communications technologies make campaign or presidential history. And as we'll see, while Trump's style of engaging with the media was highly successful during the campaign in garnering attention and an estimated $5 million in free media, in the eyes of the press and a majority of the public, it began to fail miserably once he entered the Oval Office, where expectations for how to communicate with the press and the public are quite different.[1] So, I argue that while upending historical precedents for political communication can be quite successful during a campaign, where unpredictability is expected, it can backfire once one inhabits the presidency, an institution expected to embody and ensure stability.

Trump and his associates have made it clear that they loathe and have no respect for the press: "the opposition party" as Steve Bannon called them, "very dishonest" and purveyors of "fake news" as Mr. Trump repeatedly asserts. This is nothing new; Trump is simply much more explicit, public,

and outspoken about it, which for a president is not without its perils. Ever
since George Washington's ambivalent attitudes toward and often passionate hatred of the press, many American presidents have shared this distrust
of reporters and have had to calculate how to deal with the news media
and, as communications technologies and outlets evolved and expanded,
with the broader media overall. During their campaigns and administrations, presidents seek, by turns, to set the agenda about what is and is not
important for the news media to cover, to co-opt, to censor and control, to
evade, and even to manipulate and defame. And they have had to confront
how these powerful institutions can shape, at times irrevocably and fatally,
presidential destiny. In turn, media institutions, executives, and practi-
tioners have had to recalibrate their practices and routines in response to
new communications technologies and media environments, and to presidential media management strategies. New communications technologies
can't make history on their own, but when their distinctive features, their
affordances, mesh well with a president's performance style, new phases
of and expectations for presidential messaging can take hold—as long as
they also mesh with and enhance communication traditions embraced by
the press.

Throughout presidential history, and especially with the proliferation of
electronic media, candidates and presidents have sought to manage what
the sociologist Erving Goffman famously called the "presentation of self,"
presenting a "frontstage" self, the ideal version of themselves they perform
for voters, and protecting or concealing their "backstage" self, the one out
of the public eye, who might be less than perfect. With the rise of public relations and image management, voters and journalists have become
especially suspicious of these "frontstage" presentations of politicians, and
thus have tried to gain access to unguarded backstage moments as the true
indices of what candidates are really like.[2] Trump upended longstanding
protocols surrounding such presentation of self as well.

The modern era of presidential news management began with William McKinley's 1896 campaign and his chief strategist Mark Hanna, who
organized the distribution of nearly 200 million leaflets, tracts, and post-
ers supporting McKinley and denouncing William Jennings Bryant, the
populist candidate. Anticipating the affordances of broadcasting, Hanna
backed this up with armies of "spellbinders" who went around the country
making pro-McKinley and anti-Bryant speeches. This set the precedent for

agenda-setting and for developing, repeating, and staying "on message." It was during McKinley's administration that an aide established the White House news "briefing," which Theodore Roosevelt himself took over during his famous "shaving hour" meetings, off-the-record exchanges with reporters that gave them direct access to the president and allowed the president to try to shape favorable coverage; they also formed the beginnings of the White House Press Corps. Roosevelt's secretary George Cortelyou, appreciating the increased agenda-setting power of a by-now robust and powerful press, arranged journalists' access to interviews and events, and gave them new working space inside the Executive Mansion, another precedent.[3] By 1913, Woodrow Wilson had instituted regularly scheduled press conferences—deferential by today's standards—and his successors felt compelled to follow suit. All of this was designed to curry favor with reporters who were seen as conduits to the people, and thus to public opinion.

It was Franklin Roosevelt, confronting the biggest economic crisis to face the nation and a newspaper industry overwhelming hostile to the New Deal, who pioneered in using a then-new medium, radio, to circumvent the press to speak directly to the public. He understood the intimacy radio afforded, with its emphasis on listening and the power of the human voice to convey familiarity and affinity. In both the 1936 and 1940 elections, two-thirds of the nation's newspapers editorially opposed Roosevelt's reelection, so his skilled use of radio through his "fireside chats," with his intimate "my friends" and "I–you" mode of address, was crucial to his political survival. He brilliantly exploited the affordances of this medium, and just as the radio networks were establishing their own news divisions that would now compete with the press.

Television introduced a new dynamic to campaigning, through the famous Kennedy-Nixon debates and the emphasis now on appearance and visual decorum, and to campaign advertising, more expensive than radio with the need for visuals. Dwight Eisenhower was the first president to have televised "fireside chats," and introduced the televised news conference in 1955 as a way to speak directly to the people and to counter the more conservative and critical elements of the Republican Party. These were not broadcast live, however; his media-savvy press secretary James Hagerty edited the films prior to broadcast to put Eisenhower in the best possible light. Indeed, it was Hagerty to whom the term "news management" was first applied.[4] The telegenic John F. Kennedy initiated the live, televised press conference, a forum that conveyed his ability to be both authoritative and informal, holding sixty-four of them before his assassination. And with the Bay of Pigs, the Cuban Missile Crisis, and the Civil Rights Movement, Kennedy had to develop effective television addresses to the American people that, by turns, admitted mistakes, reassured a terrified nation, and enunciated national moral standards. By the early 1960s then, the live, televised press conference and national address were established features of presidential messaging where the tug of war between the media and the administration over agenda-setting was fought out.

Despite his two successful presidential campaigns, Nixon hated the press; his and Vice President Spiro Agnew's stance was combative, overtly attacking news organizations and even placing some reporters under surveillance. Given this, and the growing oppositional social and political movements, Nixon did face an increasingly hostile and suspicious press corps, and at a time when television news had established powerful national influence and credibility. This administration demonstrated that striking out at the press could be ill-advised and provoke the news media to be even more adversarial than usual, which undid Nixon's presidency.

It was Ronald Reagan, a former movie actor and radio announcer, and his advisers, especially Deputy Chief of Staff Michael Deaver and the White House Director of Communications David Gergen, who shifted what they saw as a balance of power in favor of the media during the Ford and Carter administrations and returned that control to the presidency. Deaver and Gergen truly refined and elaborated on news management; they understood news routines, the daily needs of reporters and their deadlines, and that the "care and feeding" of the press was crucial to such control.[5] White House aides provided reporters with Reagan's itinerary every day, gave them summaries or full copies of his speeches or comments in advance, and stuck to a "message of the day" that everyone adhered to. Thus, they did at least half or more of the journalists' work for them, making their jobs easier. As a result of all this, and up until the disaster of Iran-Contra, when these techniques both became more exposed and also fell apart, Reagan enjoyed, by all accounts, much better press coverage than he deserved.[6]

By the early 1990s, presidents were subject to new time pressures, as the maturity of CNN News, broadcast 24/7, and the establishment of Fox News in 1996 meant that reporters wanted more instant answers and were constantly looking for stories—and pundits—to fill the news hole. Coverage of presidential campaigns was criticized for its emphasis on image over substance and on the "horserace"—who was ahead—instead of the issues at hand. The rising use of email and then the Internet allowed for greater exchange of political information among upstart news outlets and everyday people; the Internet also provided an additional platform for partisan commentary, like the Drudge Report, which broke the Monica Lewinsky scandal. Conservative politicians and activists began denouncing an alleged "liberal bias" in the news, which played a role—along with increased sensationalism in the 1990s—in the eroding trust in the news media. And by the turn of the twenty-first century, print journalism was facing an economic crisis as revenue from advertising declined and migrated to online sites, prompting the closure of some papers and a decline in investigative journalism.

When the George W. Bush administration succeeded, through repeated and disciplined messaging, and with the help of an overly compliant media, to convince a majority of Americans that Saddam Hussein had "weapons of mass destruction" and that Iraq should be invaded, only to have the war turn into an unmitigated disaster, the credibility of presidential public relations and the press reached new lows. What presidents learn, often the hard way, is that when the discrepancy between the public relations message and actual events or the president's actual persona or policies is too large, the public relations staging can backfire. For example, when Bush did his "top gun" landing on the *U.S.S. Abraham Lincoln* in May 2003 to announce the end of major combat in Iraq, underneath the now infamous "Mission Accomplished" banner, while the mission had not been accomplished at all, the press began to become more skeptical of the administration. The gap between how Bush handled the 2005 catastrophe of Hurricane Katrina, and what television cameras were showing to the American people, further undermined his credibility. If there is a gap between presidential performance and presidential imagery, typically the media will expose that. And over time, administrations have had to walk that line between disciplined messaging and not being so overly scripted that the press senses deception or weakness.

By the time Barack Obama ran in 2008, the explosion in the Internet's reach, and the affordances of social media like Facebook, YouTube, and texting, meant that presidents and presidential candidates were once again confronting an emerging, transitioning media environment while still also having to master traditional media, especially television. The Obama campaign exploited these new media aggressively and brilliantly, with an email list that reached 13 million people directly, creating what David Plouffe referred to as "our own television network." Over 1800 Obama campaign-related videos on YouTube garnered more than 50 million views. At the same time, with the user-generated, do-it-yourself affordances of such sites, anyone could ridicule, criticize, or contradict the president.

So, by 2016, these were some of the precedents and routines that Trump and the news media adhered to, yet overturned. Indeed, experience with publicity (Trump) met experience with news management (the media). And by now, Twitter, which Trump used to directly reach his supporters and circumvent the press, had become a major element in the new media ecosystem. Trump was newsworthy because he was a bombastic reality TV star and a wealthy real estate developer with no political experience. As a highly dramatic media performer who loved the spotlight and sensed that voters were weary of carefully scripted "frontstage" personae, Trump took unspeakable comments about race, immigrants, women, and Muslims—as well as about his opponents—out of the backstage and onto the frontstage of his rallies. Twitter, which matched his rhetorical style of short words, declarative statements, and incendiary insults, was the perfect medium for him. Twitter brought in new ways of circumventing yet engaging the news media; no candidate had used the medium the way Trump did to set the agenda and command attention, compelling the media to recalibrate their coverage to fit the novelty of the platform and the candidate. Because the tone and content of his tweets were often highly controversial (and ratings bait), the press provided him an entirely new level of free media by reporting nearly all of his tweets.

But tweets also fit into several established news routines—the use, of course, of headlines and snappy pull quotes, increasingly shorter sound-bites given to presidents (and all political candidates), and cable news' reliance on the chyron (see Zizi Papacharissi's "The Importance of Being a Headline" in this volume). Thus Trump's tweets exploited these preexisting practices while also making them more explosive, because what he said to and about fellow candidates (and celebrities) so violated political decorum, the tweets were highly newsworthy. Cable channels have to fill the 24/7 news hole and are always looking for "scoops" or exclusives, especially during a campaign, so when Trump would simply phone in, his calls were of course taken and aired. And not only were most of his rallies aired on CNN, they were also plugged with hyped-up chyrons reading "Donald Trump Expected to Speak Any Minute." Because his rallies were filled with drama, vilification, and even violence, they were often front-page or leading stories. So in this way, Trump constantly set the agenda in terms of substance, journalistic practice, and rhetoric, as well as about what was newsworthy— him. He led, and the news media followed.

After the election, there was much hand wringing, from journalists and their critics, about the extent to which the news media, and especially cable news, had enabled Trump's victory by giving him so much coverage. But reporters, accustomed to pivoting from covering someone as a candidate versus as president, and wedded to longstanding traditions about how to do so, had new expectations, based on precedent and journalistic principles, about interactions with the president. And this is where Trump, who got elected in part by breaking the rules around "politics as usual," failed to appreciate the pull of tradition, even in the face of new media platforms, or to learn from his predecessors.

By repeatedly attacking the press (along with his surrogates) as trafficking in "fake news," and disputing obvious facts (such as the size of his inauguration crowd), like Nixon he energized the news media into a frenzy of fact-checking and inadvertently resuscitated investigative reporting. And like Nixon, Trump didn't appreciate the power of angered anonymous sources. By failing to honor and by attacking intelligence agencies, he converted what might have been recalcitrant sources for the press into widespread and serial leaks by people eager to see incompetent or possibly criminal people exposed. (Indeed, the more leaks the weaker the presidency, and the weaker the presidency the greater the leaks).[7] In utter contrast to the Reagan team's "message of the day," or Bush's tightly coordinated PR machine, there was no disciplined messaging at all, with the President, primarily through Twitter, contradicting members of his own administration. As a result, press briefings (which he has threatened to eliminate) have become even more chaotic and contentious. In his first five months, Trump held only one solo press conference in which, as CNN's Jake Tapper (among many others) noted, Trump "said things that were not true" and seemed "unhinged."[8] Nor did Trump, in his first five months, address the nation about any of the serially unfolding scandals surrounding his administration.

While Trump's tweets remained covered, 140 characters—attention-getting during a campaign—are inadequate to laying out complex policy issues, leading news organizations to differ on whether and how to cover them.[9] More to the point, while there has been, so far, minimal "backstage" coverage of Trump's marriage or personal life, his pre-dawn tweets, titillating during a campaign, provide unnerving backstage access to his state of mind, interpretation of facts, and paranoia.

The press have of course over the years become quite wary of and savvy about news management—the staged photo ops, the message of the day, and the like. But in the face of minimal, confused, and failed news management, where nearly every precedent, however suspect, has been ignored or overturned, the news media confront a vacuum that they need to fill. Here, tradition and established practices matter, especially, as Twitter has shown, when new communications technologies and their uses can be so disruptive to existing, respected, and comforting habitual conventions.

Breaking the rules of media engagement and presentation of self was one of the factors that made Trump seem fresh and new to some and thus helped him get elected. But once in office, he was dealing with decades-old traditions of presidential messaging and coverage that his preferred (and often only) mode of communication, Twitter, could not upend. He was also dealing with a press stung by their abdication of agenda-setting during the campaign, and determined to reclaim it, especially from a president whose goal was to undermine their very legitimacy. And, finally, he was dealing with a dispersed bureaucracy with various power centers, not his own business or crowds at a rally. All Trump's rule-breaking thus produced an unstable political environment that Washington's established institutions, especially the press corps, both feed on yet seek to rebalance. Thus, even with the very latest communications technologies, presidents can only do so much to countermand the pull of history and precedent without undermining their own authority, legitimacy, and power.

Notes

1. As of this writing, Trump's approval rating, according to Gallup, is 37 percent. http://news.gallup.com/poll/201617/gallup-daily-trump-job-approval.aspx.

2. Erving Goffman, *The Presentation of Self in Everyday Life* (New York: Doubleday, 1959), 7.

3. Susan J. Douglas, "Managing the President's Public Persona," in Niki Hemmer, ed., *Crucible: The President's First Year* (Charlottesville: The University of Virginia Press, 2017).

4. Susan J. Douglas, "Managing the President's Public Persona."

5. Mark Hertsgaard, *On Bended Knee: The Press and the Reagan Presidency* (New York: Farrar Straus and Giroux, 1988).

6. Ben Bradlee of the *Washington Post* said, "We have been kinder to President Reagan than any President I can think of since I've been at the *Post*," cited in Mark Hertsgaard, *On Bended Knee*.

7. Herbert J. Gans, *Deciding What's News: A Study of CBS Evening News, NBC Nightly News,* Newsweek *and* Time (New York: Vintage Books, 1980), 119.

8. http://www.cnn.com/videos/politics/2017/02/16/trump-press-conference-jake -tapper-unhinged.cnn/video/playlists/donald-trump-press-conference-2-16-17.

9. Michael M. Grynbaum and Sydney Ember, "If Trump Tweets, Is It Always News? A Quandary for the News Media," *New York Times*, November 30, 2016, A16.

18   Trump on Twitter: How a Medium Designed for Democracy Became an Authoritarian's Mouthpiece

Fred Turner

On its face, Twitter appears to be a quintessentially democratic medium. It promotes individualized expression; helps build social networks; and, until recently, seemed to epitomize the decentralized, highly individualized public sphere long called for by liberal theorists and digital utopians alike. During Donald Trump's campaign for president, however, it became an engine of authoritarianism. Day after day, Trump spit out bits of fiction and hyperbole. They piled up like tiny bricks, slowly but surely walling off the landscape of reality. In its place, Trump hung billboards depicting his own imagined magnificence. The mass media pointed to Trump's tweets, ridiculed their lies, lampooned their tone—and spread them far and wide. Slowly but surely, Trump succeeded in doing what every fledgling totalitarian must. He made the world look chaotic and dangerous. And through Twitter, he put himself at the center of the storm.

But how did this happen? Only twenty years ago, many scholars and journalists agreed: the Internet and the World Wide Web were sure to bring about more democracy. Virtual communities would be hubs of collaborative intimacy. Blogs would give the average person a voice. The strangleholds of corporate media centralization and state censorship would finally be broken and a new, benevolent era of free expression would emerge. Now those hopes have now been well and truly dashed—not only by Donald Trump's use of Twitter, but by the failures of the Egyptian spring, the revelations of Edward Snowden, and the Russians' hacking of America's elections. All of these events have challenged our faith that the technologies of free expression necessarily bring democracy in their wake.

During his campaign, however, Trump went a critical step further. He successfully fused two elements that Americans have long regarded as implacably opposed: the authoritarian's will to centralize power and the democrat's faith in decentralized communication. When Trump tweeted, he demonstrated that the faith of a generation of twentieth-century liberal theorists—as well as their digital descendants—was misplaced: decentralization does not necessarily increase democracy in the public sphere or in the state. On the contrary, the technologies of decentralized communication can be coupled very tightly to the charismatic, personality-centered modes of authoritarianism long associated with mass media and mass society. More frightening still, Trump's tweets have demonstrated that the technologies of individualized expression may not always stand as bulwarks against totalitarian power. They can, in fact, be made *cornerstones* of such power. In short, Trump has turned our understanding of the relationship between democracy and communication on its head. He has perhaps even ushered in a new era, an era of authoritarian individualism.

World War II and the Roots of Social Media

If so, Trump has overturned the intellectual consensus that gave rise to our faith in social media in the first place. To see how, we need to return to the start of World War II. In the late 1930s, American intellectuals, politicians, and journalists marveled at the rise of fascism in Europe, and particularly in Germany. Many had long thought of Germany as the birthplace of Beethoven and Goethe and so as the epicenter of European high culture. How, they wondered, had this most sophisticated of nations fallen under the sway of a short, mustachioed former clerk, Adolf Hitler? Many worried too at the rise of fascism in America. Although we have largely forgotten the fact today, the racism and anti-Semitism that characterized Nazi doctrine were widespread in the United States at the same time. In 1938, for instance, the Catholic demagogue Father Coughlin broadcast his venomous anti-Semitism to a weekly radio audience of 3,500,000. In 1939, the Amerikadeutscher Volksbund drew 22,000 American fascists to a rally at Madison Square Garden in New York. An enormous banner reading "Stop Jewish Domination of Christian America" looked down on the stage. Later that year, after Hitler had marched into Poland, hundreds of American fascists marched down East 86th Street in New York behind American flags and Nazi swastikas as large crowds looked on without protest.

To observers at the time, the question was, why?

Today, most historians would probably look for an answer in the economic chaos of the era. But at the time, many Americans pointed to the power of the mass media. They made two distinct though often overlapping cases. The first was primarily structural and made by American journalists and German refugee intellectuals such as Shepard Stone and Theodor Adorno. The second was primarily psychological and made by anthropologists and psychologists such as Margaret Mead and Gordon Allport. Both groups noted that the leaders of Germany and America had taken hold of large, centralized media systems. The structuralists believed that the one-to-many design of mass media technologies in and of themselves forced audiences to tune their senses toward a single, powerful source. When they did, these analysts argued, they became vulnerable to whatever charisma the source might possess. Moreover, simply by turning together in a single direction, audiences rehearsed the one-to-many structure of fascism. In the process, the structuralists suggested that they ceased to reason and became members of an unthinking mass.

Figures such as Mead and Allport feared this process too. In 1940, they helped form the Committee for National Morale, a group of sixty scholars who aimed to advise President Roosevelt on the best ways to establish democratic unity as war loomed. Members of the Committee generally subscribed to the theories of Franz Boas and the culture and personality school of anthropology. That is, they believed that every society had a modal personality type. It was the role of the family to cultivate this type in their children and so help them to adjust to their culture. When children left the family, Committee members believed that media tended to sustain the socialization process begun at home. Most of them agreed with the structuralists that mass media tended to produce an authoritarian personality style. They also associated that style with German culture and with fascism more generally. How, they asked, could Americans produce a mode of media that would cultivate a democratic form of personality? And what would such a personality type look like anyway?

Their answers to these questions laid the cultural groundwork for social media. A democratic person, they argued, would be a psychologically whole individual, able to freely choose what to believe, with whom to associate, and where to turn their attention. A democratic personality would embrace others and celebrate their differences, while retaining their own sense of separateness. Members of the Committee believed that insofar as mass media promoted undifferentiated experience, it also promoted an undifferentiated, mass society. They argued that if they were to defeat the Axis, media makers would have to develop a multi-source medium for propaganda. Only among an *array* of images and sounds could Americans cultivate the diversity of views that might sustain both unity and individuality.

In 1942, Bauhaus refugee Herbert Bayer and American photographer Edward Steichen brought the Committee's ideas to life in *Road to Victory*, a huge exhibition of pro-American images at New York's Museum of Modern Art. There they hung photographs above, below, and around museum-goers with the aim of democratizing their perceptions. As they moved among the pictures, viewers were meant to choose the ones they found most individually meaningful, but to do it together. If the structure of mass media modeled the one-to-many structure of fascist government, the many-to-many nature of the encounters promoted by *Road to Victory* modeled its egalitarian alternative.

Road to Victory was the first in a long line of such exhibitions that stretched across the Cold War. By the 1960s, these exhibitions had become models for the multimedia performances of the San Francisco counterculture. On the shores of California, audiences again surrounded themselves with media in order to liberate their minds. But now the critique of fascism and mass media had become something subtly different: a critique of bureaucracy and mass society. Before long, locals like Steve Jobs seized on this new critique, and on the idea that decentralized media technologies could democratize their users' perceptions, to promote computers as tools of democratic revolution. Today the founders of Bay-area social media firms from Facebook to Twitter make the same claims: social media will allow us to present our authentic selves to one another, they say, to "connect," and so by implication form an egalitarian, even potentially anti-authoritarian, solidarity.

Authoritarian Individualism

Trump's capture of the presidency has visibly betrayed the anti-authoritarian promise of digital media. It has also revealed a critical flaw in the thinking that underlies it. Since World War II, many Americans have imagined that totalitarian societies are by definition regimented, hyper-bureaucratized, hierarchical, and emotionally numb. The emblems of such societies are the gulag and the concentration camp. Particularly after the 1960s, we have tended to imagine free societies as just the opposite: unregimented, antibureaucratic, egalitarian, and suffused with feeling. The emblems of a free society today, at least on the left, are the open-air rock concert and the sit-in. We are free, we believe, when we speak our individual truths together.

Yet, anyone who sat in the mud at Woodstock knows how far from utopia a rock concert can be. And anyone who has ever had successful surgery at a hospital will respect the value of hierarchy, bureaucracy, and disinterested reason. The critique of mass society and mass media that so animated Americans during and after World War II has left us blind to the ways in which individualism itself can be summoned to serve authoritarian ends. The Committee for National Morale, for instance, saw authentic individuality and the interpersonal sphere of action as key sources of resistance to fascism. The commune builders of the 1960s did too. Today both the performance of individual authenticity and the interpersonal sphere have become weapons in Donald Trump's assault on the institutions of American democracy.

Consider the question of Donald Trump's character. During the election, Hillary Clinton criticized his tempestuous, bullying style, assuming that it would alienate voters. It didn't. To many voters, Trump's carefully cultivated ability to wear his feelings on his sleeve made him appear more authentically himself. Trump mastered the idiom of mediated authenticity on reality TV's *The Apprentice*. There he depicted himself not only as a masterful manager, but as a man flung here and there by his anger, his drive, his affections. Today on Twitter he repeats the performance. Trump's Twitter stream alternates between self-congratulatory announcements of his achievements and bombastic attacks on those he sees as enemies. Senator Charles Schumer is "Cryin' Chuck Schumer." Former FBI Director James Comey is a "phony." And of course, the mainstream media are "Fake News."

Many see these outbursts as signs of a president who can't control his emotions and thus, of Trump's unsteadiness. But to many of his supporters, the outbursts are signs of his just being himself. On Twitter, Trump's tempestuousness is a sign of his authenticity as a person. Displaying that authenticity is one of the ways he claims the right to our attention and, with it, our political support. The historical irony is almost overwhelming: Trump has taken the logic of individual authenticity that animated the New Left in 1968 and American liberalism for thirty years before that and put it to work as a new mode of authoritarian charisma. Thirty years ago, anti–Vietnam War protestors presented themselves to those in Washington as authentic individuals bent on challenging a state gone off the rails. Today, their place has been taken by Donald Trump.

To be clear, I'm not trying to equate Trump's name-calling with mass marches on the Capitol. What I'm trying to do is make visible the consequences of an intellectual logic left over from the fight against fascism. The performance of authentic individuality does not necessarily free us from authoritarianism. Nor does authoritarianism always stalk us in the uniforms of German troops. On the contrary, the performance of individuality can help make the case that a particular individual represents a set of political interests *in their bodies*. In the 1960s, the notion that the personal is political drove any number of social movements. But the notion of an embodied, personalized politics is also central to authoritarianism. In settings ranging from Franco's Spain to Putin's Russia, authoritarian leaders have claimed to uniquely manifest the will of the people in their facial expressions, the strength of the people in their own muscles, the anger of the people in their voices. In fact, they have often offered this ability to personalize the political as a justification for seizing power.

Trump has done the same thing on Twitter. In the twentieth century, mass media theorists often believed that charismatic authoritarian leaders had to first bring the bodies or minds of their audiences together in one place before they could work their hypnotic magic. That place might be a Nuremberg-style rally, or a one-to-many, geographically dispersed radio listening experience. Today however, when Trump tweets, he presents himself as if he were part of a conversation among friends. Part of that presentation is a function of the medium's structure. Individual tweets arrive on a feed that almost certainly contains a wide array of sources. Depending on how users configure their Twitter streams, those sources may very well include friends, family, and colleagues. Much as mid-century authoritarians could use radio to broadcast their voices into the intimacy of the family living room, so now Trump can use Twitter to insert himself into the company of a user's chosen conversation partners. Trump also works hard to suggest to that his intimate circle—and through Twitter, yours—includes the rich and powerful. "Great meeting with a wonderful woman today, former Secretary of State Condoleezza Rice!" he tweets.

Here Trump's performance of individual authenticity, his raw emotionalism, make perfect sense. Trump tweets like a teenaged girl—not just in frequency, but in genre and diction. On July 25, 2016, for instance, he tweeted "I was @FoxNews and met Juan Williams in passing. He asked if he could have pictures taken with me. I said fine. He then trashes on air!" The blend of name dropping ("Juan Williams") and the "He-wanted-to-be-with-me-but-then-he-dissed-me" framing is straight from the High School Mean Girl Power Play Handbook. In the mass media era, few presidential candidates would have spoken in such a casual, petulant idiom, at least not in public. To do so would have been to diminish their power. Like a mid-century authoritarian, Trump builds his claims to power on constructing the sense that he feels the pain of his audience. Trump has married the rostrum-pounding emotionalism of the twentieth century dictator to the interpersonal intimacy of our new media era. On Twitter, his petulance is par for the course. By showing it, he demonstrates that he is a human being like his readers and like the friends whose tweets surround his in their feeds. He is a person like them.

Except of course, he isn't. That's the tyrant's trick: to pretend to act on behalf of the people while leading them down a dark alley and robbing them blind. The trick is as old as time. And it was a trick that twentieth-century scholars, journalists, and media makers hoped to prevent by breaking up one-to-many media and replacing them with multi-source media surrounds. As he speaks on Twitter, a descendant of those surrounds, Trump undermines the assumptions at the heart of their work. Authoritarian charisma is not medium-dependent. Nor are authentic individuality, the intimate social sphere, or flexible, collaborative networks necessarily enemies of totalitarianism. Today, it is only key bureaucracies—the courts, the press, and even the FBI—who stand in the way of Trump's becoming a charismatic autocrat in the mold of Vladimir Putin. These bulwarks remind us that in an era of authoritarian individualism, what democracy needs first and foremost is not more personalized modes of mediated expression. It is a renewed engagement with the rule of law and with the institutions that embody it.

19   Tweeting All the Way to the White House

Josh Cowls and Ralph Schroeder

The argument of this chapter is simple: Donald Trump's use of Twitter, transformed into dominance of the mainstream media, plus populism, caused his victory.[1]

The longer version is as follows: From June 16, 2015, when Trump announced his candidacy, until he won the Republican nomination on July 20, 2016, he sent a series of controversial tweets that secured him far more attention on television and in newspapers than his rivals, often more than all the others put together. Mainstream media, starved for news and competing for audiences, eagerly seized on Trump's 140-character pronouncements. In this way, Trump set the agenda: he dominated the attention space, which blocked out all the other candidates. Populism also played a role. Trump presented himself as being anti-establishment, including being against his own party. After he won the nomination, his use of Twitter was no longer crucial to the explanation: both candidates were guaranteed a roughly equal share of media attention. But between his announcement and his nomination, populism became crucial. He painted his opponents as part of the Washington establishment and in league with Wall Street elites. There has been a populist undercurrent in American politics for a long time, but on this occasion, propelled via Twitter, which bypassed the gatekeepers of traditional media, populism could emerge interstitially to win out over the ideological and organizational stranglehold of the two parties.

Populism has been defined as the belief that the true and virtuous people are underrepresented. Populists, in Mueller's (2016) view, claim that they are the "100%" and want to exclude "others." They are also anti-elite—against the media and the political establishments in the case of right-wing populists and against wealthy economic elites in the case of left-wing populism (represented in 2016 by Bernie Sanders). In addition to the "100%

people" and anti-elitism, a third characteristic of populists is that they espouse the ideal that the government should more adequately represent the people. And populist ideology is not just domestic: external enemies are also supposedly threatening the nation, economically and geopolitically; in this case, illegal immigrants and Islamic terrorists. Trump's populist agenda promised to overcome these threats and, in doing so, to "make America great again."

Trump became the Republican Party's nominee even though he was an outsider—a political novice and businessman—and the party favored insider candidates. His positions were far from the political mainstream, including, most controversially, his strident anti-immigrant stance. And many of the stories in the media were critical of Trump's positions. But for a newcomer, even negative attention can be a plus, and drawing most of the attention while leaving little else for others is even better. Trump's views received completely disproportionate coverage in the media. The relation between the number of tweets in which Trump and other candidates are mentioned and their coverage in mainstream media over the course of the campaign has been tracked (at viz2016.com) and shows a clear correlation: Trump is mentioned in tweets far more than any other candidate in both parties, often more than all other candidates combined, and the volume of tweets closely tracks his outsize coverage in the dominant mainstream media (which, in the tracking analysis, include CNN, Fox News, MSNBC, ABC, CBS, NBC, and local news). Polling data confirms that Trump pulled ahead of other Republican candidates in synchrony with his dominance of the media attention space, again despite the fact that his nomination as the Republican candidate was opposed by the party up until the party's convention and beyond.

The evidence for how Trump's tweeting translated into dominance of traditional media goes beyond counting how tweet mentions are converted into traditional media mentions. We can also look, for example, at content, or at how Trump used Twitter as a megaphone for his message: the most common phrase in his tweets was "Make America Great Again"—the significance of which is expounded by Sonnevend (this volume)—and in second place, announcements of campaign events and media interviews. But he also used Twitter in three stages to attack his enemies: first, taking aim at his primary opponents; then, with the race reduced to two, his Democratic opponent; and since the election, his new main enemy, the media.[2]

Twitter increasingly amplified his message: he had gained 13 million Twitter followers by the time of the election, but compared to when he announced his campaign, his tweets were by then also being retweeted five times as often—holding the number of followers constant. Furthermore, he made savvy use of the @ (or "mention") function in his tweets, primarily pointing his supporters to news programs on sites such as Fox News, which would send them to favorable TV coverage, or to defend himself against negative news coverage by the "failing New York Times." Again, these tweets may not have mattered much among those on Twitter, but they did in terms of how they received extensive mainstream media coverage, especially when they stoked controversy.

Our argument can also be proved "ex negativo" (since we both work at Oxford, we have to throw in some bad use of Latin!): using Media Cloud (https://mediacloud.org) data, it is possible to compare how often Trump's Twitter handle is mentioned compared with those of his nearest primary rivals (Ben Carson, Jeb Bush, Marco Rubio, and Ted Cruz) in the mainstream media between June 1, 2015, and May 31, 2016, when his rivals had conceded. These data show that after he entered the race, Trump mentions dwarf the mentions of all the others, with the single exception of Cruz mentions at the end of January just before his Iowa victory (which is perhaps no coincidence).

Yet another way to support our argument is to use the GDELT campaign television tracker, which makes use of the Internet Archive's Television News Archive.[3] Using this tool, it can be shown that Trump receives more mentions on CNN than on its rival 24-hour news stations, Fox News and MSNBC. Similarly, we can look just at CNN and compare how Trump fares against his rivals in the primaries. In the first half of 2015, there is much speculation about a number of potential candidates. But within the space of two weeks of the announcement of his candidacy in mid-June, Trump pulls far ahead of all the other candidates in references, almost never relinquishing his dominant position. Furthermore, during the primary, Fox News had more weeks than CNN during which Trump's rivals had more mentions. Trump even had vastly outsized coverage on CNN compared to Hillary Clinton once the race started after the party conventions and up until the election—even though Clinton was typically ahead in the polls.

Trump did not use sophisticated technology. His opponents, and especially the Democratic presidential campaign, were stronger in using advanced data analytics and social media targeting, which Trump outwardly scoffed at. But he did use a simple technology in a new way to get his message across unfiltered, bypassing gatekeepers. (This should remind us that uses of old technology can be innovative, and that innovation can be put to maleficent uses). And it is also worth highlighting the novelty of this use of technology: before 2016, apart from data analytics, the main effect of the Internet on campaigning had been on fundraising and on targeting campaign ads at social media users. Trump was an innovator.

But this innovation could only work in the highly competitive context of traditional news media seeking audience share. News producers on television and in newspapers were forced to give a lot of time to Trump's views since the American media system is characterized by horserace politics: the focus of elections is on personalities, and coverage of TV debates, for example, is driven by who won or lost—much like reality TV shows—not by weighing policies. And the 2016 election was good for traditional media. Tomasky (2016) quotes the television executive Les Moonves who said during the primaries that the Trump phenomenon "may not be good for America, but it's damn good for CBS." Or again, in October 2016 at a forum at Harvard University, Jeff Zucker, president of CNN, boasted that in 2016 his network had come closer to Fox News in ratings than in the previous eight years—a tacit acknowledgment of the commercial pressures that news organizations face, as Pickard (this volume) shows. This extensive "free" media coverage also meant that Trump had to spend far less on political advertising than his rivals.

Furthermore, journalists covering the campaign, themselves extensive users of Twitter, eagerly picked up newsworthy tweets. Perhaps, Hamby (2013) argues, they have become too insulated in the Twitterverse. They used to spend a lot of time with the candidates—as in *The Boys on the Bus* (Crouse 1973)—and also used to get a sense of the public's concerns and their responses to the candidates. Hamby documents that in recent campaigns, by contrast, journalists rely on Twitter as a major source, not just following candidates and campaign teams but also by following each other. They are also under pressure by their editors to feature these "breaking news" (or tweets!) in their stories, especially attention-grabbing ones that increase audience share. Trump was, therefore, able to set the agenda by tweeting positions that were guaranteed a wide audience in mainstream media—in large part because of, not in spite of, their controversial nature.

As Douglas (this volume) demonstrates, presidential candidates seeking to influence the media agenda are nothing new. But compared with previous media platforms, tweets are unfiltered—put the other way around, there is less editorial control—and can spread around the network rapidly, which allows minor incidents to gain widespread attention quickly. Here it can be noted that Trump's tweets also went against the grain of tighter management of campaign messages on social media that has characterized the campaigns of other candidates (see Kreiss 2016): he tweets himself, and the controversial nature of many of his messages means that they are a boon to news-starved journalists. Hamby describes the often desperate search among journalists to find something worthwhile to report on, and Trump provided plenty of tweets that were considered newsworthy enough to be reproduced in full in the news.

Trump's position could not have been achieved without the support of a substantial proportion of the electorate. His base of support consisted of a part of the population that considers itself left out by the country's media elites and its established party elites (Cramer 2016). There is an economic aspect to the demographic of this support, but it is also among the less-educated, more male, more rural, and more white population, as Hampton expands upon (this volume). Trump supporters share a distrust of government, a deep-rooted tradition in American politics (Hall and Lindholm 2001). Their anti-immigrant, anti-refugee, and anti-Muslim stances are more to do with excluding undeserving "others" from the citizenship rights of the "100%" and with economic nationalism than purely with economic disadvantage or uncertainty—consider, by contrast, the very low rates of support for Trump among economically disadvantaged voters of color.

Again, Trump's success cannot be explained by reference to Twitter alone. Trump did not directly speak to his audience via Twitter—too few Americans are on Twitter for this to have been an effective tactic. But he could rely on traditional media to broadcast his new media messages. The explanation relies on how Trump's political message—his unconventional remarks on Twitter—received a level of attention which would have been impossible had he relied on press conferences or traditional broadcast coverage. In other words, by communicating via Twitter, Trump was able to bypass the conventional gatekeepers of journalists and mainstream TV and newspapers because they were compelled to report his views in a competitive environment, which relies on audience share. As Karpf (2016) argues:

In a world with digital media, but less analytics, this election drama would have un-folded differently ... journalists and their editors would have been less attuned to the immediate feedback of Trump's daily ratings effects, and this would have led them to spread their coverage more evenly (as they always have in the past). Trump's me-dia dominance isn't just driven by our attention, it's driven by the media industry's new tools for measuring and responding to that attention.

The role of the media and of Twitter was decisive inasmuch as other factors that typically play a role can be ruled out: the argument that the party and its elites "decide" on the candidate (Cohen et al. 2016) did not apply on this occasion (though arguably, they applied to Hillary Clinton's nomination). Second, Trump had fewer resources; he spent far less than other candidates during the primaries and during the general election cam-paign (and there was less overall spending than in previous campaigns). Third, Trump did not have as effective a data analytics–driven or ground campaign; in this respect, his campaign was less sophisticated than that of his competitors.

Populists have traditionally been adept at using the mass media of their day. But the reach of their media was limited, as with direct mail and mag-azines or latterly email (Kazin 1998, 259–260), unless populists could also obtain sufficient attention in the mainstream media. Other populists have had a critical attitude to the mainstream media, and Trump also main-tained a critical—even conspiratorial—attitude toward the establishment-dominated media throughout the election and accused the media of being "rigged" against him. He still does. The extent to which this attitude drove his supporters to alternative media and social media has not been system-atically examined (to our knowledge). But the key is that Trump was able to continue to have this and other messages relayed from his tweets to the mainstream media, even though the mainstream media often cov-ered him negatively (and covered his claims that the media were biased against him).

Trump is in a long line of right- and left-wing populism in America. Yet as Kazin (1998) points out, populism has generally moved rightward after World War II. Populism as an ideology has waxed and waned in the post-war period, though in terms of voter support for a populist ideology, it has often been just as strong as left, right, moderate, and libertarian ideologies (Clagget, Engle, and Shafer 2014). Trump's language was strongly populist; only Bernie Sanders rivaled him on the left and Ben Carson on the right for populist language, as Oliver and Rahn (2016) have shown. They also show that the strong support among voters for his populist views have not been taken into account by parties, and by the Republican Party in particular, which they say constitutes a "representation gap": "Donald Trump's simple, Manichean rhetoric is quintessentially populist ... the opportunity for a Donald Trump presidency is ultimately rooted in a failure of the Republican Party to incorporate a wide range of constituencies" (Oliver and Rahn 2016, 202). In other words, his populist appeal mattered too. Together with Trump's use of Twitter, and how his tweets translated into dominating mainstream media attention, this provides a sufficient explanation for why he now sits—tweeting—in the White House.

Notes

1. Longer versions of the argument, and full supporting documentation, visualizations, and references, can be found in Cowls (2017) and Schroeder (2017).

2. http://www.nytimes.com/interactive/2016/12/06/upshot/how-to-know-what -donald-trump-really-cares-about-look-at-who-hes-insulting.html.

3. http://television.gdeltproject.org/cgi-bin/iatv_campaign2016/iatv _campaign2016.

20 Social Media or Social Inequality: Trump's "Unexpected" Election

Keith N. Hampton

Since at least the United States election of 2000, scholars have debated the role of the Internet in the electoral process. Most often, and without much supporting evidence, pundits have argued that the Internet provides new forums for political engagement and increased voter participation among groups previously less likely to participate—notably young people. The 2016 presidential election has spurred a very different discussion. Although pundits have continued to suggest that the Internet, and in particular social media, played a role in deciding the outcome of the election, the discourse has taken a negative tone. The defeat of Democratic candidate, Hillary Clinton, at the hands of Republican candidate, Donald Trump, has generated an outcry from scholars who now point to the deleterious role of social media in influencing the result of the election.

Arguments as to why social media might have contributed to President Trump's election have included the sway of "fake news," algorithms that create filter bubbles, the influence of strong political opinions expressed through social media, and how social media sorts people into echo chambers that limit their exposure to different points of view. Although these issues should not be entirely dismissed, there is no evidence that these forces worked in favor of a particular presidential candidate. By focusing on the potential harmful effects of social media, scholars have largely ignored how the unique historical context of the 2016 presidential election (primarily changes in patterns of inequality and immigration) and the absence or limited use of social media by specific segments of the population contributed to the election's outcome.

In Context

The 2016 election took place on the heels of the Great Recession, a period of general economic decline, high rates of foreclosures, and declines in home values. Americans have felt the subsequent, ongoing, economic recovery unequally; income growth has been concentrated among the highest income earners, whereas most others have experienced income stagnation or decline. Income inequality is at its highest since a peak in the late 1920s (Sommeiller, Price, and Wazeter 2016).

At the same time, the composition of the American population is changing. At nearly 40 million people, the total, foreign-born population of the United States represents a larger proportion of the population than at any time since the 1920s (Grieco et al. 2012). Opinions about the value of immigration and its impact on America are strongly divided by class and political affiliation. Those from the middle class, those with more years of formal education, and Democrats generally express a positive view of immigrants. Those from the working class, those with fewer years of education, those with low incomes, and Republicans are much less likely to believe that immigrants benefit the country (Doherty, Tyson, and Weisel 2015).

It was economic inequality and unfavorable attitudes toward immigrants—both concentrated in the white working-class—that created the context for the election of Donald Trump, not the use of social media. Evidence as to why these two factors mattered more than others can be found in an analysis of who switched their vote, from supporting the Democratic candidate for President in 2012, to the Republican candidate in 2016.

Who Switched Their Vote?

Data collected from actual voters suggest that a very narrow segment of the population shifted its vote from the Democratic candidate for president in 2012 to the Republican candidate in 2016. The National Election Pool, a consortium of media companies, has been collecting exit poll data from voters since 2003. In 2016, on behalf of the National Election Pool, Edison Research conducted a national probability survey that consisted of approximately 16,000 phone interviews with early and absentee voters and, on

Election Day, in person interviews with 85,000 voters as they exited nearly 1,000 polling stations.

An analysis of exit poll data conducted by the Pew Research Center (2016) found deep divisions among demographic groups and their preference for presidential candidates. However, for the most part, these divisions were consistent with historical trends. For example, women were more likely to vote for Clinton than for Trump (54% to 42%). Yet, women supported Clinton by about the same margin as women had voted for the Democratic candidate over the Republican candidate in 2012 (55% to 44%) and 2008 (56% vs. 43%). Men were more likely to support Donald Trump— by a 12-point margin, which was only modestly higher than the 7-point advantage men gave the Republican candidate in 2012. Clinton lost white voters by a margin that was nearly identical to what occurred in 2012. In 2016, white, non-Hispanic voters favored Trump by 21 percentage points (58% vs. 37%), not unlike the 2012 Republican candidate who won white voters by 20 points (59% to 39%).

One key demographic changed its vote from the Democratic candidate in 2012 to the Republican candidate in 2016. In comparison with recent presidential elections, a wide partisan gap emerged in 2016 between those with and without a college degree. In 2012, those without a college-degree showed near equal support for Democratic and Republican candidates (51% to 47%). In 2016, there was an 8-point margin in favor of Trump (52% to 44%). However, when looking only at white voters without a college degree, a 39-point margin emerged in favor of Trump (67% to 28%). Although whites without a college education had also preferred the Republican candidate in 2012 (61% to 36%) and 2008 (58% to 40%), it was by smaller margins. Trump's margin of support among white, working-class voters, who are concentrated in less urban areas, was the largest since 1980. It was this shift in voter loyalty that swayed the election in favor of Donald Trump.

Digital Inequality

Evidence of votes shifted from the Democratic to the Republican candidate in the 2016 presidential election points to a small segment of the population, primarily white, working- class voters without a college degree. The very people who switched their allegiance in 2016 from the Democratic to the Republican presidential candidate are the most likely to be removed from those forces of social media argued to have influenced the vote.

According to a national survey conducted by Pew Research Center (2015), this group is more disconnected in its online and offline media activities than most segments of the American population. An examination of its overall media use shows that this demographic is much less likely to access information on a variety of topics, including education, finances, government services, health care, job information, and their local community. They use less diverse sources of traditional media, like the television, radio, and newspapers, and they access less information online. Of the 15 percent of Americans who do not use the Internet at home or on a mobile device, two-thirds are white and do not have a college degree.

The reason why this demographic is so digitally disconnected is the result of a confluence of forces. Because they are more likely to live in rural areas and small towns, they are less likely to have access to broadband Internet service. Working-class Americans have less disposable income, and the price of broadband Internet can be prohibitive. Individually, they often place less value and priority on Internet use. White, working-class Americans who do have Internet access also tend to use the Internet differently than most Internet users. They access the Internet less frequently and are less likely to use social media, including Facebook, Twitter, and Instagram.

Given low rates of penetration and use, social media likely had very little influence on these voters. The argument that "fake news" or other aspects of social media were persuasive, to the extent that they were responsible for vote switching, ignores the fact that those who switched from the Democratic to the Republican candidate tended to be the most disconnected. Far stronger and more ubiquitous social forces than social media drove votes to Donald Trump. However, the Internet may still have played a role, or more accurately, the absence or limited use of social media by this demographic, may have paved the road to Donald Trump's victory

Community

Many of the factors that scholars who study social media have suggested were influential in the 2016 presidential election were present long before the Internet. One example is echo chambers or the tendency for people to self-select into groups who share their views and to avoid opportunities for discussion with those who have competing opinions. There is a natural tendency to find people with similar backgrounds and beliefs in similar places and for people who are similar to become friends. When communities have few relationships that extend to diverse outsiders, they become extreme examples of echo chambers. Echo chambers can be a source of insularity and intolerance to outsiders. They are found on- and offline.

In the contemporary world, mobility dilutes echo chambers. That is, as a result of education attainment and economic opportunity, people move geographically and mix with people of different backgrounds and beliefs. Finding similarity that is based on more than a shared location, new friendships form, and many old social ties go dormant and dissolve. In America, widespread mobility accelerated in the 1800s with large-scale rural to urban migration. It increased with the introduction of technologies, such as the telephone and automobile. More recently, the Internet pushed this trend still further, providing additional mobility as a result of the ease of communication. Mobility encourages the formation of diverse relationships and the exposure to different types of people, opinions, and beliefs.

To understand why white, working-class Americans voted for Trump, we need to recognize that members of these communities often have limited exposure to diverse media content, experience less mobility, and as a result, often live in echo chambers with narrow exposure to diverse opinions. These forces, in a situation of economic insecurity generated the ideal context that would sway votes to Donald Trump.

Roots of Intolerance

Donald Trump campaigned on a message targeted to the white working class. He appealed to a demographic that felt especially left behind in the wake of and recovery from the Great Recession. In large part, Trump focused on the presence of immigrants and other minority groups, whom many from the white working class consider to be in direct competition for jobs and economic success. In the words of Mark Sanford, a former Republican governor of South Carolina and member of the US House of Representatives, "Trump fanned the flames of intolerance."

Middle-class Americans, particularly those with more years of formal education, tend to be more tolerant of immigrants and minorities for a number of reasons. Education increases knowledge about the positive aspects of different groups and encourages people to think critically about stereotypes. Educational institutions and the mobility associated with educational attainment provide for social mixing across groups. Personal, positive, social contact in settings where groups are cooperative builds positive attitudes. The middle class is also less likely to see themselves in direct economic competition with immigrants. As Côté and Erickson (2009) show in their seminal work on "Untangling the Roots of Tolerance," one of the strongest predictors of tolerance is the diversity of people's personal networks—ties that break down echo chambers. However, not all diversity is the same; people with diversified ties to middle-class people are more tolerant, but those with ties limited to the working class tend to be significantly less tolerant. It was a campaign message that supported the attitudes of those who view minorities and immigrants as undesirable that persuaded voters.

Escaping the Echo Chamber

Although the use of social media may not have directly influenced the election—certainly not as much as inequality and intolerance—digital technologies are changing the structure and insularity of community. They are influencing the diversity of networks. Social media not only support mobility—increased contact at a distance—but increasingly provide for relational persistence and pervasive awareness (Hampton 2016a). This change has significant implications for how people receive information and view the world around them.

Pervasive awareness results from the short, asynchronous exchanges that typify social media. One outcome of these exchanges is increased exposure to the events, activities, beliefs, and opinions shared by friends and family. Internet users and especially social media users report more diverse social networks (Hampton et al. 2011). It is not clear if their networks become more diverse over time, or if they are simply exposed to more diversity that was always present but previously hidden in their personal network. Relationships are dynamic, and some of this newfound diversity may be a result of the persistence of relationships, which makes information from established ties more visible.

Persistent contact is an outcome of communication technologies that allow people to articulate their association and maintain contact over time. Previously ties would have gone dormant or dissolved as a result of mobility, but now, when people move neighborhoods, go away to school, change jobs, and so on, their relationships persist over time both online and often offline. Persistence has the potential to link lives across generations and over the life course in ways that previously would have been difficult or impossible to sustain.

These affordances of relational persistence and pervasive awareness may have important influences on rural, small town, working-class Americans. These communities have experienced a long net loss of young adults migrating out to cities for education and new economic opportunity (Smith, Winkler, and Johnson 2016). This migration results in an expected increase in diversity within the personal networks of those who leave, as they advance into the middle class and experience a corresponding boost in tolerance. But it has traditionally done little for the small town ties they leave behind; their relationships do not experience a similar boost in diversity; their attitudes toward external groups, such as immigrants and minorities, often remain intolerant. However, with social media, relational persistence may provide rural working-class people with access to diverse middle-class ties. These ties consist of rural emigrants and the ties they visibly maintain through social media, ties that previously would have been unobserved, and relationships that may have dissolved due to distance and infrequent contact. Through an awareness of the activities and attitudes of these ties, maintained through social media, they have increased exposure to middle-class opinions and attitudes toward immigrants and minorities.

Leave No One Behind

Intolerance and isolation are not limited to or inherent to the white, rural, and small town working class. Rather, intolerance and its consequences are a result of failures of government policy. There is a failure to reduce competition between minorities and working-class people by intervening with remedies, such as affordable higher education, job retraining, and accreditation of foreign-trained professionals. There is a failure to develop national and regional policies aimed at valuing multiculturalism. These failures have allowed inequality to reach levels not seen in America for nearly one hundred years. Inefficient policies fail to create the conditions for rural areas to have equal access to broadband infrastructure. They fail to provide adequate subsidies for those with low incomes to obtain broadband home Internet access and training. The conditions that allow intolerance to persist come not from the working class but from the middle and upper classes. The consequences of intolerance are felt not just by minority groups and expressed through public opinion, but are experienced by all Americans as cynicism and lower levels of informal helping behavior (Hampton 2016b).

Social media may not be the reason why Donald Trump was elected as the 45th President of the United States, but they may help eliminate the conditions that have allowed a message of intolerance to sway American voters. Access to and use of social media can increase contact between the working and middle classes. This may increase contact with minorities, enhance local knowledge of the value of different groups of people, and, through diverse networks, influence white working-class Americans to find increased tolerance. Social media may not only influence those who see themselves in direct economic competition with minority and immigrant groups, but they may serve the dual purpose of increasing middle-class voters' understanding of the concerns of working-class Americans.

21   How Interactivity Can Build Transparency: What Tech Can Teach Us about Rebuilding Media Trust

Nikki Usher

On the night of the 2016 election, the *New York Times* launched a feature that had never been used on the site before: a pictorial data interactive with live updates. The technological sophistication was admirable—even the most ambitious newsrooms during the election season had attempted only real-time text-based interactives, such as NPR's automatic transcription of debates. In fact, the closest newsrooms had gotten to live-time graphical displays were rudimentary stock charts. However, *what exactly* this *Times* visualization meant was unclear for anyone looking for information about the election. A Gizmodo author, J. K. Trotter, chronicled the confusion, writing, "*The New York Times* is currently tracking the state of tonight's presidential election with what appears to be a pressure gauge … ?"[1] Trotter chronicled his colleagues' reactions: "an IV drip of election drugs"; "they figured out how to shoot election heroin into our veins"; and perhaps the most apt description, "a meaningless representation of nothing."

This particular interactive held no clear takeaway for the news consumer to learn something about the election. Nonetheless, this "meaningless representation of nothing" kept Gizmodo writers and other election junkies tuned to the *New York Times* election web page, a boondoggle as far as optimizing analytics for "time spent online," and while pennies per person, in aggregate, the graphic itself was likely as much a money-maker as a digital effort can ever be. This pressure-gauge graphic epitomized the worst of what interactive journalism has become, but Nate Silver's FiveThirtyEight, The Upshot, Real Clear Politics, and a host of other data-visualizing, interactive-generating sites used to chronicle the election also represent the bastardization of what this form of journalism promised for the news industry and news consumers.

The election of Donald Trump revealed a dangerous issue with interactive journalism: interactive journalism provides alluring certainty to journalists and the public alike thanks to its quantification and visualization of information, but is as liable to mislead as it is to inform. And without real changes and a reevaluation of the limits of these interactives, news organizations will continue to follow the economic incentives to produce more of them without stopping to think of the damage that has been done—and might be done in the future. The salvo for interactive journalism, however, is also within reach: a return to its normative roots in open source and its focus on transparency can not only reorient newsrooms' approach to this type of journalism, but may also provide grounding to reshape journalism as a whole for the better.

Interactive journalism looked quite different when it first appeared in newsrooms, holding a promise for new kinds of storytelling that aimed to take advantage of the best that digital journalism could offer. But as election 2016 reveals, it became a victim of its own success, where its most useful contributions were normalized into newsroom routines while interactive journalism's more idealistic promise receded into the background. Interactive journalism—a visual presentation of storytelling through code for multilayered, tactile user control for the purpose of news and information—builds upon existing web and mobile properties and includes more than data visualization.[2] Interactives have indeed advanced digital storytelling: ideally, they provide users with visual "nut grafs," and on the other hand, they enable self-exploration and possibly deeper engagement with the content.[3]

When interactive journalism was first introduced in newsrooms, it was hyped as yet another solution to save the news. Early discussions of interactive journalism positioned these journalists as outsiders who would supercharge newsrooms with their introduction of open source culture, hacker culture, and "making." The programmers in the newsrooms and the data geeks (often one and the same) would usher in in a world of immersive storytelling and spur a move toward quantification in editorial content thanks to their ability to render large data sets understandable. These interactive journalists also would be translators of a different and admired tech culture.[4] This promise was what initially excited funders like the Knight Foundation and Mozilla, inspired grassroots groups like Hacks/Hackers, and promoted evangelism by techies who had become journalists.

Between 2000 to the early 2010s, interactive journalists were a source of wonder and fascination to institutional journalism. In 2005, the *New York Times* "ideas" section, its year-end review of the most interesting inventions and intellectual contributions, named a Google maps interactive "mashup" with Chicago crime data as a crowning achievement. The Knight Foundation articulated a vision of the "Journalist 2.0" in 2011, an uber-journalist that paired the hacker culture found in technology startups with the underlying editorial principles of journalism—and even put together a diagram replete with a hacker wearing a t-shirt with html on the left and a journalist wearing a v-neck sweater on the right to illustrate the point. (The "Journalist 2.0" was bearded and wearing flannel.)

Also compelling for the news industry was that interactive journalists could also be an answer to journalistic authority under threat. Through quantification afforded by data journalists, news organizations could move beyond the anecdotal journalism that had dominated news and provide greater certainty to their claims through numeracy. Quantification was not only a way to respond to accusations about bias, but it was also a way to articulate the importance of professional journalism—journalists with special skills could make complicated data knowable and easily understood for people—something ordinary people armed with a cell phone or a blog could not. Some of the most famous figures in Internet culture became advocates for data journalism, including Tim Berners-Lee, who argued:[5]

Data-driven journalism is the future. Journalists need to be data-savvy. It used to be that you would get stories by chatting to people in bars, and it still might be that you'll do it that way some times. But now it's also going to be about poring over data and equipping yourself with the tools to analyze it and picking out what's interesting. And keeping it in perspective, helping people out by really seeing where it all fits together, and what's going on in the country.

What was overlooked, however, was that data is laden with assumptions, and is itself socially constructed—problems with data would result in problems with its presentation, too. The extent to which data, visualized in interactive, clickable, and customizable ways, could misinform as well as inform was rarely acknowledged. (In this volume, C. W. Anderson makes a slightly different point: that journalism is more exact than ever before, but we are more partisan than ever before, making this quantification moot).

However, what had started as an effort to rethink journalism through new ways of storytelling got pushed to the side, while the opportunity for a source of alternative revenue and a reclamation of jurisdictional dominance became more important. Both of these motivations deserve serious criticism. News economics may have resulted in the oversaturation of election-focused interactives. Elections have set dates known in advance for years, and as such offer a chance for interactive journalists to engage in the long-term planning required to create sophisticated interactives. There was ample support for this inside newsrooms, as the 2008 and the 2012 elections provided support that election interactives and predictions would and could drive traffic. According to Digiday, when Nate Silver left the *New York Times* in 2013 to found FiveThirtyEight, his work was responsible for 20 percent of nytimes.com traffic and accounted for 71 percent of visits to the site's politics coverage; moreover, The Upshot, the *Times*'s replacement for Silver's content, was responsible for ten of the most-read stories in 2014.[6] David Leonhardt, the head of The Upshot, was quoted by Digiday saying, "Among readers, there's really big appetite for smart stuff that isn't words."

The 2016 election would be a chance to show off and make money, then. Even local newspapers were in the game: top teams from Gannett, McClatchy, the AP, and beyond were working from Washington and New York to syndicate their interactives across company and client sites. A whole constellation of digital-native blogs and news sites also added to the mix of interactive elections content. Ultimately, these interactives could be sticky—or encourage time spent online engaged with the content, as well as spreadable—and shared across social networks, and could drive traffic to other parts of the site.[7] For some news consumers, some interactives were even an obsessive ritual, "election heroin."

This stuff that wasn't words were often numbers, maps, stats that portended to have predictive power to accurately forecast the outcome of the election. This particular claim to certainty that news organizations invoked, though implicit, set apart their unique contribution to understanding the political landscape, arguably absent accusations of bias or anecdotal cherry-picking. While some of these interactives represented sophisticated polling aggregation, the interactives obscured their complexity. The blues, light blues, and shades of red that one could scroll over, as well as the sliding horizontal shaded lines that rejiggered electoral combinations, however, masked the sophistication of the underlying methods used to make these predictions. It is not that Nate Silver, Ezra Klein of Vox, or the political scientists and statisticians contributing for The Upshot whose work was then visualized, and beyond, didn't know there were issues with these polls—they wrote about (some of) them. However, these doubts did not seep into the interactive visualizations, which for some partisans may have provided a false sense of security or a driving rationale for action.

Even into the night of the election, Nate Silver's NowCast had forecasted that Hillary Clinton's chances of winning the election at more than 70 percent. The lack of certainty could only be seen in various shades of red and blue, some not visible on mobile devices or on screens set to a particular darkness ratio. The *New York Times* live election crack certainly didn't give a sense of what was happening throughout the night. And in the days after the election (and to present), the misleading interactives continued to come from newsrooms that have since published post-mortems and hot takes about how the "news media got it wrong." On the *Washington Post*, an electoral map showed red and blue states, with Virginia a solid blue. The story accompanying the map, however, underscored the slim margin of Clinton's victory in the state.

You can find a representation of misleading data interactives on almost any site, but the most pervasive might be the large map of countywide results across the United States. On first glance, it appears that essentially, the entire US is red save for a few (yes) more coastal areas (and the African American blue belt in the Deep South). But this map misleads too, and one would have to scroll over these counties to see that these red counties have very little population (in fact, populations low enough to lead to poor sampling)—and the fewer blue counties represent huge cities with large populations.

There are more pernicious effects of data presented as more certain and with less nuance than it deserves. Trump made it perfectly clear that he thought the polls were fake. The visualizations were particularly far from Trump's favor—the NowCasts and The Upshot and Real Clear Politics poll aggregations strongly favored a Clinton win, as told in images of blue states across the country. When we live in a political environment where facts are under assault, news organizations simply can't afford to screw up quantification—and more specifically, present certainty in visualizations of data when certainty cannot be claimed.

As a corrective, with risk of sounding as inappropriately nostalgic as the Trump campaign itself, it's worth thinking about how interactive journalism can reclaim its roots. What was—and continues to be—most interesting about interactive journalists is their alignment with open source values. As such, it's worth thinking about how some of this normative influence on newswork can be claimed—and in fact, positioned as a different way of securing journalistic authority.

Open source culture at its best presents an alternative model for collaboration and innovation from proprietary cultures focused on closed-system practices. Although only some aspects of open source are truly noncommercial, showing work, sharing code, and inviting community to build upon ideas is at the heart of open source programming. Unlike antisocial hackers, most hackers use the term to express their commitment to solving problems (often, at least initially, in inelegant ways) and making frustrating processes simpler.[8] The hacker ethic is closely aligned with maker culture, with the aspiration of trying and creating something new because it is fun and because it just might improve the world. Transparency is a key commitment in open source culture; open source code is not only shared but also documented—how and why things have been implemented and how they should work is open to anyone who is looking to use this code (though the election has also revealed perversions of this ethic, too).

These journalists are still very much engaged in open source culture, but their influence as normative translators has yet to be felt within most newsrooms. Interactive journalists from newsrooms all over the world share their work on GitHub, the largest repository for open source code. There are professional groups around the world, such as Hacks/Hackers meetups and Online News Association affiliate groups that bring together interactive journalists and also facilitate dialogues with startups, programming experts, and data visualization professionals. The NICAR annual conference, which now draws an international audience of interactive journalists, facilitates "tinkering"—with workshops on how to build sensors for news, how to rapid prototype a news game, and beyond. Interactive journalists (despite their flaws) are now respected members of major newsrooms—and as members of the in-crowd have an opportunity to start explaining how what they do is not just provide an alternative for storytelling and economic revenue but also represents a different normative framework.

What is needed most in journalism's relationship with its audience is a conversation about how stories come to be made; what facts, data, and interpretations drive story creation; and the process through which journalists go about doing their work. This sort of transparency and dialogue is endemic to the work interactive journalists do every day—but it remains siloed within the subprofession's own culture. Now, however, as news organizations look once more for answers to the latest "media failure,"[9] interactive journalists are well-poised to explain how they benefit as professionals from a culture of transparency and how the newsroom is already benefitting, unwittingly to some, from open source values. While efforts to "regain trust" of those who have abandoned mainstream media as an information source are dubious, efforts to keep the trust of those who remain are meaningful—and thinking more broadly about how to create "open journalism" that translates beyond interactive journalism may facilitate a better public understanding of how news gets made.

Notes

1. J. K. Trotter, "*The New York Times* Live Presidential Election Meter Is Fucking with Me," Gizmodo, http://gizmodo.com/the-new-york-times-live-presidential-meter-is-fucking-w-1788732314.

2. Nikki Usher, *Interactive Journalism: Hackers, Data, and Code* (Chicago: University of Illinois Press), chapter 1.

3. Nick Geidner and Jackie Cameron, "Use Patterns of Interactive Graphics: A Case Study of a *New York Times* College Debt Graphic," *Journal of Digital and Media Literacy* 5, no. 1 (2014): http://www.jodml.org/2014/06/17/use-patterns-of-interactive-graphics-a-case-study-of-a-new-york-times-college-debt-graphic; Nick Geidner, Ivanka Pjesivac, Imre Iveta, Iona Coman, and Dmitry Yuran, "The Role of Interactive Graphics in Reducing Misperceptions in the Electorate," *Visual Communication Quarterly* 22, no. 3 (2015): 133.

4. Seth C. Lewis and Nikki Usher, "Open Source and Journalism: Toward New Frameworks for Imagining News Innovation," *Media, Culture & Society* 35, no. 5 (2013): 602; Seth C. Lewis and Nikki Usher, "Code, Collaboration, and the Future of Journalism: A Case Study of the Hacks/Hackers Global Network," *Digital Journalism* 2, no. 3 (2014): 383; Seth C. Lewis and Nikki Usher, "Trading Zones, Boundary Objects, and the Pursuit of News Innovation: A Case Study of Journalists and Programmers," *Convergence* 22, no. 5 (2016): 543.

5. Jonathan Gray, Liliana Bouegru, and Lucy Chambers, *The Data Journalism Handbook* (Sebastopol, CA: O'Reilly, 2012), chapter 1.

6. Ricardo Bilton, "FiveThirtyEight vs. The Upshot: Who's Winning the Data Journalism War?" *Digiday,* April 4, 2015, https://digiday.com/media/fivethirtyeight -vs-upshot-whos-winning-data-journalism-war.

7. Henry Jenkins, Sam Ford, and Joshua Green, *Spreadable Media: Creating Value and Meaning in a Networked Culture* (New York: NYU Press, 2013).

8. Gabriella Coleman, *Coding Freedom: The Ethics and Aesthetics of Hacking* (Princeton, NJ: Princeton University Press, 2013).

9. Matt Carlson, "Gone, But Not Forgotten: Memories of Journalistic Deviance as Metajournalistic Discourse," *Journalism Studies* 15, no. 1 (2015): 33.

IV   Pathways Ahead

22   The Center of the Universe No More: From the Self-Centered Stance of the Past to the Relational Mindset of the Future

Pablo J. Boczkowski and Seth C. Lewis[1]

What happened to the strength of American news media? How is it possible that journalists collectively missed the outcome of the 2016 electoral process and subsequently became the targets of repeated attacks by a presidential administration at a scale unseen in recent US history? How did journalists become so disconnected from the people and communities they are intended to serve that they misread not only the recent election but also their cultural authority in a society that increasingly distrusts them? We argue that, for the better part of the twentieth century, mainstream media organizations implicitly took their strong market positions—with the concomitant large audiences and significant profit margins—as an indicator of how much the public and government officials valued their reporting. In short, as a measure of authority and influence. But, by doing so, they overestimated the value of their editorial products and underestimated the extent to which their audience size and profit margins were also an artifact of a limited information environment: advertisers supported and the public consumed these editorial products in part because there were not many other options available.

This structural configuration led to the emergence of a culture of self-centeredness—a decades-long conviction about the inherent value of journalism in society and an assumption that exploring new relationships was unnecessary if not even detrimental. This, in turn, led media organizations to downplay competitive challenges; miss collaborative initiatives for editorial and technological innovation; and erode their standing as a social institution. This self-centeredness has resulted in a media system that is increasingly disconnected from its publics and marginalized in the information ecology. Thus, journalism has become institutionally weak in the face of contemporary challenges such as the Facebook-Alphabet duopoly that has a chokehold on the digital market, leaving news organizations fighting for the crumbs of display advertising revenues.

Building upon a brief historical account of self-centeredness in mainstream media, we argue that journalism can begin to rebuild trust among audiences, stand firm against powerful actors, and find its digital bearings by developing a more "relational" orientation—one focused on news as a distinctly networked enterprise, drawing on the resources of crowds, communities, and even intra-occupational competitors. By becoming more reflexive, responsive, and relational, journalism can restore its institutional relevance for the long game, in the President Trump era and beyond.

Self-Centeredness in US Journalism: Culture, Markets, and Structure

For most of the twentieth century, mainstream media organizations in America enjoyed limited competition in their respective markets. For instance, in terms of local news, the vast majority of markets had only one newspaper by the mid-1990s. Regarding national news, during the second half of the twentieth century only a handful of newspapers and television networks vied for the attention of hundreds of millions of Americans. This meant that those organizations enjoyed a privileged position connecting audiences to advertisers, marked by the twin pillars of relatively large audiences and large profit margins for the majority of news outlets. Most managers, editors, and reporters took this situation for granted, and interpreted it as an indication of how much both powerful actors and the general public valued their products—rather than as largely a function of media organizations' strong market positions. Over time, this translated into the development and deepening of a culture of self-centeredness: if such high levels of audience and commercial success could be achieved by going it alone, why would it be potentially advantageous to open up and partner?

The first encounter with digital alternatives to print and broadcast media in the United States took place in the early 1980s. Executives and editors from some of the leading media organizations probed what technologies such as videotex and teletext meant for the future of journalism. The dominant stance was one of trying to figure out whether these technologies could harm the status quo, rather than also—or perhaps only—explore what new commercial and narrative opportunities might emerge from them. The most ambitious, and costly, initiative in this regard during this period was Viewtron, a videotex system developed by a now-defunct corporation, Knight-Ridder, initially joined by AT&T. This initiative, which lasted between 1980 and 1985, took place in the greater Miami area, which was then headquarters of the corporation and home to one of its flagship newspapers, the *Miami Herald*.

Viewtron was a system that delivered news and information to subscribers who owned a dedicated terminal. Some of its novel features previewed applications that later became staples of the digital age, such as electronic commerce and user-to-user communication. The latter was particularly appealing to consumers, according to data collected by Knight-Ridder. However, rather than partnering with technology actors or listening to the users to build new products and services, the overriding goal of the company was to determine whether videotex presented "clear and present danger" to its core business. When Knight-Ridder executives concluded that it did not, they shut down Viewtron. Technology actors were treated as vendors rather than partners, the audience as clients rather than a source of novel practices, and innovation as a threat rather than an opportunity. Had they approached innovation differently and stayed in the game through failure, like entrepreneurs often do, news organizations such as Knight-Ridder, the *Los Angeles Times*—through its Gateway videotex project—and those that participated in the videotex experiment undertaken by the Associated Press and CompuServe could have had a preview of the future. Instead, they retreated to their small and large empires, content with remaining the center of the universe … for just another decade or so.

The 1990s saw a significant increase in the rate of innovation in the digital realm, from the revival of online services providers such as America Online to the commercialization of the Web to the emergence of some of today's dominant players such as Amazon, Craigslist, eBay, and Google. Self-centeredness continued to be a prevailing stance among mainstream media companies, even as they saw their prominence dwindle slowly but steadily. This led them to often overestimate the value of their reporting and underestimate the potentially devastating consequences that were going to arise from a weakening of their market position by new competitors more attuned to listening to the audience and engaging in true partnerships.

Perhaps there is no better parable of the perils of self-centeredness than the relationship between the Tribune Corporation and America Online.

In the early 1990s, the latter was a small technology firm making inroads into the market through its popular chat forums. Needing an infusion of cash and also local brand recognition, in 1991 America Online sold an 8-percent stake to Tribune for an alleged $10 million. They also partnered in providing localized information services in the cities where Tribune had newspapers. America Online took advantage of the cash to develop products and services that catered to unmet needs in the population—mostly allowing people to communicate with each other. Tribune took advantage of the appreciating stock of America Online to invest in a series of initiatives that hardly paid off. When the decade was coming to a close, America Online acquired Time Warner while Tribune was already seeing its fortunes decline. Had Tribune developed a full-fledged partnership with America Online, one premised on incorporating technology as a core element of the journalistic mission and in listening to the audience and its information needs, perhaps it would have entered the twenty-first century in a much stronger position, better prepared for the coming broadband and mobile eras. Instead, like most mainstream media companies, Tribune used profits from the deal to protect its steadily diminishing territory, altogether losing significant relevance in the national conversation.

The Decentering of Mainstream Media in Contemporary America

During the late twentieth century, most news companies in America were not only arrogant about their economic position as natural information monopolies or oligopolies, but that same attitude of imperviousness influenced the cultural assumptions that journalists developed in the course of their work. They saw themselves not only as public stewards but as uniquely powerful and important ones—possessing even a "calling" that was theirs and theirs alone to fulfill. The same conditions of scarcity, exclusivity, and control in the information market on which the traditional news business model thrived also facilitated an occupational worldview of distinctiveness. Thus, as decades of ethnographic research has shown, journalists in the US developed an occupational persona at odds with outsiders: resistant to change; reluctant to listen to audiences; and reliant on a set of norms, routines, and reporting styles that positioned them "above the fray" relative to others, largely detached from the communities and people they covered. In a sense, journalists cared deeply about serving society—but preferably on their own terms, thank you very much.

While this culture of self-centeredness is not exclusively a problem of journalism—one could find it in law, medicine, and other areas of work—it led journalists to overestimate the value that their news reports generated for society and underestimate the potential contribution of other relevant actors. Moreover, this cultural stance had particularly disastrous consequences when the economic conditions upholding it unraveled in the 2000s.[2] During that decade, the eroding market position of news companies in a universe of expanded information options online not only undercut the business model of mainstream media—it also carved away at the sense of self-importance that journalists had constructed. The rise of blogging, for example, was as much a perceptual threat as an actual one. Even while bloggers never "replaced" journalists, as many feared, their emergence signified that publishing capabilities were no longer so exclusive and that journalistic functions could be performed by non-journalists, too. The widespread adoption of social media in the latter 2000s only reinforced this point, reshaping how public communication works and where journalists fit in a rapidly expanding information ecology. Thus, as social media platforms become *the* space for media discovery and distribution, perhaps the central challenge for journalism is one of perceived and actual loss of control: a slipping cultural authority over what counts as "news," and a weakened hold on how news and information move from producer to consumer with certain predictable consequences.

American journalism, in effect, has been decentered.[3] After the decades-long self-centered party, the mainstream press has found itself in a state of decentered hangover. Indeed, there is also something deeply awry with journalism's status quo in society. In the US, trust in the news media has fallen to all-time lows—around 1 in 5 say they trust local or national news organizations "a lot" (Mitchell et al. 2016). Americans appear to feel increasingly disconnected from journalism as an institution, much as their trust has waned in institutions such as government, organized religion, and professions generally.

This gnawing disconnection between journalists and their communities has been festering for decades, but previous attempts to resolve it have mostly failed. For example, and perhaps most notably, the public/civic journalism movement of the 1990s encouraged journalists to hold town-hall meetings in their communities and otherwise seek to understand if the style and substance of their news coverage matched the actual needs and interests of their readers. Some editors experimented to good success in this vein, but most journalists saw this outward orientation as a threat to their occupational autonomy—a pattern that would continue with the emergence of the citizen journalism movement in the mid-2000s. Self-centeredness may have thus emboldened journalists to be crusading truth-tellers, but it also blinded them to the damage that such aloofness has had for the very communities they have been supposed to serve—the people on whose behalf they have crusaded.

Relational Journalism as a Way Out of a State of Decentering

The time has come for rethinking journalism itself: who gets to take part, on what terms, and by what means. This requires recognizing the networked potential for journalism, thus moving beyond thinking of news as one-way linear information transfer controlled by reporters and editors. What should emerge in its place is a *relational* form of news work—one that conceptual-izes news as a distinctly networked enterprise, drawing on diverse resources such as crowds, communities, and even intra-occupational competitors. Relational journalism is not slavishly beholden to outside interests; instead, it is about doing journalism with an outward rather than inward orienta-tion, realizing the generative potential that may exist in combining forces with stakeholders who have an interest in journalism's success: from fellow journalists at rival news organizations to contributors who care about their communities.[4] While such idealized notions are not always practical or even beneficial—investigative journalists often keep their reporting secret for a reason, for instance—there is nevertheless growing evidence that a relational approach can strengthen the institutional bearings of journalism. Consider but three areas of network potential: cross-organizational, crowd-based, and listening-oriented.

1. *Cross-organizational ties*: A familiar element of journalism is the rivalry among news organizations for "scoops," or the distinction of being first on breaking news or an exclusive interview. However, in an era of declining resources for reporting, and at a time when a rush to be first increases the chances of being wrong, there is a growing oppor-tunity for journalists to collaborate across organizational boundaries around the pursuit of a shared investigation. Such cooperation can be micro or macro, fast or slow. At one extreme, there is the 2016 Panama Papers investigation, involving a tightly coordinated effort among 107

news organizations representing 80 countries to analyze 11.5 million leaked documents detailing bribery, tax evasion, financial fraud, and other misdeeds by politicians and public officials. At the other extreme, there is the flash collaboration that occurred during a "Friday night news dump" in March 2017: at that time, the Trump White House made many of its staffers' financial disclosure forms "available," but not without painstaking hassle for journalists to discover. The nonprofit site ProPublica, a leader in partnership-oriented journalism, had an idea: "Why not call our friends at other outlets and coordinate." Within minutes, the Associated Press and the *New York Times* were on board. Using shared Google documents, together they retrieved and publicized the key files in a fraction of the time it would have taken them working solo (Umansky 2017). "[A] new level of solidarity and cooperation is needed among the fourth estate," the journalists who led the Panama Papers investigation said. "American journalists should stop [Trump] from dividing their ranks—however hard their professional competition may be. They should do the opposite: unite, share, and collaborate" (Obermaier and Obermayer 2017).

2. *Crowd-based relationships:* The same desire for being first on a story often leads journalists to keep their reporting private (and often for good reason). But relational journalism recognizes that doing journalism "in the open" might offer help in generating news tips and suggestions, yes, and also a higher level of authenticity and transparency about how journalism works. This could ultimately lead to greater trust and thus willingness to share with journalists—developing a virtuous cycle of contributions from crowds. As Adrienne Russell argues in chapter 25, this can have liberating effects for journalists. For example, as journalists become more comfortable on social media, more of them can use platforms such as Twitter to crowdsource the reporting process. During the 2016 presidential election campaign, *Washington Post* reporter David Fahrenthold wanted to track Trump's claims of giving millions of dollars of his own money to charities, but he needed help knowing which of thousands of charities to contact. On Twitter, he asked for advice. He began posting photos of his pen-and-paper notes that documented which charities he had contacted and what they reported about Trump donations ("never" was the answer from most). His resulting investigation of the gap between image and reality in

Trump's philanthropy, assisted along the way by his Twitter followers, resulted in the 2017 Pulitzer Prize for National Reporting, with
the prize committee noting that Fahrenthold had "created a model
for transparent journalism in political campaign coverage" (Hazard
Owen, 2017).

3. *Listening-oriented initiatives:* Beyond collaborating across boundaries
with organizations or social media crowds, relational journalism is about
developing more meaningful connections within communities—a
point also underscored by Sue Robinson and Rod Benson in chapters
23 and 26, respectively. Does the public feel appreciated and understood? Do people have the impression that journalists are responding
to their concerns? Such a journalism may be reciprocal in nature, seeking to develop more mutually beneficial relationships between journalists and audiences (Lewis, Holton, and Coddington 2014). At the
very least, it may seek to make *listening* a critical component of what
news organizations do by creating deliberate, visible opportunities for
the public to participate during key phases of the news process. An
emerging example is Hearken, a platform and consultancy that helps
news organizations "listen to the public as a story develops from pitch
through publication," based on what it calls "public-powered journalism." Hearken provides tools for news organizations to gauge reader
interest on key topics, determine questions that the public would like
to have answered, and develop opportunities for follow-up engagement
post-publication. Unlike the traditional model of allowing readers
mainly to react to news after publication (through online comments),
the Hearken approach seeks to give the audience "a seat at the editorial
table ahead of publication" (Bilton 2017). Such an arrangement puts
journalists in a listening role, not simply a lecturing one.

Conclusion

American journalism has been going through a decades-long process of
weakening as a social institution, as evidenced by its diminished economic
foundations, its loosening grip on the audience, and its declining perception of trustworthiness. The role of the media during the 2016 presidential electoral campaign, the ascent to power of Donald Trump as the 45th
President of the United States, and the press–government relations during

his first months in office should be understood in connection with this process of institutional weakening. We have argued that, moving forward, the longstanding stance of self-centeredness that emerged and evolved during the second half of the twentieth century should give way to a relational mindset. We see indications of this new mindset in a host of recent developments, and their successes have been encouraging. Although this new mindset will not be a cure-all, and additional successes should not be taken for granted, we think that it could be essential to the media's institutional bearings for the future by giving journalists greater collective strength against powerful interests that would like to divide and conquer. This would also enable journalism to acquire greater social currency with communities that see opportunities for more mutually beneficial relationships. Ultimately, relational journalism is about developing better connections within the news and social media; across technology spaces and platforms where the users devote an increasing portion of their attention; and in connection with the neighborhoods, towns, and cities where people live. Paraphrasing what Kenneth Gergen (1994) wrote more than two decades ago, all news that is meaningful grows out of relationships.

Notes

1. Author order is alphabetical; both authors contributed equally to this article.

2. As Victor Pickard argues elsewhere in this volume (chapter 24), the historic naturalization of the advertising-supported model for mainstream media also left them with fewer alternatives moving forward once the economic downturn of the industry acquired full force.

3. We are not claiming that the economic and technological transformations created this decentering, but that, to a certain degree, they exposed a crisis in power and authority that already existed. (We thank C. W. Anderson for bringing this issue to our attention.).

4. In a related vein, Matt Carlson (2017) calls for a "relational" approach to journalistic authority, one that recognizes the inherently complicated and interconnected nature of authority that is claimed by and granted to journalists. Journalistic authority, in this view, is not an object that journalists automatically possess; rather, it's expressed in the dynamic and complicated relationships that exist among journalists and various actors, such as sources and audiences.

23   Trump, Journalists, and Social Networks of Trust

Sue Robinson

The strategic, deliberate work to undermine the authority of the American mainstream journalism profession by US President Donald Trump and his administration seeks to annihilate the Fourth Estate as a major underpinning of American democracy. The institutional relationships of legacy media organizations that depended on access to power are collapsing—and have been for some time. Mainstream information exchange is being subsumed by fake news driven by highly polarized networks that keep people from having dialogue across differences. As a media scholar, I see this as distressing but also as a tremendous opportunity to reconfigure the ways in which American citizens engage in informed public discourse. Professional journalists entered this time period with historically low levels of trust from their audiences—a reaction against institutional and organizational constructs that journalism had developed over the last century. Yet, this negative commercial relationship also comes with surging digital innovation, a plethora of new actors vying for credibility in a new information world, and a web of networks that have potential to bypass hostile institutional actors such as Trump.

This essay explores how digital technologies—and the networked infrastructure they facilitate—can be used by journalists to counter Trump's aggressive move to further dismantle trust in professional reporting. Drawing from a huge body of empirical work around transformed information networks that have spurred experimental journalistic enterprises, my argument will consider a group-oriented, connected response within this fractured media environment. The key to this argument will be the strategy of building trust through local networks across groups of Americans for fact-based journalism. When traditional institutional relationships break down, journalists must turn to the local to connect multiple publics and to remain relevant, rebuild trust, and reinvigorate community. My research suggests that using digital networks to connect to otherwise disparate niche publics, paired with offline community building exercises and an explicit commitment to bridging divide, can counter those who would see journalism die.

Institutional Distrust

During the first week after taking office as President of the United States in February 2017, Donald Trump spent more than an hour attacking the press's "dishonesty" in one of his first press conferences. This kicked up a grand narrative that had already been playing out in many communities for decades. This storyline emerged again and again in interviews we conducted with citizens who felt marginalized by the press: "They talk nice, and sometimes they do good. But their interests are not your interests. The media is rarely your friend," one person posted in part of the Facebook sample from my research. A reverend of a midwestern church attended by mostly African Americans explained to me how that distrust between marginalized communities and mainstream journalists had built up after years of disconnect and perceived apathy by reporters. In one example, he tried to get local reporters to come to a celebration of the first gay wedding in the church and was met with silence. But when journalists sniffed conflict brewing between him and other religious leaders in town, suddenly his phone calls were returned. He declined comment, saying, "Trust is earned. It is not just handed over." And then the 45th President of the United States began working to sever what remained of the citizen–journalist relationship, calling all news content "fake" and categorizing journalists as "the enemy of the American people." He tapped into another marginalized group (or at least people who perceived they were marginalized)—that of working-class, rural Americans who felt displaced economically, culturally, and politically. These people's intense distrust of US institutions had led them to further apathy and disconnect.

Trust in the press and other key US institutions is at historic lows and continuing to drop: only 32 percent of Americans report confidence in news organizations, according to a 2016 Gallup poll.[1]. The new sharing economy has helped this downward trend along as "fake news" can be circulated widely through the networked digital information infrastructure.

People are turning toward their trusted social circles to figure out what's what. Whether in the "Make America Great Again" Fox-watching community or the "I Stand with Her" *New Yorker* niche, whether among whites or people of color, citizens still seek trusting relationships within community but find them only within polarized spaces. President Trump feeds on these polemic divisions and he fans the flames of distrust about the media. This work establishes Trump as a major, uncontested information source for otherwise informationally isolated groups.

By the time of Trump's media attacks in 2017, information flow had already moved away from institutionally determined constructs of authority. In new information networks, political ideology and personal identity had become dimensions of trust. In other words, if I am friends with you on Facebook and I know you are liberal and I identify as liberal too, I view the links and information you post as more credible than when my conservative friend posts something political. Our identities inform our decisions on information credibility. We have seen a resurgence of interest in news publications, particularly liberal-leaning outlets such as the *Washington Post* and the *New Yorker*, but the interest corresponds with one's identity ties; much scholarly research has demonstrated the prevalence toward seeking information that align with one's worldview. Furthermore, today's digital infrastructure allows polemic segregation to thrive. Such a situation evokes a quote from philosopher John Dewey, who argued that individual participation in multiple groups created a sense of community because the push and pull of those groups forced an individual to be tolerant of others with whom he or she fraternized. When that social diversity and cohesion dissolves, "Liberty is then thought of as independence of social ties, and ends in dissolution and anarchy," Dewey warned in 1927 in *The Public and Its Problems*. Dewey viewed journalists as essential bridges for difference in uniting communities into greatness. But for journalists to be bridges, they need to find connections on either side.

Solutions: Group-Oriented, Networked Responses in Consideration of Multiple Publics

In early 2017, just before the inauguration of President Donald Trump, the *Texas Tribune* posted an ad for a community journalist whose beat would be "Texas" and who would be tasked with going out into the rural parts of the state to listen and report on a marginalized constituency. My research suggests that journalists at the *Texas Tribune* or anywhere else must recommit to the fundamental tenet of journalism to build community as *part of the community*. My work demonstrates that today's reporters should utilize digitally evolving social networks of trust to bring in new information, and through these interactions, to facilitate dialogues that spill over into offline interactions. Consider the following two projects:

1. In October 2016, Monica Guzman helped co-found the newly launched Seattle blog called *The Evergrey* newsletter, which sought to explore the liberal city's identity crisis and reconnect citizens into community. Changing demographics, an influx of development, and nationally polarizing politics were creating feelings of disconnect and chasms of distrust throughout the Northwest. In one of the newsletter's projects, Guzman and her co-founder identified a city of similar size but with a conservative predilection; where Seattle's urban King County had gone 74 percent for Democrat Hillary Clinton in the 2016 presidential election, rural Sherman County, Oregon, had gone 74 percent for Republican Donald Trump. Guzman took 20 King County residents on a 10-hour road trip to meet up with 16 people who called Sherman County home to explore the difference—and find commonalities. Said one Sherman County citizen, "I wasn't sure what to expect. I can't lie— there was a little trepidation. I was afraid it'd be a lot more Clinton/ Trump stuff," according to *The Evergrey* post about the trip. But in the end, she added, "Instead what we got was some really nice guided discussions on the fact that even though how we approach problems is very different, in the end we truly are looking for the same thing."[2] Guzman and her colleagues made some pivotal decisions during the planning of this journalistic endeavor: (1) instead of rolling cameras for the entire trip, they opted for the less conspicuous note-taking to facilitate ease of conversation; (2) they worked the phones, email, and social platforms hard before the trip, making connections with key influencers in the area to ensure a critical mass of participation; and (3) their primary aim was not to stoke dissension or elicit copy for the newsletter but rather to fuse connections among citizens. In other words, their motivation centered on building community, and their result was a budding trust between the citizens of two very different places. "No one went out in the street and protested or had a baseball

bat and did bad things," said another Sherman County resident. "That was the positive of the day—having a civil conversation."[3]

2. Halfway across the country, in liberal Madison, Wisconsin, *Capital Times* editor Paul Fanlund wanted to open a dialogue in mainstream progressive circles about race, especially the county's terrible racial achievement disparities—generational problems that had created stark division between the Midwestern capital's white population and its communities of color. Since he began his efforts in 2013, Fanlund has faced discomfort from his fellow white progressives as well as pushback from some segments of the African American community. A local reverend, who had at one time worked as managing editor of *Capital Times* with Fanlund, connected the news organization with a few community leaders of color. The result was a webpage dedicated to the dialogue, several front-page columns written by African American leaders about their experiences being black in Madison, regular co-hosted public forums around topics that involve race with people of color leading the panels, and several other decidedly nontraditional (at least in a journalistic sense) experiments for the news organization that included live blogs and Facebook events. These conversations also spurred an internship program and an intense hiring campaign to attract more reporters of color to the overwhelmingly white newsrooms.

In both of these anecdotes, we see the common thread of advantageous networking to bridge chasms born from identity politics and distrust that have permeated over the course of years. If they have any hope of fulfilling their core missions, journalists can no longer operate in a sender–receiver manner that simply pushes information into people's various media channels. Nor does it suffice to rely on built networks with government officials and community leaders for representative, credible commentary. Rather, journalists should tap into social networks' key influencers—those people who serve as bridges between groups and who can rally their constituents for civic action when necessary. Too often, reporters use these people as punctuation points, as representatives for their entire groups rather than as direct conduits to other perspectives. In the Seattle example, Guzman and her staff networked ahead of the event to identify citizens willing to come talk and to ensure participation across divide. In Madison, Fanlund offered community leaders space—both physically in forums and digitally on the website—to talk so Madison citizens could really hear. One activist told me in an interview for my research: "The key thing that [the editor] did was he let me write my story myself. He didn't interview me. There was no ghostwriter. ... They let me tell my story without censoring me, and that was huge. I will not forget the *CapTimes* for that. That was risky." That risk-taking on the part of the news organization translated into trust for this activist of color, and he opened his networks to reporters who connected them to the white progressives that made up the *Capital Times*'s audiences.

The other common thread I found in successful projects like these is the emphasis on the hyperlocal and a renewed commitment to connecting multiple publics. In his 1927 *The Public and Its Problems,* Dewey lamented the lack of integration of emergent multiple publics. Ever prescient, Dewey even suggested that when government institutions inhibit communication, "to form itself, the public has to break existing political forms." This resonates today as the President and his aides themselves have circulated "fake news" intentionally (see any number of examples, from the inauguration numbers to policy details about Obamacare). This work destroys democracy for it casts a malignant impediment for any authentic cross-deliberation to happen. This is where hyperlocal news comes in. In the hyperlocal— like the projects above—the journalist operates from within community, as opposed to maintaining critical distance apart. This fosters relationships between multiple publics where diverse citizens and journalists share experiences and develop trust. Citizens collaborating with reporters "at work, socially" create social bonds that would not adhere in traditional sender– receiver relationships. When this happens, democracy is exercised as citizens become more civically engaged and participate in public life.

Finally, it is noted that both projects entail offline work that is facilitated via a digital, networked infrastructure. With citizens sharing in the civic work of public information exchange via a road trip or forums at the public library, the news organizations boost interest for their online content. Social spaces such as Facebook and Twitter provide alternative sites for journalistic endeavors that also represent "safe" spaces where trusting relationships might begin to flourish. Monica Guzman and her co-founder conducted a live video chat on Facebook—taking comments, posting conversations, and archiving the video on YouTube—to fill out the textual, mediated spaces around the trip to Sherman County, offering a rare behind-the-scenes view for citizens. The staff of the *Capital Times* also conducted live interactions on social platforms during their many forums, tagging those individuals who were taking part and thus opening up their conversation to other networks not in the *Capital Times*'s "friend" group. The digital infrastructure offers opportunities to invite citizens into social spaces where credible journalism lives. Grassroots relationships can form here because citizens feel comfortable with people they trust already in the space.

In conclusion, I believe that networked-reporting principles, emphasis on multiple publics, and online–offline facilitation are a few group-oriented, connected responses to the current environment of declining information authority due to distrust. It is the job of the professional communicator today to learn the best ways to manipulate social networks so as to build connecting and connected bridges instead of exacerbating rampant distrust that nurtures isolation and polarization. Journalists undercut fake news where it lives—in the social fabric—with a keen sense of locality. These news organizations have reconceptualized the *product* of journalism, understanding it as a *process of community building* engaging with *multiple publics* that will result in larger markets ultimately. In this transformation there dawns a new, less-institutionalized infrastructure for journalism, one centered on citizens as the scaffolding. As such, Trump as an institutional obstacle for fact-based information to circulate and exchange might become obsolete.

Notes

1. http://news.gallup.com/poll/195542/americans-trust-mass-media-sinks-new-low.aspx.

2. https://theevergrey.com/took-10-hour-road-trip-cross-political-divide-heres-happened.

3. https://theevergrey.com/took-10-hour-road-trip-cross-political-divide-heres-happened.

24 When Commercialism Trumps Democracy: Media Pathologies and the Rise of the Misinformation Society

Victor Pickard

The commercialism driving much of the American media system counts among the many factors that contributed to Donald Trump's election. From imbalanced, sensationalistic coverage in traditional news media to the proliferation of "fake news" in social media, commercial imperatives drove news organizations to popularize a dangerous politics. Trump received more media attention than all of the other republican candidates, and during a critical period in the primary season he received nearly three times more coverage than Hillary Clinton and 16 times more than Bernie Sanders (Tyndal Report 2016). Various estimates show Trump receiving free advertising worth billions of dollars in the run-up to the elections (Confessore and Yourish 2016; Harris 2016; Schroeder 2016). Despite such wide coverage, relatively little serious media attention was given to scrutinizing Trump's policy positions. Content analyses show a near-complete absence of substantive coverage of policy issues prior to the elections among major news outlets (Patterson 2016). Informational deficits occurred in mainstream news media as torrents of misinformation were flowing through social media.

These data points reflect a depressing portrait of the American news media system. Although awareness and criticism of these problems has risen since the election, too little analysis penetrates to the structural origins of these media failures. What is it about the American media system that encourages such socially irresponsible coverage? What are the historical conditions that led Americans to inherit such a system? What are the policies and ideologies that keep this system intact? While I have addressed some of these questions in previous writings (e.g., Pickard 2016), this essay further reflects on the diagnosis of specific media failures and recommends potential remedies. The essay concludes with a discussion about the implications that such an analysis holds for communication research more generally.

Trump Is a Symptom of Structural Media Failures

Trump's ascendance revealed a number of structural pathologies in the American news and information systems. In a previous essay, I described three core failures that impacted the news media's coverage of the political issues that led to Trump's election (Pickard 2017). First, the news media's excessive commercialism—largely driven by profit imperatives and, thus, the need to sell advertising—manifested in facile coverage that privileged entertainment over information. For ratings-driven news outlets, the always-controversial Trump was the ultimate boon. CBS CEO Leslie Moonves admitted that "[Trump's candidacy] may not be good for America, but it's damn good for CBS." He continued: "The money's rolling in and this is fun ... this is going to be a very good year for us ... bring it on, Donald. Keep going" (Collins 2016). Jeff Zucker, the CEO of CNN, approvingly compared CNN's election coverage to that of ESPN's sports commentary (Mahler 2017). Such comments reveal how American news media typically privilege profit-seeking over public service.

A second failure in the American media system was a tremendous amount of misinformation circulating via social media platforms, especially Facebook. Many factors contributed to this problem, ranging from unscrupulous manipulators to the political psychology of partisans. But receiving too little attention are the structural enablers and commercial incentives that encourage clickbait and misinformation to flow unimpeded through Facebook's platform. Much of this is facilitated by the promise of advertising revenues, but in more general terms it also connects to Facebook's monopoly power. As a global Internet platform and an algorithm-driven editor and publisher, Facebook has significant gatekeeping power over much of the world's information system.

It has become fashionable, especially among communication scholars, to pooh-pooh concerns about fake news as little more than moral panic and social hysteria. And some of this skepticism is warranted. For example, it is true that much of the criticism aimed at fake news is unacceptably ahistorical, often stemming from a desire for simplistic, mono-causal explanations of Donald Trump's unexpected election. Nonetheless, many concerns about widespread misinformation are also legitimate. Numerous reports suggest that fake news was circulated more often than real news during the weeks leading up to the election (Silverman 2016). Indeed, given that Americans are increasingly accessing news through its platform (Gottfried and Shearer 2016), Facebook's centrality within the news media ecology has drawn well-deserved scrutiny. Unfortunately, much of this criticism continues to overlook the structural roots of this problem. With commercial incentives boosting the spread of misinformation, Facebook is not sufficiently incentivized to successfully address the problem, opting instead to rely on outside parties, crowdsourcing, and algorithmic tweaks. The rise of fake news is one more manifestation of the asymmetric relationships stemming from Facebook's status as an enormous monopoly with profound political economic power but little independent oversight—all the while shirking the responsibilities of being an actual media company (Ingram 2016).

A third systemic failure is the slow-but-sure structural collapse of professional journalism. The number of journalists has continued to decline as the market no longer supports the same levels of news production. Print newsrooms have lost more than 40 percent of their employees over the past decade. Yet, newspapers still provide the bulk of original reporting within the American news media system. It is always difficult to demonstrate what is not being covered—or how issues are being covered differently—as a direct result of this dramatic reduction in news staff and other forms of cost-cutting. But the emergence of news deserts—where entire regions and issue areas are no longer being covered within news media—is a worsening problem (Abernathy 2016). This should be seen as a major challenge for public policy, but thus far, it has not received the attention it deserves.

All of the problems described above are to some degree directly related to profit imperatives and other structural constraints within a commercial media system. Taken together, these shortcomings in the American news media system create the ideal conditions for what I call the "misinformation society"—an electorate that is increasingly fed clickbait, sensationalistic television news coverage, and degraded print news instead of informative, fact-based, policy-related news. The remainder of this essay addresses concerns stemming from the ongoing structural collapse of professional journalism, and concludes with recommendations for structural reform.

Competing Narratives about Journalism

Several meta-narratives emerged after the Trump election that largely defined discourses around journalism. The first narrative, which has begun to fade to some degree, is that professional journalism was culpable for enabling Trump's ascendance. This narrative especially pertains to television news coverage, but also applies to print news to some extent. As noted above, Trump's commercial appeal led news organizations to give him far more attention than the other candidates. News media also indulged in false equivalence by equating Trump's questionable history with that of other candidates. Typical news media coverage also sensationalized and trivialized the elections via "horserace" coverage by fetishizing polling data instead of offering critical analysis of candidates' policy positions.

The second narrative, in tension with the first, is a newfound appreciation for the fourth estate. Many people increasingly see news institutions as the last existing bulwark protecting them against fascism and fake news. For many, as Trump attacks the press, public sympathies naturally redound to news organizations (although the opposite appears true for Trump partisans). One direct result has been a "Trump bump" in which many publishers have seen a sudden and dramatic spike in subscriptions. However, this desperately needed boost in financial support for news organizations does not solve the basic economic problems facing print journalism.

This leads us to a third narrative that predates the election: despite our increasing need for public service journalism, it is precisely this kind of journalism that is economically failing. The market's failure to support journalism can be summarized in the following: as consumers and advertisers have migrated to the Web, where digital ads pay pennies to the dollar of traditional print ads (and most of that revenue is going to Facebook and Google), the 150-year-old advertising revenue model for commercial newspapers is now damaged beyond repair. Indeed, in many ways advertising was just a subsidy for the news, which was produced as a kind of byproduct or positive externality from the main exchange. But because this advertising revenue model has been around for so long, it is often assumed to be the natural order of things, with alternative models falling beyond our political imagination (see the essay by Boczkowski and Lewis in this volume).

Nonetheless, alternative models are exactly what we should be discussing. The Trump bump notwithstanding, the overall dismal picture of the newspaper industry's decline will not abate anytime soon. The Pew Research Center's 2016 annual State of the News Media report—the gold standard in terms of assessing the health of American news industries—stated that "this accelerating decline suggests the industry may be past its point of no return" (Barthel 2016). For Pew to make such a statement speaks volumes about the severity of the crisis. Such a serious social problem deserves a national conversation proportionate to the scale of the crisis. But thus far, there has been little such discussion, and virtually no public policy response.

What's to Be Done?

Now is an opportune time to discuss entirely new forms of journalism. Because these media failures are structural in nature, they will require structural reform. In particular, they will require reducing or removing commercial pressures on the media system. I have discussed many of these proposals at length elsewhere (e.g., Pickard 2015, 2017), but I will summarize several here. A number of general methods can help reduce commercial pressures on news media. These include diversifying media ownership structures by incentivizing acquisitions by minority groups, breaking up media conglomerates, and blocking mergers to prevent monopolies and oligopolies from forming; allowing for greater employee autonomy—in some cases perhaps employee ownership—so that journalists' professional norms can dictate reporting instead of commercial pressures; encouraging close community engagement to help ensure that local news reflects diverse constituencies' needs, voices, and views; allowing for independent oversight, ranging from ombudsmen to professional media watchdogs to citizen news councils; installing federal, state, and local regulations that prevent commercial imperatives from unduly shaping the form and dissemination of news and information; creating nonprofit news media institutions based on membership models and/or foundation support; and subsidizing noncommercial alternatives such as public media systems, which require government-guaranteed support systems that are entirely insulated from political pressures.

In many ways, this last approach—creating public communication infrastructures—is the surest safeguard against commercial excesses and irresponsible journalism, but it is also the option that is most politically fraught. This is especially true in the American context where such measures are easily condemned by market libertarians who see any public expenditure as a government takeover by stealth. Moreover, such measures are also financially fraught since public options require generating revenues from non-market-based sources. However, a number of creative means exist to raise the necessary capital—and in ways that are not dependent on direct government involvement.

For example, making Facebook and Google allocate a small percentage of their revenues for public service journalism is an argument that British media reformers have advanced. A rising chorus of American media critics is making similar demands that digital giants who benefit so handsomely from content created by others should help finance the production of that content. This argument gains traction when considering that Facebook and Google's domination of digital advertising further weakens the same professional news organizations they expect to help fact-check against fake news.

This money could also go toward a permanent public media trust fund (Pickard 2015), which would help support the kinds of reporting that the market will never incentivize, but that a healthy democracy absolutely requires (Hamilton 2016). Such a fund could be sustained by a combination of revenue streams that numerous reformers have proposed in recent years, including spectrum fees paid by commercial operators; a small consumer tax on electronics; a universal service fund added to monthly phone bills; transitioning already-existing international broadcasting subsidies; citizen tax vouchers; leveraging already-existing public infrastructures like post offices and libraries, and many other potential sources.

Implications for Communication Scholars

Historically the field of communication research has demonstrated a reluctance to broach questions and advance critiques that focus on the commercial structure of our media system. The reasons for this evasion are many, including fears of being too critical of the market and sounding Marxist; the role of the social scientific "dominant paradigm" that emphasizes description and explanation over prescription and normative commitments in its analyses; the tendency to celebrate new technological affordances; the belief in "consumer sovereignty" and the growing emphasis on new modes of resistance and other agency-related considerations. The end result is that the commercial nature of our media system is most often taken for granted, with relatively few scholars questioning its legitimacy or broad systemic vulnerabilities. This is unfortunate, because neglecting such questions undercuts reform efforts. A more balanced approach to both structure and agency allows us to analyze what is wrong with our media system and what we need to do—as scholars and citizens—to create better alternatives.

Among the many possible analyses of Trump's election and media performance, one point is clear: when it mattered most, too many American media institutions privileged profit over democracy. This does not mean that people working within the media industries are bad. It does suggest, however, that the incentive structures driving these media institutions are skewed. To contest a thriving ecosystem of misinformation, we need to redesign our news media system so that different logics are guiding it. Therefore, any attempt to address these problems for media and for democracy should include ideas for radical structural reform. But such remedies hinge on a better understanding of the core problems. Communication scholars have a key role to play in clarifying what these problems are, what is at stake, and what can be done to make things better.

25 Making Journalism Great Again: Trump and the New Rise of News Activism

Adrienne Russell

Send the interns.

—Jay Rosen

The idea was to send newsroom interns to Press Secretary Sean Spicer's spin-session White House briefings to avoid wasting journalism resources. It was first articulated by New York University media professor Jay Rosen, and he expanded upon it in an essay published two days after the inauguration of Donald Trump. "Recognize that the real story is elsewhere, and probably hidden."[1]

The proposal perfectly pulled together a line of critique of the dominant mainstream media political coverage that over the last decades has in repeated and glaring instances failed to watchdog and check corporate and government power. America's major news outlets instead often served up product marked by celebrity-culture insiderness and team-tracking, sports-style reporting that played down citizen protest, legitimized war propaganda, glossed torture and mass-surveillance, demonized whistleblowers, ignored the high crimes of high finance, sustained support for discredited trickle-down economics, muddied the debate around the science of climate change, and fretted and giggled all the way to the bank as Trump tweeted and blustered his way into the presidency. People in the United States and around the world have suffered and will suffer tragic consequences tied to the major public-interest stories bungled by the news media.

The good news is that these failures have fueled reflection among journalists about how they have approached their work, leading to perhaps the most important shift in the culture and practice of news reporting in the last century, where the priority placed on pursuing objectivity is giving way to a form of activism based on conviction that journalism in the United States must reclaim its role as a defender of democracy.

How Not to Die in the Darkness

So far, not a single news outlet appears to have taken up the Rosen plan, but it is still early days in the Trump era and, remarkably, anything suddenly seems possible. Major news media figures and outlets have responded to the Trump administration with new-level reflection on the professional mission of news journalism and with what has seemed to be partly instinctive experimentation around the kind of norms and practices that might best produce journalism today that serves the public interest. There is growing sentiment that "normal" rules no longer apply:

"The news media are not built for someone like [Trump]," said James Fallows at the *Atlantic* after the election.[2]

"I feel we face an existential crisis, a threat to the very relevance and usefulness of our profession," CNN's Christiane Amanpour told journalists earlier the same week at a press freedom award ceremony.[3]

In the months since the election, the topic has been taken up in countless articles, essays, advice pieces, open letters, and at forums whose participants include journalists, scholars, technology developers, and constitutional lawyers. Commentary includes rethinking what for decades has been accepted as common practice, explorations about the value of concepts such as neutrality and objectivity. Here's Amanpour again, from the same speech:

Much of the media got itself into knots trying to differentiate between balance, objectivity, neutrality, and crucially, truth. We cannot continue the old paradigm—let's say like over global warming, where 99.9 percent of the empirical scientific evidence is given equal play with the tiny minority of deniers. I learned long ago ... never to equate victim with aggressor, never to create a false moral or factual equivalence. ... I believe in being truthful, not neutral. And I believe we must stop banalizing the truth.[4]

At the risk of celebrating way too soon, and without articulating a list of legitimate caveats that could fill another essay, it appears that mainstream media figures are embracing an activist approach to their work—an approach in which they see being a reporter above all else as working as an activist on behalf of the facts. That is different than the approach that has prevailed for decades, and such a shift of mentality across the mainstream industry could be enormously significant. Working as an activist of any kind is a whole different kind of work than trying to produce "all the news that's fit to print," pretending to be "fair and balanced," committing to "always taking the lead," or otherwise attempting to fulfill the news-team slogans that mostly underline the mission confusion that has gripped the industry and that suddenly seem outdated, even as promotional branding. The *Washington Post*'s new tag, "Democracy Dies in Darkness," has been mocked as overblown, but few would argue against its value as a news media artifact of the era. Where the *Times*'s slogan, "All the News That's Fit to Print," signals a commitment to impartiality, the *Post*'s new tagline signals a commitment to democracy.

Many forces—cultural, economic, political, technological—surely have combined to move mainstream news media to this new place, however temporarily, but it already seems likely that at the center of the story lies the Trump administration's distinctly "alternative" approach to facts and its related new-level disdain for and attacks on the news media. At the risk of overstating and understating at the same time, Trump has made it personal—and at a time when the fourth estate in the United States might feel more vulnerable to attack than at any time in the nation's history.

Trump has famously called the news media "the enemy of the American people," has described the *New York Times* as "evil." He has targeted individual reporters for abuse. His administration has excluded CNN, the *New York Times*, Politico, BuzzFeed, and other outlets from press briefings. He refers to the mainstream media as "fake news." His reelection campaign (launched in early 2017 for the 2020 election) attempted to run an ad at CNN that included the words "fake news" superimposed over the faces of journalists from most of the nation's top cable and network stations, including CNN, where the ad was meant to run, and the nation's Public Broadcasting Service.

Watergate reporter Carl Bernstein said Trump's war on the media "may be more insidious and dangerous than Richard Nixon's attacks on the press."[5]

Hinting at what makes the Trump administration's lies different than the spinning "truthiness" and mendacity of administrations past, Vox founder Ezra Klein wrote that the constant petty falsehoods sold and defended so zealously by the Trump administration are part of a larger communications strategy. He argued that the administration has "created a baseline expectation" among supporters that nothing the mainstream media reports can be trusted. "Delegitimizing the institutions that might report inconvenient or damaging facts about the president is strategic for an administration that has made a slew of impossible promises and takes office amid a cloud of ethics concerns and potential scandals."[6]

There is awareness among mainstream journalists that something has to change and, for now at least, there seem to be areas of practice that are evolving as a result. Journalists are doing things differently by telling it like it is, unhooking from power, increasing the steps they take to protect their own and their sources' online privacy, and cooperating with one another. These evolving practices are aimed to protect against the spread of falsehoods and to advocate on behalf of facts. Each are briefly elaborated below.

Telling It Like It Is

The *New York Times* front-page headline printed January 23, 2017, didn't mince words: "Trump Repeats Lie About Popular Vote in Meeting With Lawmakers."[7] It says something about shifting journalism norms that, at the time, the word *lie* tied to the president made a splash. Already, in May 2017, the paper-of-record's headline seems unsurprising. In a subsequent piece, *New York Times* writer Dan Barry felt the need to dig into the decision. After initially using the word *falsely*, the paper switched to *lie* online, and then it remained that way for the print edition.

Executive Editor Dean Baquet told Barry that he "fully understood the gravity of using the word *lie,* whether in reference to an average citizen or to the president of the United States." Baquet added that he thought the word "should be used sparingly" but that, in this case, "we should be letting people know in no uncertain terms that [what the president said] is untrue."[8]

In fact, the *New York Times* began "letting people know" during the last stretch of the campaign. At the end of September 2016, the paper ran a full-page news article entitled "A Week of Whoppers from Trump."[9] Politico that week took the same tack: "Trump has built a cottage industry around stretching the truth," the Washington-insider outlet reported. "[He] averaged about one falsehood every three minutes and 15 seconds over nearly five hours of remarks. In raw numbers, that's 87 erroneous statements in five days."[10] *US News* noted that four mainstream news organizations—the *Washington Post* and the *Los Angeles Times* as well as the *New York Times* and Politico—condemned Trump that weekend for "playing fast and loose with the facts." The paper speculated that this kind of reporting "could mark the beginning of a sea change in which mainstream news organizations depart from their traditional goal of even-handed reporting and become truth squads."[11] The *US News* piece was written by the paper's White House and Politics reporter Ken Walsh, who unwittingly demonstrated the systemic problem that has plagued mainstream media news. "A sea change," he wrote, underlining the gravity of the problem, again more profoundly for doing so without knowing he was doing it. It is difficult to imagine how the public interest was being served by a journalism that made it a "traditional goal" to place "even-handed reporting" above doggedly seeking the truth. It is just as easy, however, to imagine how well that arrangement served the interests of politicians, political parties, think tanks, and spin-room pundits.

For what it's worth as a measure of shifting mentalities, the business side has climbed on board. After the inauguration, the *Washington Post* brought out its new slogan on democracy and darkness. The *New York Times* ran an ad campaign that featured full-page, billboard, and television spots on the value of the truth—"now more than ever"—and how it takes hardworking journalists dedicated to facts to get at it. And CNN refused to run the Trump reelection campaign ad with the "fake news" labels stamped over journalists' faces, spurring the president's campaign to complain it was the victim of censorship.

Unhooking from Power

Telling it like it is appears to be liberating. Mainstream media reporters seem to be building and strengthening sources away from the celebrity-dominated main stage, working the hallways backstage, and moving more meaningfully among the audience. That is to say, they seem less dependent on and less afraid of losing access to the people at the top who are the subjects of their reporting. Administration leaks are opening at a regular clip among agency workers and civil servants. The *Washington Post*'s David Fahrenthold won a 2017 Pulitzer Prize for his crowd-sourced reporting on

Trump's philanthropy foundation. He invited his Twitter followers to help him report a string of damning stories. As Pablo Boczkowski and Seth Lewis argue in this volume, Fahrenthold's method of fostering crowd-based relationships yielded factual information in an efficient way and it also worked to build credibility among the public at a time when trust in the mainstream media is at an all-time low (see chapter 22).

Doing journalism away from the pressroom gives mainstream and often well-known reporters greater freedom, even if it's semiconsciously felt, to call a spade a spade and pursue fraught storylines. Masha Gessen, Russian-American journalist and activist, wrote a widely circulated *New York Review of Books* piece the day after the election, warning against cooperation with Trump. "Those who argue for cooperation will be willfully ignoring the corrupting touch of autocracy, from which the future must be protected," she wrote.[12] Days later, Reuters editor-in-chief Steve Adler circulated a memo to his staff comparing the challenges faced by US journalists to those faced by journalists working under authoritarian regimes. The memo reads like a rallying cry. "Don't take too dark a view of the reporting environment," he said. "It's an opportunity for us to practice the skills we've learned in much tougher places around the world and to lead by example."[13] The same week, *Time*'s Middle East bureau chief, Jared Malsin, wrote a piece on "How to Report under Authoritarianism," based on experience reporting in Egypt and Turkey.[14] "Everything changes ... the battles, the risks, the rules. All of that is at stake in a kind of struggle and negotiation between the government and the press," he wrote. "Encrypt your data. Get burner phones. Lawyer up. ... Don't give in to intimidation."

Adopting Technology Tools

Maslin was working territory that has expanded in a world shaped in part by National Security Agency whistleblower Edward Snowden. Even state and local political journalists have started taking measures to defend against intimidation by protecting themselves and their sources against digital surveillance. Technology teams are developing privacy tools and training resources for journalists. In fact, since 2016, Snowden has been president of the Freedom of the Press Foundation based in San Francisco, an organization dedicated to arming journalists with privacy practices and tools. As Snowden told *Wired* magazine, "Newsrooms don't have the budget, the sophistication, or the skills to defend themselves in the current environment. ... We're trying to provide a few niche tools to make the game a little more fair."[15] The organization's most widely used tool is SecureDrop, a Tor-based system for uploading news tips and leaked materials now being used by major news outlets that include the *Guardian*, the *New York Times*, and the *Washington Post*.

Kate Krauss, a director for the Tor Project, argued that privacy is about more than any one reporter or source. "An independent press corps cannot stay independent for long if reporters can't investigate, communicate with sources, and write without worrying that someone is looking over their shoulder. Even the fear of surveillance triggers self-censorship and influences writers' thinking, research, and writing." She points out that Google recently notified reporters at CNN, the *New York Times*, and the *Atlantic* that "a government actor" had attempted to hack their email systems.[16]

Banding Together

The collaborative spirit that drives the work of many of the technologists involved in creating tools and advocating for the adoption of increased security is increasingly reflected in the work of reporting. As also discussed by Boczkowski and Lewis in chapter 22 of this volume, Frederik Obermaier and Bastian Obermayer, the journalists at *Süddeutsche Zeitung* in Germany who broke the Panama Papers story, wrote an opinion piece for the *Guardian* calling on American journalists to collaborate rather than to compete with one another. The Panama Papers story was investigated and reported on by 400 journalists, they pointed out. "American journalists should stop Trump from dividing their ranks. However hard their professional competition may be, they should do the opposite: unite, share, and collaborate."[17] Journalists seem to be heeding the advice. Muckrock, an organization that promotes investigative journalism, created a channel on the group-messaging service Slack for reporters who want to share information about making Freedom of Information Act requests. Muckrock expected to win over a few dozen people but drew more than 3,000 participants. Media Matters launched a Moveon.org petition in January calling on news organizations to stand up to Trump's attempts to blacklist or ban critical news outlets:

If Trump blacklists or bans one of you, the rest of you need to stand up. Instead of ignoring Trump's bad behavior and going about your business, close ranks and stand up for journalism. Don't keep talking about what Trump wants to talk about. Stand up and fight back. Amplify your colleague's inquiry or refuse to engage until he removes that person/outlet from the blacklist.[18]

As of May 10, 2017, the petition contained more than 330,000 signatures.

Guideposts

At the end of May 2017, President Trump fired Federal Bureau of Investigation Director James Comey, who was busy expanding the Bureau's investigation into possible Trump campaign ties to Russia. Mainstream news reporters swarmed the story and White House accounts shifted by the hour in response. The *Washington Post* wrote a tick-tock story that officials refused to comment on but that more than 30 backstage sources filled out, effectively putting the paper's reporters next to the President over the course of the entire tumultuous weekend leading up the firing.[19] Trump's response to the damning coverage was to threaten to cancel all future White House press briefings.[20] "As a very active President with lots of things happening, it is not possible for my surrogates to stand at a podium with perfect accuracy!" he tweeted. The battle between Trump and the media continues to heat up, and the fact-chasing press seems for today to be winning the battle. Every fact-filled piece fuels more of the same. Even-handed reporting as a goal is giving way to truth squadding. It's journalism that feels like activism—the kind that can topple a political leader, and has done so, on and off throughout history.

Notes

1. Jay Rosen, "Send in the Interns," *Press Think*, January 22, 2017, http://pressthink .org/2017/01/send-the-interns.

2. James Fallows, "How to Deal with the Lies of Donald Trump: Guidelines for the Media," *The Atlantic*, November 28, 2016, https://www.theatlantic.com/notes/2016/ 11/a-reflexive-liar-in-command-guidelines-for-the-media/508832.

3. Christiane Amanpour, "Journalism Faces an 'Existential Crisis' in Trump Era," *CNN*, November 23, 2016, http://www.cnn.com/2016/11/23/opinions/christiane -amanpour-journalism-in-trump-era.

4. Ibid.

5. Michael M. Grynbaum, "Trump Calls the News Media the 'Enemy of the American People,'" *New York Times*, February 17, 2017, https://www.nytimes.com/2017/02/17/business/trump-calls-the-news-media-the-enemy-of-the-people.html.

6. Ezra Klein, "Trump's Real War Isn't with the Media. It's with Facts," *Vox*, January 21, 2017, https://www.vox.com/policy-and-politics/2017/1/21/14347952/trump-spicer-press-conference-crowd-size-inauguration.

7. Michael D. Shear and Emmarie Huetteman, "Trump Repeats Lie about Popular Vote in Meeting with Lawmakers," *New York Times*, January 23, 2017, https://www.nytimes.com/2017/01/23/us/politics/donald-trump-congress-democrats.html.

8. Dan Barry, "In a Swirl of 'Untruths' and 'Falsehoods,' Calling a Lie a Lie," *New York Times,* January 25, 2017, https://www.nytimes.com/2017/01/25/business/media/donald-trump-lie media.html.

9. Maggie Haberman and Alexander Burns, "A Week of Whoppers from Donald Trump," *New York Times*, September 24, 2016, https://www.nytimes.com/interactive/2016/09/24/us/elections/donald-trump-statements.html.

10. Kyle Cheney, Isaac Arnsdorf, Daniel Lippman, Daniel Strauss, and Brent Griffiths, "Donald Trump's Week of Misrepresentations, Exaggerations and Half-Truths," *Politico*, September 25, 2016, http://www.politico.com/magazine/story/2016/09/2016-donald-trump-fact-check-week-214287.

11. Kenneth T. Walsh, "The Truth Squad: When Donald Trump. Lies Journalists Are Telling It Like It Is," *US News*, September 30, 2016, https://www.usnews.com/news/articles/2016-09-30/journalists-are-calling-trump-out-for-lies.

12. Masha Gessen, "Autocracy: Rules for Survival," *New York Review of Books,* November 10, 2016, http://www.nybooks.com/daily/2016/11/10/trump-election-autocracy-rules-for-survival.

13. Steve Adler, "Covering Trump the Reuters Way," Reuters, January 31, 2017, http://www.reuters.com/article/rpb-adlertrump-idUSKBN15F276.

14. Jared Malsin, "How to Report under Authoritarianism," *Time*, November 16, 2016, http://time.com/4569137/president-donald-trump-authoritarianism-journalists.

15. Andy Greenberg, "Edward Snowden's New Job: Protecting Reporters from Spies," *Wired,* February 14, 2017, https://www.wired.com/2017/02/reporters-need-edward-snowden.

16. Kate Krauss, "Time for Journalists to Encrypt Everything," *Wired*, March 10, 2017, https://www.wired.com/2017/03/time-journalists-encrypt-everything.

17. Frederik Obermaier and Bastian Obermayer, "We Broke the Panama Papers Story. Here's How to Investigate Donald Trump," *The Guardian,* January 24, 2017,

https://www.theguardian.com/commentisfree/2017/jan/24/panama-papers-media
-investigation-next-donald-trump-hold-accountable.

18. Tell the White House Press Corps: Stand up to Trump's blacklist, MoveOn.org
Petition, https://petitions.moveon.org/sign/tell-the-white-house-3.

19. Philip Rucker, Ashley Parker, Sari Horwitz, and Robert Costa, "Inside Trump's
Anger and Impatience—and His Sudden Decision to Fire Comey," *Washington Post*,
May 10, 2017, https://www.washingtonpost.com/politics/how-trumps-anger-and
-impatience-prompted-him-to-fire-the-fbi-director/2017/05/10/d9642334-359c-11e7
-b373-418f6849a004_story.html.

20. David Jackson, "Trump Threatens to Cancel Press Briefings, Unhappy with
Comey Coverage," *USA Today*, May 12, 2017.

26 The Case for Campaign Journalism

Rodney Benson

Instead of allowing an autocratic-styled president to set the news agenda with his distracting and often untruthful remarks, journalists ought to focus their energies elsewhere: on alerting the public to the most important events and issues of the day.

I call this kind of proactive reporting "campaign journalism." Today, this term is often associated in the United States with electoral campaigns. Originally, however, campaign journalism referred to English and American reporting during the late nineteenth century that offered in-depth coverage of a social problem with the goal of prompting a political response.[1] This is not the same thing as partisan journalism, nor is it advocacy journalism except in the broadest sense of advocating sustained attention to a given problem.

Much of campaign journalism consists of investigative reporting, but not all investigative reporting is campaign journalism: to count as a campaign, the coverage has to be sustained over a substantial time period, at least several weeks, but better yet months. It is still practiced from time to time by leading national news organizations and ambitious local news media. I am suggesting that news media concentrated on breaking news shift to campaigns and that those currently sponsoring campaigns do more of them and sustain them for longer periods of time.

For example, campaign reporting in the Trump era could focus on the likely impact of the president's proposed policies (deep cuts to education, health care, antipoverty programs, etc.) or problems he is actively seeking to make worse (such as climate change); alternatively, journalistic campaigns could dig into social trends that Trump is ignoring, but that are decisively changing the country's political and social climate (globalization, economic restructuring, growing inequality, drug addiction, etc.)

Of course, President Donald Trump treats any critical coverage as a personal threat. He will hate even more being ignored. Already, he has called a press corps that has mostly only accurately relayed his remarks "an enemy of the American people." For this reason, self-respecting journalists have nothing to lose in taking a more assertive approach. To be clear, I am not calling for journalists to return insult for injury. I am not calling for more partisan opinion writing. Effective campaign journalism has to be firmly rooted in the facts. But make no mistake: it must be relentless and even ruthless in reporting—and repeating—the truth.

Lead, Don't Follow

Beliefs in media power to the contrary, research has repeatedly established that media tend to follow rather than lead the political agenda. Media "index" their coverage to what political elites are doing and saying.[2] This tendency supports democracy when there are two strong parties that also keep each other in check: in such cases, media pluralism reflects political pluralism. When one party completely dominates government, however, and there is little internal party dissent, journalists are faced with a difficult choice: either index their coverage to a one-sided discourse or else proactively present the other side themselves.

During the first year of the Trump presidency, America's leading news organizations have indeed been characterized as playing this oppositional role. But they have only done so reluctantly, wherever possible leaning on and following the political opposition (whether rare rogue Republicans or outspoken, but largely powerless, Democrats). Critical or not in their commentary, media have mostly played Trump's game by indexing their coverage to his every move.

Even so, President Trump continually attacks news organizations and prominent individual journalists. Partly as a result, public trust in the news media is at record lows, although opinions are sharply divided: In early 2017, 90 percent of Democrats and 70 percent of Independents, but only 42 percent of Republicans, believed that "media criticism of political leaders keeps them from doing things they shouldn't." These wide-ranging percentages are a dramatic change from 2016, when more than 70 percent of Republicans, Democrats, and Independents alike agreed with this statement.[3]

In this polarized environment, nothing that mainstream news organizations do would be compelling or credible to diehard Trump partisans. But let us not forget that such partisans make up well under half of voters, not to mention the total adult populace. Journalists should forge ahead and do their best to tell the truth to the majority, a group that includes many Independents and weak Trump supporters who have not yet closed their minds to factual information that puts the president in a bad light [4]

Report, Repeat, Keep It Fresh

Political campaigns know that for a message to be retained, it has to be repeated multiple times. This is why they often strive for a single "message of the week" or even better, a theme that captures the thrust of the entire campaign, such as "Make America Great Again."[5]

Psychological research has affirmed this hunch, though with a caveat. Repetition helps retention and persuasion up to a point, after which time it may actually alienate and dissuade audiences.[6] Thus, a successful campaign has to continually figure out approaches to say the same thing, but in novel, interesting ways.

There are plenty of examples of successful journalistic campaigns that suggest how it can be done.

Shortly after purchasing the *St. Louis Post and Dispatch* in 1879, Joseph Pulitzer launched a series of campaigns against the city's powerful oligarchy. Pulitzer began with a campaign against the St. Louis Gas-Light Company's efforts to re-establish the monopoly that had allowed it to charge St. Louis residents the highest utility charges in the nation. As Pulitzer's biographer, James McGrath Morris, writes:

Every day for the next two weeks, Pulitzer shoehorned into the paper articles that detailed the monopolistic practices of the gas company and featured poignant interviews with victimized customers. The flurry of articles, as well as the continuous stream of editorials—appearing, as they usually did, under the banner headline No Compromise! No Compromise! No Compromise!—caught the city's attention.[7]

Soon, however, the "paper began to sound like a one-note composition." Needing "another campaign that would goad the oligarchs and attract readers," Pulitzer's editors found a new angle to generate reader interest and fury: tax dodging. In addition to uncovering information about dishonest tax declarations by the wealthy, the *Post and Dispatch* unabashedly reminded readers of the moral issues at stake. Each day, "the paper reprinted the text of the taxpayers' oath, with the headline 'What Tax-Dodgers Swear and Swallow.'"[8] Ultimately, Pulitzer's gas campaign succeeded (the city rejected the company's plan to restore its monopoly), while the tax campaign resulted in a state investigation but no reforms. But Pulitzer had clearly hit on a successful formula for both civic and commercial success. The *Post and Dispatch* filled its "news columns with the kind of stories ... that made people talk,"[9] and built its readership as it championed the interests of the middle and lower classes.

Over the course of the past century, there have been other examples of successful campaign journalism. During the early 1980s, the French newspaper *Libération* actively helped promote the cause of the beurs, the second generation of Algerian immigrants living in France. Between October and December of 1983, the newspaper provided saturation coverage of a beur march starting in the south of France and proclaimed their arrival in the nation's capital with a front-page banner headline and photograph. In so doing, *Libération* also proclaimed the arrival of a more "multicultural" vision of French identity and of immigrants' "right to be different." *Libération*'s campaign thus provided a space for and helped legitimate arguments about cultural diversity that had heretofore received little attention in France.[10] Two decades earlier, some US newspapers' extensive and enthusiastic coverage of civil rights could also be fairly characterized as a campaign.

Doubling Down: Behind, Besides, and Beyond Trump

What could campaign journalism look like in the age of Trump? Some news organizations are already launching campaigns or proto-campaigns. They are afraid to call them as such, but they shouldn't be.

The *Washington Post*, at Jeff Bezos's prodding, has rediscovered its Watergate mojo. The paper's bold reclaiming of national political reporting began well before Trump's election. But clearly, the paper has not hesitated to aggressively cover this administration's flouting of political norms and the rule of law. The *Post*'s reporting on Trump's Russia connections has merged the categories of breaking and sustained in-depth reporting, and thus could be considered a type of campaign journalism. And similar to the results for Pulitzer, this campaign has paid off handsomely in commercial terms as the paper has aggressively increased its digital reach and revenues.[11]

The *New York Times* competes with the *Washington Post* for scoops, but it also does a different kind of campaign reporting that the *Post* tends not to do: relentless reporting on government policies and their human impact. The *Times* even has a name for this kind of reporting, as one long-time reporter confided to me: "pounding the zone." The *Times* has long pounded the zone on the immigration issue, demanding more humane treatment of arrested undocumented immigrants. It has also clearly pounded the zone in its environmental coverage, providing repeated documentation of the effects of climate change, making the case that Trump's policies will make a bad situation even worse.

Campaign journalism need not only be about Trump. This has been the approach of John Oliver's show, *Last Week Tonight*, which has focused on discovering the important issues well before the politicians do. With few exceptions, Oliver has steadfastly ignored Trump's tweets and nearly daily scandals.[12] The show provides a model for how news media can responsibly attempt to set the agenda rather than always following (even if in critical mode) the agenda of the administration in power.

But most of this reporting falls short of being a classic campaign in the Pulitzer tradition. Although in-depth, and often running to thousands of words and featuring powerful photos, the reports generally disappear after a few days only to be replaced by a new zone to be pounded. Even regular readers are likely to forget and move on. What's worse, though, is that much of this reporting fails to reach beyond those already convinced.

Excellence for Everyone

Perhaps the biggest difference between today's investigative journalism and the campaign journalism of Pulitzer's era is whom the reporting is for. At the *Post and Dispatch*, and subsequently at his *New York World*, Pulitzer created newspapers that provided excellence for everyone; in marked contrast, the current publisher of the *New York Times*, Arthur Sulzberger, Jr., has said his newspaper is about "providing quality news for quality audiences."[13] Columbia University sociologist Michael Schudson has argued that diminishing, and increasingly elite, audiences can stand in for the public as a whole.[14] The problem, of course, is that this elite may have interests and ideas that diverge substantially from the broader public. Moreover, some marginalized groups may have few elite representatives keeping an eye out for their concerns. For example, many elites may be most concerned about inside-Washington political maneuvering and legal procedural issues, whereas a significant plurality if not majority of voters are most concerned with economic inequality, jobs, education, and health care. Inside-the-Beltway coverage, of course, can be very important as it concerns the healthy functioning of democracy, but this kind of news should not be allowed to completely crowd out reporting that hits closer to the immediate and urgent concerns of average citizens.

Campaigns that are mostly targeted at the like-minded may only backfire in the end. This is what happened to *Libération*'s beur "diversity" campaign. After Jean-Marie Le Pen's National Front party consistently gained ground in local and regional elections in the mid-1980s, effectively shifting the national political debate to the right, *Libération* was among the first to backtrack and ultimately even took the lead in reframing the immigration debate around the need for "integration." Its earlier campaign for diversity thus had few lasting effects.

A similar fate could befall the nascent campaigns of US elite journalism. In deciding what to cover, journalists need to venture outside their comfort zones and not just preach to the choir. Campaign reporting will be more compelling and powerful when journalists transcend their blind spots, no longer assuming that what is most important to them and to their own social circles will be most important to a wide range of citizens.[15]

It may be that the most influential campaign journalism will not come from the prestige outlets like the *Washington Post* or the *New York Times*. The local nonprofit outlets that have spread across the country in recent years—such as MinnPost, Voice of San Diego, and Texas Tribune—could be one fount of social problem–based campaign reporting. Unfortunately, foundation policies currently push many nonprofits to pursue an elitist news strategy, following the Sulzberger mantra of quality news for quality audiences.

Local television news, when it is not focused on crime and celebrities, has the opportunity and capacity to create campaigns with real impact. As a judge for a major television news award competition over the past few years, I have viewed several excellent examples of sustained local TV news coverage that shows the human consequences of failed local government policies and effectively pushes for legislative remedies. In other words, civically effective campaign journalism may look nothing like what we have come to expect from US elite newspapers.[16] That's probably a good thing. The challenge will be to figure out how to encourage more impactful campaign journalism, whether through nonprofit or commercial means.[17]

Notes

1. See Melissa Jean Score, "The Development and Impact of Campaigning Journalism in Britain, 1840–1875: The Old New Journalism?" Ph.D. thesis, Birkbeck, University of London, 2015; and James McGrath Morris, *Pulitzer: A Life in Politics, Print, and Power* (New York: Harper Perennial, 2010).

2. W. Lance Bennett, *News: The Politics of Illusion*, 9th ed. (New York: Longman, 2011).

3. Pew Research Center, "Americans' Attitudes about the News Media Deeply Divided along Partisan Lines," May 9, 2017, http://www.journalism.org/2017/05/10/americans-attitudes-about-the-news-media-deeply-divided-along-partisan-lines.

4. See also chapter 12 by Daniel Kreiss in this volume.

5. See also chapter 11 by Julia Sonnevend in this volume.

6. John T. Cacioppo and Richard E. Petty, "Effects of Message Repetition on Argument Processing, Recall, and Persuasion," *Basic and Applied Social Psychology* 10 (1989): 3–12.

7. Morris, 164.

8. Morris, 164.

9. Ibid., 171.

10. Rodney Benson, *Shaping Immigration News: A French-American Comparison* (Cambridge: Cambridge University Press, 2013), 110–112.

11. James B. Stewart, "*Washington Post*, Breaking News, Is Also Breaking New Ground," *New York Times*, May 19, 2017, https://www.nytimes.com/2017/05/19/business/washington-post-digital-news.html.

12. Angela Watercutter, "John Oliver Returns to Out News the News—By Ignoring Trump," *The Wire*, February 10, 2017, https://www.wired.com/2017/02/john-oliver-trump-agenda.

13. Morris, 212–215; remarks by Arthur Sulzberger, Jr., at Columbia School of Journalism, April 6, 2011, author notes.

14. Michael Schudson, *Why Democracies Need an Unlovable Press* (Cambridge: Polity Press, 2008), 14.

15. See also chapter 22 by Pablo Boczkowski and Seth Lewis in this volume.

16. Rodney Benson, "Can Foundations Solve the Journalism Crisis?," *Journalism* (2017): 1–19, first published online August 31, doi:10.1177/1464884917724612.

17. For a sympathetic critique of campaign journalism by Scottish elite and tabloid newspapers and the articulation of a new normative framework in support of demo-cratically efficacious campaign journalism, see Jen Birks, "The Democratic Role of Campaign Journalism," *Journalism Practice* 4 (2010): 208–223.

18. See also chapter 24 by Victor Pickard in this volume.

27 We All Stand Together or We All Fall Apart: On the Need for an Adversarial Press in the Age of Trump

Dave Karpf

There is an old saying about bankruptcy. "How do you go bankrupt? Slowly at first, then all at once."[1]

When evaluating the challenges facing political journalism in 2017, a similar categorization scheme springs to mind. There are slow problems—problems driven by changing information technologies, and by the political economy of news operations, and by the slow evolution of behavioral norms that govern how political actors and political journalists interact with one another. Compelling individual cases—a trolling operation hosted in Russia or Macedonia, a new fact-checking website supported by the Knight Foundation, or a politician's insistence that an unflattering story is "fake news"—can serve to illustrate these slow problems. But the slow problems are systematic in nature. They would remain largely the same regardless of the results of a single election, and regardless of the choices of a single media or technology company.

But there are also all-at-once problems. The relationship between the American government's first estate and its fourth estate is radically different in a Trump presidency than it would have been in a Clinton presidency. Donald Trump lies with impunity about matters large and small. He demands loyalty, not accuracy or honesty, from the members of his administration. He casts American press organizations as the central villains in the narrative of his presidency, and speaks frequently about pursuing legal strategies that could bankrupt independent media. And Trump's victory was not the inevitable culmination of the slow problems in political journalism. History is both deeply contingent and brutally path-dependent. One can imagine a thousand scenarios in which some minor shift in campaign events produced a Clinton victory, or some earlier shift produced a different Republican nominee. Trump's relationship with the media poses an unprecedented all-at-once problem.

Academics have a tendency to focus on the slow problems, ceding the all-at-once problems to public intellectuals and commentators. Slow problems, after all, move at the same (glacial) pace as academia itself. But in so doing, we often make a categorical error by assessing all public problems as though they were rooted in the slow-moving processes we are best suited to studying. This is a tendency that we ought to recognize and, in this particular instance, reject. We have entered a unique moment in American history; one in which established norms, institutional routines, and behaviors are being upended.

There is reason for genuine concern that the Trump administration will undermine the political press. This may come through the dissolution of press norms, relations, and institutions. It may come through the creation of (quasi-) state news organizations. Or it may come through financial and legal challenges to independent press organizations. This essay discusses these threats to a free and functional fourth estate. It concludes by arguing that the President's attacks on the press *as an institution* require a new commitment to collective behavior that defends the values of a free and functional press. Donald Trump has cast the independent press as his adversaries. The fourth estate must recognize and respond to this new role.

A Few Observations

Elite political behavior is governed more by norms than by laws. Presidents, judges, and legislators are legally *required* to do very little. Most of their interactions are instead governed by shared expectations of what they *ought* to do. Norms only maintain their force so long as either (a) they are obeyed jointly by all or (b) some negative consequences meet those who break them.

The relationship between the executive branch and the media, in particular, has always been premised upon informal norms and shared understandings. Although we often speak of the media as the "fourth estate," and scholars have long discussed the vital role that a free press plays in a functioning democracy, the text of the constitution asserts no positive role for the press. It solely offers the negative rejoinder against congress making laws abridging the freedom of the press.

Donald J. Trump is a president who prides himself on challenging informal norms and shared understandings. For his supporters, this is one of his greatest strengths. For his critics, it is his greatest flaw. This was evident throughout the long presidential campaign, where Trump refused to release his tax returns, revoked press access from news outlets that provided unfavorable coverage, and encouraged supporters to verbally accost the press pen as a set piece of his rallies. PolitiFact judged nearly 70 percent of his statements to be "mostly false," "false," or "pants on fire" (by comparison, Hillary Clinton received one those ratings on only 24 percent of her statements). It was evident during the transition, when Trump refused to hold press conferences and cast ("fake news") CNN and the ("failing") *New York Times* as the central villains opposing his administration.

It has become even more apparent in the early months of his presidency. Trump's presidency began with a verifiable lie regarding the crowd size at his inauguration. President Trump then went on to publicly claim that the Hillary Clinton received 3–5 million illegal votes in the 2016 election—a claim that his press secretary was forced to repeatedly defend while lacking a shred of evidence. It has descended further since then, including the president's early morning tweet that Barack Obama had wiretapped Trump Tower and other explicit falsehoods that have been directly contradicted by all knowledgeable parties.

These statements from the President and his press secretary are distinct from the normal interactions between the executive branch and the White House press corps. Presidents often complain about press coverage. They often seek to strategically frame the news to promote preferred narratives. Republican presidents since Nixon have, in particular, complained in general terms about the biases of the "liberal media establishment." And if we consider a counterfactual universe in which a Jeb Bush, a Marco Rubio, or a Ted Cruz had become president, we could reasonably expect that they would take issue with their coverage by mainstream media outlets. But presidents and their press secretaries go to great lengths to avoid being caught in an outright lie. This is a major norm governing the press–president relationship: if a president is caught lying, then Something Bad Will Happen. The presumptive norm is that *spin* is acceptable, but lying crosses a line. That norm has now been violated. Nothing, so far, has happened. Trump has instead taken to labeling all unflattering reporting as "fake news." Time and again, the President has placed established media organizations (rather than Democrats) in the central adversarial role.

And while this administration seeks to cast CNN and the *New York Times* in the role of the villain, it has simultaneously promoted and given unprecedented access to a range of conservative media organizations. This extends well beyond the relationship between the Republican Party network and Fox News/conservative talk radio. Although Trump has spoken favorably about Fox News, has a well-reported penchant for watching *Fox and Friends* to start his day, and has even gone out of his way to defend embattled Fox personality Bill O'Reilly, Trump's ties to more extreme elements of the conservative media network are even more troubling. This includes Breitbart News, which (Trump's former chief strategist/Breitbart executive chairman) Steve Bannon once referred to as "the platform for the alt-right." Trump has also engaged repeatedly with Alex Jones, who has used his "Infowars" radio program to promote outlandish conspiracy theories.

As the Trump White House continues to antagonize and demonize the White House press corps, it is also promoting and rewarding with increased access this set of allied conservative media organizations. This raises the real possibility of the emergence of a quasi-state media apparatus, in which independent media are attacked, undermined, and denied access while Trump-allied media are promoted, rewarded, and given (formal or informal) governmental approval. It is worth noting that two of Trump's most trusted advisors—Steve Bannon and Jared Kushner—have no experience working in government, but each has run a media property (Kushner owned the *New York Observer* until January 2017).

Meanwhile, another Trump advisor and supporter—Peter Thiel—spent 2016 demonstrating a viable strategy for attacking and shutting down media organizations that a billionaire dislikes. After Terry "Hulk Hogan" Bollea's successful lawsuit against Gawker resulted in a $140 million verdict that bankrupted the media organization and its owner, it came to light that Bollea's case was one of several that had been bankrolled by Thiel, the culmination of a nearly decade-long vendetta against Gawker Media. Importantly, the Bollea case was structured so that Gawker's insurance would not cover the claims, resulting in bankruptcy even though there was a strong likelihood that the judgment would have been reduced or overturned on appeal. In an interview at the National Press Club, Thiel later remarked that "single-digit millionaires" like Bollea have "no effective access to our legal system."

Thiel's successful legal gambit against Gawker Media raises the concern that it could be replicated and deployed by Thiel and other Trump-aligned billionaires against media organizations that provide unfavorable coverage of the President and his agenda. Another conservative billionaire, Frank VanderSloot, nearly bankrupted *Mother Jones* magazine through a 2012 defamation lawsuit that took three years and $2.5 million to defend against. Although the suit was eventually dismissed, VanderSloot announced in the aftermath that he was setting up a $1 million fund to pay the expenses of people who wanted to sue *Mother Jones*. The looming threat of such lawsuits raises the cost of legal insurance for news organizations, and can potentially render them uninsurable.

For roughly a decade, journalism and political communication scholars have focused on a set of "slow" threats to American journalism: The infrastructure necessary to support high-quality reporting is expensive, and we have entered a long period of uncertainty regarding the viability of any one particular revenue model. Meanwhile, a range of new communications technologies incentivize the spread of cheap hot-takes over painstaking research and fact-checking. We must now grapple as well with these new "all-at-once" threats. The press as an institution is now facing not only a funding crisis, or a popularity crisis, or a readership crisis. It is now facing an existential crisis: the external threat of a hostile administration attempting to undermine and replace it.

A Few Implications

What is stopping Trump and his allies from lying to or shutting out traditional media organizations, constructing a quasi-state media apparatus, and strategically attacking independent media organizations through the legal or regulatory system? These are new questions for the Trump era, ones that would have seemed absurd under a different president. Scholarship in the fields of comparative media and comparative government has taken on a newfound vibrancy and relevance, as researchers draw connections to the role of media suppression in the democratic decline of Latin American countries, in Berlusconi's Italy, and in Putin's Russia. If the Trump administration pursues this type of antagonistic stance, there are three areas where we should pay particularly close attention: press access, press accountability, and press reprisals.

In the area of press access, we must ask whether the administration is following established practices for allowing the fourth estate room to cover the administration and inform the public. Where the administration moves away from established routines, we should pay close attention and ask why and who benefits. We should also pay attention to the relationships between the administration and new conservative media outlets. There are reasonable arguments for expanding press access beyond the traditional members of the White House press corps. But if GatewayPundit and Breitbart are receiving exclusives while CNN and the *Washington Post* are having their press access revoked, then there is cause for serious alarm. Small individual episodes such as Secretary of State Rex Tillerson's stating that he's "not a big media press access person" and restricting press access during his first major mission to Asia, Press Secretary Sean Spicer shutting CNN and other news organizations out of a closed press briefing, and Spicer expanding the White House press briefings to focus on "floaters" from far-right publications should be read within this broader context.

Regarding press accountability, it is incumbent upon us as scholars, journalists, and citizens to take seriously the question of what happens if the administration simply chooses to repeatedly lie to the media and, through them, the American public. There is reason to believe that the Trump administration has crossed the line between political spin and outright untruth. If journalists do not collectively impose a cost for this lying, then they cannot individually expect the claims made by Trump and his spokespeople to have any lasting truth-value. CNN's brief foray into denying Kellyanne Conway any airtime can be read as a positive step in this direction. So too can the (slowly) emerging habit of White House press corps members following up on each other's questions. Media organizations and key journalists will need to collectively create new adversarial habits that exact a normative penalty for White House misinformation.

And regarding press reprisals, we should pay particular attention to regulatory and legal threats to news organizations coming both from the Trump administration and from his network of allies. To date, President Trump has spoken frequently about loosening libel laws. Libel statutes are established at the state level, not the federal level, so this threat does not fall directly within the powers of the presidency. But news organizations may also be endangered through aggressive lawsuits by Trump-allied billionaires like Peter Thiel, or by partisan regulatory oversight. The Gawker lawsuit in 2016 was viewed largely as a referendum on Gawker.com. But it also could be a template for undermining independent media.

A Simple Proposal: Collective Action in Defense of a Free Press

If the fourth estate is going to continue to fulfill its democratic duty during the Trump era, it is going to have to unlearn some old habits. Most importantly, the longstanding ideal of journalists as iconoclasts and individualists, competing with one another on their way to grab *the story*, probably needs to change. As Boczkowski and Lewis note in chapter 22 of this volume, the American news media has developed a self-defeating "self-centeredness." That self-centeredness reveals itself in the odd pride journalists take in being difficult to organize. They don't have a robust history of collective action, and they view this as a badge of honor.

The ideal of the striving, independent reporter was ensconced within the old norms of press–political relations. Reporters were not demonized or denied access as a distinct group. Quite the opposite: the American tradition has long treated them with deference and given them preferential treatment. This reportorial independence is absent in other countries and other contexts, where it is abundantly clear that the press has collective interests that require collective defense.

In present-day America, it is not enough for press critics to write think pieces in industry outlets, or for public intellectuals to voice concerns from the sidelines. Formal industry associations like the White House Correspondents Association, the Reporters Committee, and the Online News Association must play an active coordinating role in asserting expectations, addressing violations, and coordinating responses. This will strike some observers as crossing the line from journalism into activism. It will make some reporters fret. But it is an appropriate and proportional response—as Adrienne Russell writes in her essay for this volume, journalists must prepare themselves to become "activists on behalf of the facts." The American Medical Association defends the interests of doctors. The American Political Science Association defends the interests of political scientists. Journalistic associations have not historically played an active role defending the interests of journalists from political attack, because those interests have not often been directly threatened. The Trump administration has selected "the media" as the central villain in its public narrative. The associations that represent the media must adapt to the adversarial role this creates for them.

If individual news organizations and individual reporters view themselves as competitors fighting for the administration's favor, then they will be party to the erosion of press freedom, press access, and government accountability during the Trump years. It is time for American press organizations to take their shared social role and responsibility seriously, and to act collectively to defend it. Threats and vulnerabilities should be assessed. Norms and routines should be evaluated. Red lines should be drawn, and responses considered. Journalists will need to abandon their prideful resistance to collective action. They will need to stand together if they want to avoid falling apart.

Notes

1. It is a paraphrase of Hemingway in *The Sun Also Rises* (1926): "How did you go bankrupt? Two ways. Gradually, then suddenly."

2. http://www.politifact.com/personalities/donald-trump and http://www.politifact.com/personalities/hillary-clinton.

Contributors

Mike Ananny is Assistant Professor at the University of Southern California's Annenberg School for Communication and Journalism, and Affiliated Faculty with USC's Science, Technology and Society research cluster.

C. W. Anderson is Professor of Media and Communication at the University of Leeds.

Rodney Benson is Professor of Media, Culture, Communication, and Sociology at New York University.

danah boyd is Principal Researcher at Microsoft Research, Founder and President of Data & Society, and Visiting Professor at New York University.

Pablo J. Boczkowski is Professor in the Department of Communication Studies at Northwestern University.

Robyn Caplan is Researcher at Data & Society Research Institute and PhD Candidate at Rutgers University's School of Communication and Information.

Josh Cowls is Research Assistant in Data Ethics at the Alan Turing Institute, and a Research Associate at the Oxford Internet Institute, University of Oxford.

Michael X. Delli Carpini is Dean of the Annenberg School for Communication at the University of Pennsylvania.

Susan J. Douglas is Catherine Neafie Kellogg Professor of Communication Studies at the University of Michigan.

Keith N. Hampton is Professor in the Department of Media and Information at Michigan State University.

David Karpf is Associate Professor in the George Washington University School of Media & Public Affairs.

Daniel Kreiss is Associate Professor in the School of Media and Journalism at the University of North Carolina at Chapel Hill.

Seth C. Lewis holds the Shirley Papé Chair in Emerging Media in the School of Journalism and Communication at the University of Oregon, and is Affiliated Fellow of the Information Society Project at Yale Law School.

Zoey Lichtenheld is a graduate student at George Washington University.

Andrew L. Mendelson is Professor and Associate Dean at the CUNY Graduate School of Journalism.

Gina Neff is Associate Professor and Senior Research Fellow at the University of Oxford's Department of Sociology and Oxford Internet Institute.

Zizi Papacharissi is Professor and Head of the Communication Department and Professor of Political Science at the University of Illinois at Chicago.

Katy E. Pearce is Assistant Professor in the Department of Communication at the University of Washington.

Victor Pickard is Associate Professor at the University of Pennsylvania's Annenberg School for Communication.

Sue Robinson holds the Helen Franklin Firstbrook Professor of Journalism at the University of Wisconsin-Madison's School of Journalism & Mass Communication.

Adrienne Russell is Mary Laird Wood Professor in the Department of Communication at University of Washington.

Ralph Schroeder is Professor at the Oxford Internet Institute, University of Oxford.

Michael Schudson is Professor of Journalism at Columbia University.

Julia Sonnevend is Assistant Professor of Sociology and Communication at the New School for Social Research in New York.

Keren Tenenboim-Weinblatt is Senior Lecturer at the Department of Communication and Journalism at the Hebrew University of Jerusalem.

Tina Tucker is a PhD student in the Department of Political Science at Duke University.

Fred Turner is the Harry and Norman Chandler Professor of Communication at Stanford University.

Nikki Usher is Associate Professor at The George Washington University.

Karin Wahl-Jorgensen is Professor in the Cardiff School of Journalism, Media and Cultural Studies.

Silvio Waisbord is Professor in the School of Media and Public Affairs at George Washington University.

Barbie Zelizer is the Raymond Williams Professor of Communication at the University of Pennsylvania's Annenberg School for Communication.

Bibliography

Abernathy, Penelope Muse. *The Rise of a New Media Baron and the Emerging Threat of News Deserts.* Center for Innovation and Sustainability in Local Media, University of North Carolina School of Media and Journalism, 2016. http://newspaperownership .com/newspaper-ownership-report.

Achen, Christopher H., and Larry M. Bartels. *Democracy for Realists: Why Elections Do Not Produce Responsive Government.* Princeton, NJ: Princeton University Press, 2016.

Adler, Leslie. *The Red Image: American Attitudes Toward Communism in the Cold War Era.* New York: Garland, 1991.

Anderson, C. W. *Apostles of Certainty: Data Journalism and the Politics of Doubt.* New York: Oxford University Press, 2018.

Arceneaux, Kevin, Martin Johnson, and Chad Murphy. "Polarized Political Communication, Oppositional Media Hostility, and Selective Exposure." *Journal of Politics* 74 (1) (2012): 174–186. doi:10.1017/s002238161100123x.

Arendt, Hannah. "Truth and Politics." *New Yorker,* February 25, 1967. http://www .newyorker.com/magazine/1967/02/25/truth-and-politics.

Barthel, Michael. "5 Key Takeaways about the State of the News Media in 2016." Pew Research Center, June 15, 2016. http://www.pewresearch.org/fact-tank/2016/ 06/15/state-of-the-news-media-2016-key-takeaways.

Beck, Ulrich. "The Sociological Anatomy of Enemy Images." In *Enemy Images in American History*, eds. Ragnhild Fiebig-von Hase and Ursula Lehmkuhl, 65–87. Providence, RI: Bergahn, 1997.

Benkler, Yochai, Robert Faris, Hal Roberts, and Ethan Zuckerman. "Study: Breitbart-Led Right-Wing Media Ecosystem Altered Broader Media Agenda." *Columbia Journalism Review,* March 3, 2017. https://www.cjr.org/analysis/breitbart-media -trump-harvard-study.php.

Bernhard, Nancy. *U.S. Television News and Cold War Propaganda, 1947–1960.* New York: Cambridge University Press, 1999.

Berry, Jeffrey M., and Sarah Sobieraj. *The Outrage Industry: Political Opinion Media and the New Incivility*. New York: Oxford University Press, 2014.

Bilton, Ricardo. "With Open Notebook, Hearken Wants to Help News Orgs Do More of their Reporting in Public." *Nieman Lab*, April 24, 2017. http://www.niemanlab .org/2017/04/with-open-notebook-hearken-wants-to-help-news-orgs-do-more-of -their-reporting-in-public.

Boczkowski, Pablo, Eugenia Mitchelstein, and Mora Matassi. "Incidental News: How Young People Consume News on Social Media." Paper presented at the 50th Hawaii International Conference on System Sciences (HICSS), Waikoloa, HI, January 4–7, 2017.

Borah, Porismita. "Does It Matter Where You Read the News Story? Interaction of Incivility and News Frames in the Political Blogosphere." *Communication Research* 4 (6) (2014): 809–827. doi:10.1177/009365021244935.

Boulding, Kenneth E. "National Images and International Systems." *Journal of Conflict Resolution* 3 (1959): 120–131. http://www.jstor.org/stable/173107.

Brady, Anne-Marie. "Mass Persuasion as a Means of Legitimation and China's Popular Authoritarianism." *American Behavioral Scientist* 53 (3) (2009): 434–457. doi:10.1177/0002764209338802.

Brooks, Deborah J., and John G. Geer. "Beyond Negativity: The Effects of Incivility on the Electorate." *American Journal of Political Science* 51 (1) (2007): 1–16. http:// www.jstor.org/stable/4122902.

Brophy, Enda, Nicole Cohen, and Greig de Peuter. "Practices of Autonomous Communication." In *The Routledge Companion to Labor and Media*, ed. Richard Maxwell, 315–326. London: Routledge, 2015.

Cappella, Joseph N., and Kathleen H. Jamieson. "News Frames, Political Cynicism, and Media Cynicism." *Annals of the American Academy of Political and Social Science* 546 (1996): 71–85. http://www.jstor.org/stable/1048171.

Carlson, Matt. *Journalistic Authority: Legitimating News in the Digital Era*. New York: Columbia University Press, 2017.

Cheme, Leo. "How to Spot a Communist." *Look*, March 4, 1947.

Chen, Jidong, and Yiqing Xu. "Information Manipulation and Reform in Authoritarian Regimes." *Political Science Research and Methods* 5 (1) (2017): 163–178. doi:10.1017/psrm.2015.21.

Claggett, William J., Pär Jason Engle, and Byron E. Shafer. "The Evolution of Mass Ideologies in Modern American Politics." *Forum* 12 (2) (2014): 223–256. doi:10.1515/ for-2014-5005.

Cohen, Marty, David Karol, Hans Noel, and John Zaller. "Party Versus Faction in the Reformed Presidential Nominating System." *PS: Political Science & Politics* 49 (4) (2016): 701–708. doi:10.1017/S1049096516001682.

Collins, Eliza. "Les Moonves: Trump's Run Is 'Damn Good for CBS.'" *Politico*, February 29, 2016. http://www.politico.com/blogs/on-media/2016/02/les-moonves -trump-cbs-220001.

Confessore, Nicholas, and Karen Yourish. "$2 Billion Worth of Free Media for Donald Trump." *New York Times*, March 15, 2016. http://www.nytimes.com/2016/ 03/16/upshot/measuring-donald-trumps-mammoth-advantage-in-free-media.html.

Côté, Rochelle R., and Bonnie H. Erickson. "Untangling the Roots of Tolerance." *American Behavioral Scientist* 52 (12) (2009): 1664–1689. doi:10.1177/ 000276420933153.

Cowls, Josh. "From Trump Tower to the White House, in 140 Characters: The Hyper-Mediated Election of a Paranoid Populist President." MSc. thesis, MIT, 2017.

Cramer, Katherine J. *The Politics of Resentment: Rural Consciousness in Wisconsin and the Rise of Scott Walker.* Chicago: University of Chicago Press, 2016.

Crouse, Timothy. *The Boys on the Bus.* New York: Ballantine, 1973.

Delli Carpini, Michael X., and Scott Keeter. *What Americans Know about Politics and Why It Matters.* New Haven, CT: Yale University Press, 1996.

DiFonzo, Nicholas, and Prashant Bordia. *Rumor Psychology: Social and Organizational Approaches.* Washington, DC: American Psychological Association, 2007.

Doherty, Carroll, Alec Tyson, and Rachel Weisel. *Broad Public Support for Legal Status for Undocumented Immigrants.* Washington, DC: Pew Research Center, 2015.

Dourish, Paul. *The Stuff of Bits: An Essay on the Materialities of Information.* Cambridge, MA: MIT Press, 2017.

Durkheim, Émile. *The Division of Labor in Society.* New York: Simon and Schuster, 2014. First published 1893 in French.

Entman, Robert M. "Framing: Toward Clarification of a Fractured Paradigm." *Journal of Communication* 43 (4) (1993): 51–58. doi:10.1111/j.1460-2466.1993.tb01304.x.

Etkind, Alexander, and Andrei Shcherbak. "The Double Monopoly and Its Technologists: The Russian Preemptive Counterrevolution." *Demokratizatsiya* 16 (3) (2008): 229–239.

Finlay, David J., Ole R. Holsti, and Richard R. Fagen. *Enemies in Politics.* Chicago: Rand McNally, 1967.

Gandhi, Jennifer, and Adam Przeworski. "Authoritarian Institutions and the Survival of Autocrats." *Comparative Political Studies* 40 (11) (2007): 1279–1301. doi:10.1177/0010414007305817.

Gans, Herbert J. *Deciding What's News*. New York: Random House, 1979.

Geddes, Barbara. *Why Parties and Elections in Authoritarian Regimes?* Washington, DC: American Political Science Association, 2005. http://www.scribd.com/doc/133702645/Barbara-Geddes-Why-Parties-and-Elections-in-Authoritarian-Regimes-2006.

Gergen, Kenneth J. *Realities and Relationships: Soundings in Social Construction*. Cambridge, MA: Harvard University Press, 1994.

Gerschewski, Johannes. "The Three Pillars of Stability: Legitimation, Repression, and Co-Optation in Autocratic Regimes." *Democratization* 20 (1) (2013): 13–38. doi:10.1080/13510347.2013.738860.

Gitelman, Lisa. *Always Already News: Media, History, and the Data of Culture*. Cambridge, MA: MIT Press, 2006.

Gold, Hadas, and Alex Weprin. "Cable News' Election-Year Haul Could Reach $2.5 Billion." *Politico*, September 27, 2016. http://www.politico.com/media/story/2016/09/media-tv-numbers-004783.

Gottfried, Jeffrey, and Elisa Shearer. 2016. "News Use across Social Media Platforms." Pew Research Center, May 26, 2016. http://www.journalism.org/2016/05/26/news-use-across-social-media-platforms-2016.

Graves, Lucas. *Deciding What's True: The Rise of Political Fact-Checking in American Journalism*. New York: Columbia University Press, 2016.

Green, Donald P., Bradley Palmquist, and Eric Schickler. *Partisan Hearts and Minds: Political Parties and the Social Identities of Voters*. New Haven, CT: Yale University Press, 2004.

Greenwald, Glenn. "Greenwald on Democracy, Trump and the Ongoing Dangerous Refusal to Learn from Brexit." *Democracy Now!*, November 10, 2016. https://www.democracynow.org/2016/11/10/greenwald_on_democrats_trump_and_the.

Grieco, Elizabeth M., Yesenia D. Acosta, Partricia de la Cruz, Christine Gambino, Thomas Gryn, Luke J. Larsen, Edward N. Trevelyan, and Nathan P. Walters. *The Foreign-Born Population in the United States: 2010*. Washington, DC: U.S. Department of Commerce, May 2012. https://www.census.gov/prod/2012pubs/acs-19.pdf.

Groshek, Jacob, and Karolina Koc-Michalska. "Helping Populism Win? Social Media Use, Filter Bubbles, and Support for Populist Presidential Candidates in the 2016 US Election Campaign." *Information Communication and Society* 20 (9) (2017): 1389–1407. doi:10.1080/1369118X.2017.1329334.

Grusin, Richard. *Premediation: Affect and Mediality after 9/11*. New York: Palgrave, 2010.

Hall, John A., and Charles Lindholm. *Is America Breaking Apart?* Princeton, NJ: Princeton University Press, 2001.

Hamby, Peter. "Did Twitter Kill the Boys on the Bus? Searching for a Better Way to Cover a Campaign." *Shorenstein Center Report*, August 28, 2013. http://shorensteincenter.org/d80-hamby.

Hamilton, James T. *Democracy's Detective: The Economics of Investigative Journalism*. Cambridge, MA: Harvard University Press, 2016.

Hampton, Keith N. "Persistent and Pervasive Community: New Communication Technologies and the Future of Community." *American Behavioral Scientist* 60 (1) (2016a): 101–124. doi:10.1177/0002764215601714.

Hampton, Keith N. "Why Is Helping Behavior Declining in the United States but Not in Canada?: Ethnic Diversity, New Technologies and other Explanations." *City & Community* 15 (4) (2016b): 380–399.

Hampton, Keith N., Lee Chul-joo, and Eun Ja Her. "How New Media Afford Network Diversity: Direct and Mediated Access to Social Capital Through Participation in Local Social Settings." *New Media & Society* 13 (7) (2011): 1031–1049. doi:10.1177/1461444810390342.

Harris, Mary. "A Media Post-Mortem on the 2016 Presidential Election." *MediaQuant*, November 14, 2016. http://www.mediaquant.net/2016/11/a-media-post-mortem-on-the-2016-presidential-election.

Hartley, John. *Communication, Cultural and Media Studies*. London: Routledge, 2002.

Hazard Owen, L. "David Fahrenthold Goes from Tweeting Pictures of His Notepad to Winning a Pulitzer Prize." *Nieman Lab*, April 10, 2017. http://www.niemanlab.org/2017/04/david-fahrenthold-goes-from-tweeting-pictures-of-his-notepad-to-winning-a-pulitzer-prize.

Hepp, Andreas, and Nicholas Coultry. *The Mediated Construction of Reality*. London: Polity, 2017.

Hixson, Walter L. *Parting the Curtain: Propaganda, Culture and the Cold War, 1945–1961*. New York: St. Martin's Press, 1996.

Hobsbawm, E. J. *The Age of Extremes: A History of the World, 1914–1991*. New York: Pantheon Books, 1994.

Hochschild, Arlie Russell. *Strangers in Their Own Land: Anger and Mourning on the American Right*. New York: The New Press, 2016.

Hofstadter, Richard. "The Paranoid Style of American Politics." *Harper's Magazine*, November 1964. https://harpers.org/archive/1964/11/the-paranoid-style-in-american-politics/.

Huang, Haifeng. "A War of (Mis)Information: The Political Effects of Rumors and Rumor Rebuttals in an Authoritarian Country." *British Journal of Political Science* 47 (2) (2017): 283–311. doi:10.1017/S0007123415000253.

Hyun, Ki Deuk, and Jinhee Kim. "The Role of New Media in Sustaining the Status Quo: Online Political Expression, Nationalism, and System Support in China." *Information Communication and Society* 18 (7) (2015): 766–781. doi:10.1080/1369118X.2014.994543.

Ingram, Mathew. "Sorry Mark Zuckerberg, but Facebook Is Definitely a Media Company." *Fortune*, August 30, 2016. http://fortune.com/2016/08/30/facebook-media-company.

Karpf, Dave. "Schrodinger's Audience: How News Analytics Handed America Trump." *Civicist*, May 4, 2016. http://civichall.org/civicist/schrodingers-audience-how-news-analytics-gave-america-trump.

Kazin, Michael. *The Populist Persuasion: An American History*. Ithaca, NY: Cornell University Press, 1998.

Kreiss, Daniel. *Taking Our Country Back: The Crafting of Networked Politics from Howard Dean to Barack Obama*. Oxford: Oxford University Press, 2012.

Kreiss, Daniel. *Prototype Politics: Technology-Intensive Campaigning and the Data of Democracy*. Oxford: Oxford University Press, 2016.

Ladd, Jonathan M. *Why Americans Hate the Media and How It Matters*. Princeton, NJ: Princeton University Press, 2011.

Lepore, Jill. "The Party Crashers." *New Yorker*, February 22, 2016. http://www.newyorker.com/magazine/2016/02/22/did-social-media-produce-the-new-populism.

Levitsky, Steven, and Lucan Way. "The Rise of Competitive Authoritarianism." *Journal of Democracy* 13 (2) (2002): 51–65. doi:10.1353/jod.2002.0026.

Lewis, Seth C., Avery E. Holton, and Mark Coddington. "Reciprocal Journalism: A Concept of Mutual Exchange Between Journalists and Audiences." *Journalism Practice* 8 (2) (2014): 229–241. doi:10.1080/17512786.2013.859840.

Liebovich, Louis. *The Press and the Origins of the Cold War, 1944–1947*. New York: Praeger, 1988.

Lu, Jie, John Aldrich, and Tianjian Shi. "Revisiting Media Effects in Authoritarian Societies: Democratic Conceptions, Collectivistic Norms, and Media Access in Urban China." *Politics & Society* 42 (2) (2014): 253–283. doi:10.1177/0032329213519423.

MacNeal, Caitlin. "Obama Critiques Media." *Talking Points Memo*, September 13, 2016. http://talkingpointsmemo.com/livewire/obama-clinton-trump-no-equivalence.

Mahler, Jonathan. "CNN Had a Problem. Donald Trump Solved It." *New York Times*, April 4, 2017. https://www.nytimes.com/2017/04/04/magazine/cnn-had-a-problem -donald-trump-solved-it.html.

Mann, Thomas E., and Norman J. Ornstein. *It's Even Worse Than It Looks: How the American Constitutional System Collided with the New Politics of Extremism*. New York: Basic Books, 2016.

Markel, L. "The Case for 'Interpretation.'" *ASNE Bulletin*, April 1, 1953, 1–2.

Meraz, Sharon, and Zizi Papacharissi. "Networked Gatekeeping and Networked Framing on #Egypt." *International Journal of Press/Politics* 18 (2) (2013): 138–166. doi:10.1177/1940161212474472.

Mitchell, Amy, Jeffrey Gottfried, Michael Barthel, and Elisa Shearer. "The Modern News Consumer: Trust and Accuracy." Pew Research Center, July 7, 2016. http://www.journalism.org/2016/07/07/trust-and-accuracy.

Mueller, Jan-Werner. *What Is Populism?* Philadelphia: University of Pennsylvania Press, 2016.

Mutz, Diana C., and Byron Reeves. "The New Videomalaise: Effects of Televised Incivility on Political Trust." *American Political Science Review* 99 (1) (2005): 1–15.

Nielsen, Rasmus K. Digital News as Forms of Knowledge: A New Chapter in the Sociology of Knowledge. In *Remaking the News: Essays on the Future of Journalism Scholarship in the Digital Age*, ed. Pablo Boczkowski and C. W. Anderson. 91–110. Cambridge, MA: MIT Press.

Nyhan, Brendan, and Jason Reifler. "When Corrections Fail: The Persistence of Political Misperceptions." *Political Behavior* 32 (2010): 303–330.

Obermaier, Frederik, and Bastian Obermayer. "We Broke the Panama Papers Story. Here's How to Investigative Donald Trump." *The Guardian*, January 24, 2017. https://www.theguardian.com/commentisfree/2017/jan/24/panama-papers-media -investigation-next-donald-trump-hold-accountable.

Oliver, J. Eric, and Wendy M. Rahn. "Rise of the Trumpenvolk Populism in the 2016 Election." *Annals of the American Academy of Political and Social Science* 667 (1) (2016): 189–206. doi:10.1177/0002716216662639.

Ortmann, Stefanie, and John Heathershaw. "Conspiracy Theories in the Post-Soviet Space." *Russian Review* 71 (4) (2012): 551–564. doi:10.1111/j.1467-9434.2012.00668.x.

Ott, Brian L. "The Age of Twitter: Donald J. Trump and the Politics of Debasement." *Critical Studies in Media Communication* 34 (1) (2017): 59–68. doi:10.1080/15295036 .2016.1266686.

Oxford English Dictionary. "The Word of the Year Is. ..." November 16, 2016. https://www.oxforddictionaries.com/press/news/2016/12/11/WOTY-16.

Papacharissi, Zizi. *Affective Publics*. New York: Oxford University Press, 2014.

Pariser, Eli. *The Filter Bubble: How the New Personalized Web Is Changing What We Read and How We Think*. New York: Penguin Books, 2012.

Pasek, Josh, Tobias H. Stark, Jon A. Krosnick, and Trevor Tompson. "What Motivates a Conspiracy Theory? Birther Beliefs, Partisanship, Liberal-Conservative Ideology, and Anti-Black Attitudes." *Electoral Studies* 40 (2015): 482–489. doi:10.1016/j.electstud.2014.09.009.

Patterson, Thomas E. "Harvard Study: Policy Issues Nearly Absent in Presidential Campaign Coverage." *The Conversation*, September 20, 2016. https://theconversation.com/harvard-study-policy-issues-nearly-absent-in-presidential-campaign-coverage-65731.

Pearce, Katy E. "Democratizing Kompromat: The Affordances of Social Media for State-Sponsored Harassment." *Information Communication and Society* 18 (10) (2015): 1–17. doi:10.1080/1369118X.2015.1021705.

Pearce, Katy E., and Adnan Hajizada. "No Laughing Matter: Humor as a Means of Dissent in the Digital Era: The Case of Authoritarian Azerbaijan." *Demokratizatsiya* 22 (443) (2013): 67–85. doi:10.5210/fm.v18i7.3885.

Perlstein, Rick. "Outsmarted: The Liberal Cult of the Cognitive Elite." *The Baffler*, March 2017. https://thebaffler.com/salvos/outsmarted-perlstein.

Pew Research Center. "March 17–April 12, 2015—Libraries and Technology Use" dataset. http://www.pewinternet.org/dataset/april-2015-libraries-and-technology-use.

Pickard, Victor. *America's Battle for Media Democracy: The Triumph of Corporate Libertarianism and the Future of Media Reform*. New York: Cambridge University Press, 2015.

Pickard, Victor. "Media and Politics in the Age of Trump." *Origins: Current Events in Historical Perspective* 10 (2) (2016). https://origins.osu.edu/article/media-and-politics-age-trump/page/0/0.

Pickard, Victor. "Media Failures in the Age of Trump." *The Political Economy of Communication* 4 (2) (2017): 118–122.

Pompeo, Joe. "*Wall Street Journal* Editor to Face Critics." *Politico*, February 9, 2017. http://www.politico.com/media/story/2017/02/gerry-baker-wall-street-journal-trump-newsroom-tensions-004928.

Postman, Neil. *Amusing Ourselves to Death: Public Discourse in the Age of Show Business*. New York: Penguin, 2006.

Robinson, Sue. "Searching for My Own Unique Place in the Story: A Comparison of Journalistic and Citizen-Produced Coverage of Hurricane Katrina's Anniversary." In *Journalism and Citizenship: New Agendas in Communication*, ed. Zizi Papacharissi, 166–188. New York: Routledge, 2009.

Rosen, Jay. "Asymmetry between the Major Parties Fries the Circuits of the Mainstream Press," *PressThink*, December 25, 2016. http://pressthink.org/2016/09/asymmetry-between-the-major-parties-fries-the-circuits-of-the-mainstream-press.

Schatz, Edward. "The Soft Authoritarian Tool Kit: Agenda-Setting Power in Kazakhstan and Kyrgyzstan." *Comparative Politics* 41 (2) (2009): 203–222. doi:10.5129/001041509X12911362972034.

Schedler, Andreas. "The Nested Game of Democratization by Elections." *International Political Science Review* 23 (1) (2002): 103–122. doi:10.1177/0192512102023001006.

Schedler, Andreas. *The Politics of Uncertainty.* Oxford: Oxford University Press, 2013.

Schroeder, Ralph. *Social Theory after the Internet: Media, Technology, and Globalization.* London: UCL Press, 2017.

Schroeder, Robert. "Trump Has Gotten Nearly $3 Billion in 'Free' Advertising." *MarketWatch*, May 6, 2016. http://www.marketwatch.com/story/trump-has-gotten-nearly-3-billion-in-free-advertising-2016-05-06.

"Second Guessing." *ASNE Bulletin*, January 1, 1955, 1.

"Security Problem." *Editor and Publisher*, April 3, 1948, 36.

Shafer, Jack, and Tucker Doherty. "The Media Bubble Is Worse Than You Think." *Politico*, June 29, 2017. http://www.politico.com/magazine/story/2017/04/25/media-bubble-real-journalism-jobs-east-coast-215048.

Shirky, Clay. *Here Comes Everybody: The Power of Organizing Without Organizations.* London: Penguin Books, 2008.

Siebert, Fredrick S., Theodore Peterson, and Wilbur Schramm. *Four Theories of the Press: The Authoritarian, Libertarian, Social Responsibility, and Soviet Communist Concepts of What the Press Should Be and Do.* Champaign: University of Illinois Press, 1963.

Silverman, Craig. This Analysis Shows How Fake Election News Stories Outperformed Real News on Facebook. *BuzzFeed*, November 16, 2016. https://www.buzzfeed.com/craigsilverman/viral-fake-election-news-outperformed-real-news-on-facebook.

Smith, Miranda N., Richelle L. Winkler, and Kenneth M. Johnson. *How Migration Impacts Rural America.* Madison: Applied Population Lab, University of Wisconsin-Madison, 2016.

Sobieraj, Sarah, and Jeffrey M. Berry. "From Incivility to Outrage: Political Discourse in Blogs, Talk Radio, and Cable News." *Political Communication* 28 (1) (2011): 19–41.

Sommeiller, Estelle, Mark Price, and Ellis Wazeter. *Income Inequality in the U.S. by State, Metropolitan Area, and County.* Washington, DC: Economic Policy Institute, 2016.

Spillmann, Kurt R., and Kati Spillmann. "Some Sociobiological and Psychological Aspects of 'Images of the Enemy.'" In *Enemy Images in American History*, ed. Ragnhild Fiebig-von Hase and Ursula Lehmkuhl, 44–63. Providence, RI: Bergahn, 1997.

Stein, Elizabeth A. "The Unraveling of Support for Authoritarianism: The Dynamic Relationship of Media, Elites, and Public Opinion in Brazil, 1972–82." *International Journal of Press/Politics* 18 (1) (2012): 85–107. doi:10.1177/1940161212460762.

Stroud, Natalie Jomini. *Niche News: The Politics of News Choice.* New York: Oxford University Press, 2011.

Sunstein, Cass. *Republic.com.* Princeton, NJ: Princeton University Press, 2001.

Tomasky, M. "Can He Be Stopped?" *New York Review of Books*, April 21, 2016. http://www.nybooks.com/articles/2016/04/21/can-donald-trump-be-stopped.

Trump, Donald J. (@realDonaldTrump). "Did Crooked Hillary help disgusting (check out sex tape and past) Alicia M become a U.S. citizen so she could use her in the debate?" Twitter. September 30, 2016, 5:30 a.m. https://twitter.com/realdonaldtrump/status/781788223055994880.

Tyndal Report. "Campaign 2016 Coverage: Annual Totals for 2015." 2016. http://tyndallreport.com/comment/20/5773.

Tyson, Alec, and Shiva Manian. "Behind Trump's Victory: Divisions by Race, Gender." Pew Research Center, November 9, 2016. http://www.pewresearch.org/fact-tank/2016/11/09/behind-trumps-victory-divisions-by-race-gender-education.

Umansky, Eric. "How We're Learning to Do Journalism Differently in the Age of Trump." *ProPublica,* May 8, 2017. https://www.propublica.org/article/how-were-learning-to-do-journalism-differently-in-the-age-of-trump.

Uscinski, Joseph. "The 5 Most Dangerous Conspiracy Theories of 2016." *Politico*, August 22, 2016. http://www.politico.com/magazine/story/2016/08/conspiracy-theories-2016-donald-trump-hillary-clinton-214183.

Vos, Tim P., and François Heinderyckx. *Gatekeeping in Transition.* New York: Routledge, 2015.

Whitten-Woodring, Jenifer, and Patrick James. "Fourth Estate or Mouthpiece? A Formal Model of Media, Protest, and Government Repression." *Political Communication* 29 (2) (2012): 113–136. doi:10.1080/10584609.2012.671232.

Williams, Bruce A., and Michael X. Delli Carpini. *After Broadcast News: Media Regimes, Democracy, and the New Information Environment.* Cambridge: Cambridge University Press, 2011.

Wilson, Andrew. *Virtual Politics: Faking Democracy in the Post-Soviet World.* New Haven: Yale University Press, 2005.

Wodak, Ruth. *The Politics of Fear.* London: Sage, 2015.

Zelizer, Barbie. "How the Cold War Drives the News." Unpublished manuscript, n.d.

Index